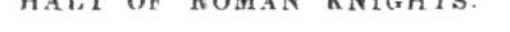

HALT OF ROMAN KNIGHTS.

THE CAPTAINS OF THE OLD WORLD;

AS COMPARED WITH

THE GREAT MODERN STRATEGISTS,

THEIR

CAMPAIGNS, CHARACTERS AND CONDUCT, FROM THE PERSIAN, TO THE PUNIC WARS.

BY

HENRY WILLIAM HERBERT.

NEW YORK:
CHARLES SCRIBNER, 145 NASSAU STREET.
1852.

C. W. BENEDICT,
Stereotyper and Printer
201 William Street.

TO

C. C. Felton,

REGENT OF HARVARD UNIVERSITY,

&c., &c., &c.

IN MEMORY

OF MANY PLEASANT HOURS HERETOFORE SPENT TOGETHER,

AND HOPE OF MORE SUCH HEREAFTER,

NOR LESS IN TOKEN

OF CORDIAL REGARD FOR HIMSELF,

AND SINCERE RESPECT FOR HIS TALENTS AND ATTAINMENTS,

THIS VOLUME

IS DEDICATED, BY HIS FRIEND,

THE AUTHOR.

LIST OF EMBELLISHMENTS.

DESIGNED BY THE AUTHOR,

AFTER THE BEST AUTHORITIES.

PREFACE.

My Dear Felton:

It is generally the custom, and a custom, I think, like comparatively few others, more honored in the observance than the breach, that an author should say a few words for himself preparatory to his book; not as an apology for writing, since if that written be so impertinent as to require an apology, it had better never have been writ at all, but as an explanation of his motives and object in writing it.

This is, perhaps, more than usually necessary, when he selects a subject, as I have done, from the annals of those ancient classic times, the vein of which is, in the opinion of many, already worn out and exhausted; while it is too apparent to you, that I should need to point it out, that the rich and pregnant soil is scarcely stirred as yet, much less the treasures brought to light from its unfathomed and almost unfathomable mines of wealth.

Until the beginning of the present century, I may

almost say that to a few secluded and solitary scholars, only was a glimpse revealed of the inner life of the men, and the true history of the nations of antiquity; while to the rest of mankind, nothing was disclosed by the weak, drivelling compilers, who called themselves—Heaven save the mark!—historians, but the crudities, the absurdities, the fables, and the falsehoods of the old annalists, presented to them in one crude and undigested mass.

Much, indeed, has been done of late days in this branch; and had Arnold and Niebuhr survived to accomplish their immortal histories of Rome; and should Grote be spared to finish his labors on the fertile field of Hellas, little more would be left to desire, so far as those two great nations, perhaps the two greatest of all time, are regarded. But still, as no one is better aware than yourself, we are all taught in our youth, at our primary schools, and in all, save our very best colleges, the old *crambe repetita* of Romulus and Remus and the she-wolf, of the golden fleece of Theseus, and the dragon teeth of Kadmos, not as beautiful myths and poetic legends of the old time when poetry was half the life of the young untarnished earth; but as facts just as authentical as the burning of Moscow, the victory of Trafalgar, or the battle of Bunker's Hill; thus spending half our lives in learning what, if we desire to follow literature with any profit, we must spend the other half of it in unlearning.

Nor would it, I believe, be too much to state that, to

this very day, nine-tenths of the readers of England and America, who know a little of such things, imagining that they know a good deal, possessing neither means nor inclination to make such things the study and business of their lives, regard the sieges of Troy and Veii, just as veritable events as those of Syracuse or Carthage; and Camillus and Kodros just as authentic persons as Julius Cæsar and Epaminondas.

Anything, therefore, that tends to popularize history, and to bring matters, generally too abstruse, too dry, and embodied in works too formidable and too voluminous to be largely popular; into such a form as shall be acceptable to the masses, is in my opinion something gained, and, at all events, involves no waste of time or labor.

This little volume does not pretend, therefore, to be either exactly history, or historical disquisition; least of all, does it desire to be classed with that most contemptible species of book-making, usually termed popularized history; which consists, for the most part, either in conveying good matter in a low and vulgar manner, or in compiling all the gossiping trash and verbiage of twaddling chroniclers, with a careful avoidance of everything solid, salutary, or permanent of ancient or modern literature.

Such is not the course I have adopted in this work, in which it has been my object to produce authentic details concerning the great generals of antiquity, with the particulars of their campaigns and conduct, more elaborate and fuller than the pages of general history will spare from other matters of graver import, perhaps not of less engrossing interest; to elucidate their feats and exploits by comparison with the rules and principles of modern warfare; to illustrate them by keeping up a parallel of modern geography—so that they can be verified by the aid of any common map; to give them life and reality by accurate accounts of dress, scenery, and habits; and to ascertain their real merits and comparative degrees of skill and excellence, by comparison with the greatest strategists and tacticians of the latter ages.

I have not, of course, dreamed of including, in my list of captains, all the men who set battalions in the field, or fought gallantly, whether for patriotism or ambition; but have selected those only who were, in my opinion, really eminent, really worthy of continued remembrance, really entitled to be enrolled in the annals of all time as great generals.

That which I have looked to most in thus estimating their value as soldiers, and ranking them in the order of merit, is the development of warfare into a science, the originating new principles of strategy or tactics, and the producing great effects and lasting influences on the progress, rise, and fall of nations, and on the comparative growth and disappearance of various races of mankind.

None, who do not comply with one or other of these propositions, are mentioned in this volume; and this may account, to my readers, for the omission of several great and heroic names of Greek history, such as Leonidas, Lysander, Phormion, Chabrias, Iphikrates, Agesilaos, Pyrrhos of Epiros, and others; who, although good soldiers and gallant officers, were distinguished by hardihood and valor—qualities common and natural to most men, and all animals, when aroused by adequate causes—rather than by skill and science; or operated on too small a scale, and with results too limited, to be considered in the light of great generals.

There is another class, much more worthy of remark than these, as possessing abilities equal, if not superior, to most of those herein cited, who are also excluded from this volume; as, though not inferior to many in military talent, they yet owe their celebrity to statesmanship, more than to soldiership; and attained greatness rather by the extent of their forecast and the prudence of their councils, than by their prowess in the tented field. Such men I mean, as Alkibiades, Perikles, Philip of Makedon, and many other great and shining characters, to whom I propose, hereafter, to introduce my readers in another volume, or series of volumes, each in itself complete and unconnected with its predecessor or successor. The next of them will be the Captains of Rome, from the Punic wars to the division of the empires; for it will be remarked, doubtless, that no Roman makes his appearance on the stage during this period; for the simple reason, that, aside from the meagreness and falsehood of the Roman legends and the absence of all contemporaneous history, Rome was, at the period to which only this volume comes down, barely emerging from barbarism; and, although she had produced scores and hundreds of brave soldiers, had sent forth no general, until the days of Scipio Africanus. He just falls within the cycle comprised in this volume, which, indeed, he might have terminated; but that I preferred, for the sake of uniformity, to defer him till he can appear in what seems to me his more appropriate place among the greatest men—Niebuhr says, THE GREATEST—of his own great country.

The other volumes of the contemplated series, to which I have alluded, should the time be spared to me, and popular favor not prove too niggard of encouragement, will be the Captains of the Eastern Empire; The Captains of Barbarians, including all Paganism and Heathenism; the Captains of the Middle Ages, and the Statesmen and Orators of each of these periods in succession; to which may be added the Hero Kings and the Tyrants of Greece. Of course, no promise of these is intended; nor is such a promise necessary; for as every volume will be complete, and will comprise a period in itself, wherever the series may terminate, it will in no respect be an unfinished work.

Only on two points farther, have I to weary your attention. The first, you will perceive at once, as you peruse the work, to be the orthography of the Greek names, which are given invariably and consistently in all respects as they were spelt, and, I am satisfied, pronounced by the Greeks; though the forms may look quaint and the sounds of some familiar names ring strangely at first in a modern ear. I have, as you know, since we have often spoken on this head, always deemed it an utter absurdity to adopt the Latin names of Greek gods, who were not synonymous, or the same in the two mythologies; and the Latin spelling of Greek names. The practice is no more defensible, than it would be to write Italian or Spanish names in Russian or Magyar orthography, and it should not be tolerated in this age when Greek is as familiar to all well educated scholars as Latin was in the days of Pope, or more so; and when truth is, or ought to be, the token of all research. You will find, therefore, that I have adopted the hard Greek *k* instead of the soft Roman *c;* the Greek termination *os* and *e* and *h*, instead of the Latin *us*, *a;* and, to conclude, the Greek diphthongs *ai* and *oi*, instead of the Latin *æ* and *œ*, as approximating at least to the nomenclature by which, in their own days, those herein named knew, and were known to, one another.* I have done this from no love of innovation or of neo-

* The reader will, I regret to say, perceive in this introduction and the life of Miltiades, a few variations from this rule have occurred through inadvertence, and the natural tendency to hang unconsciously to antiquated, even if improper usages.

logy, much less from any affectation of doing something new; but from a real conviction that a reform in this faulty habit is needed, and from a confidence that it will be generally adopted, since it is sanctioned and used by a scholar so ripe and rare as Grote, the last and best historian of Hellas.

Farther than this, I have only to add, that whatever else you may find in this volume, and whether you regard it as a defect or a merit, you will find no dish warmed up from the cold meat of other English writers; no facts assumed, no dates quoted on the authority of others, who have themselves investigated, borrowed, quoted; not a description selected, or an opinion adopted from any English or American author, unless it be a few thoughts from my favorite Arnold in the case of Hannibal, for which due credit is given. Right or wrong, my facts are deduced, my arguments drawn, my translations made, my dates verified, and my conclusions adopted, from a careful and dispassionate examination of the contemporaneous writers whose names will be found in the ample references I have made at the foot of my pages, to enable others, who may think it worth the while, to verify my facts or my opinions; for the former of which, I can at least assure you, I have not drawn on my imagination, more than for the latter on my memory.

Should you approve the tenor and spirit of this volume in general, though I may hardly hope that you will coincide with all its opinions in particular, I shall feel more sanguine than I do now of meeting some meed of popular approbation.

If I succeed in inducing a few of those who have hitherto confined themselves to lighter studies, and the more ephemeral fictions of the day, to turn to the deeper and purer well of history, which is truth, science, and experience, with as much pleasure as profit to be derived from it, all in one, I shall have gone far to have attained my highest object. If I merely succeed in averting a weary hour, soothing a sleepless night, or occupying the restless ear of pain, my time will not have been lost, nor wholly ill employed—for I am secure, at least, that there is not a line here written adverse to morality or truth; nor one which may not be read aloud in the domestic circle before the purest ears, without one moment's hesitation, or the fear of calling up one blush on the cheek of chariest virtue.

Pray, believe me, my dear Felton,

Ever and most faithfully yours,

HENRY WILLIAM HERBERT.

THE CEDARS, Sept 16, 1851.

CONTENTS.

I.

INTRODUCTORY.

II.

MILTIADES, THE SON OF CIMON.

III.

THEMISTOKLES.

IV.

PAUSANIAS, THE SPARTAN.

V.

XENOPHON, THE ATHENIAN.

VI.

EPAMINONDAS, THE THEBAN.

VII.

ALEXANDER OF MAKEDON.

VIII.

HANNIBAL.

INTRODUCTORY.

I.

THE MILITARY ART AMONG THE GREEKS AND ROMANS; BEING AN EXAMINATION OF THE SERVICES, ARMATURE, ARRAY AND TACTICS OF THEIR ARMIES; AS COMPARED BETWEEN THEMSELVES, AND WITH THOSE OF MODERN NATIONS.

CONSIDERING the vast influence which the wars of the two great nations of antiquity have exercised over the present condition, it would scarcely be incorrect to say over the actual fate, of modern Europe, and through her of the world at large, it will be neither an unpleasant nor an unprofitable mode of passing an hour, even to those who care not to prosecute deep and dry historical researches, to inquire a little into the military means by which the two powers produced results so incalculably great and important. It cannot, I think, have escaped the observation of the most superficial reader, that, while some wars, although long, bloody, well contested and conducted with equal courage and ability, have in no wise affected the condition or permanent interests of humanity, because waged between identical or kindred races and tending only to the extension of power and territory on the one side or the other—there have been other wars of conquest and extermination, by the decision of which the fate not only of empires, but of races, but of humanity itself, has been determined.

Of these, the first, and scarcely the least important, was the attempt on the part of the oriental nations, under the great Persian kings, to subjugate and enslave all Western Europe; a conclusion averted, under Providence, in the first instance by the repulse of the invaders at Marathon, Plataia, Salamis, and Thermopylæ, and finally rendered impossible by the retaliatory expedition of Alexander, and the domination of the Eastern peoples by Greek arms and Western dynasties.

The second is to be found in the famous struggle of the Punic wars, between Rome and Carthage; the termination of which set the question at rest whether the dominion of the civilized world should belong to the Caucasian or the Semitic Race; whether Greek arts and Latin arms should be the inheritance of Europe and America, or the corruption, idolatry and cruelty of Canaanitish Carthage.

The third and last and greatest contest of this nature, as regards Europe and European civilization—for China, India, and the Eastern isles, have undergone many such—is the long-protracted warfare between the Saracenic Mahommedans, and the nations of Christendom; which may be said to have commenced with the destruction of a Saracen host at Tours, in the heart of France, by the battle-axe of Charles Martel in 732; to have continued throughout the crusades of the middle ages; and to have been determined only by the artillery of Don John of Austria at Lepanto, and the lances of John Sobieski before the walls of Vienna, so lately as the years, respectively, of 1571, and 1683.

Of these three great struggles, it is impossible not to see, that the decisions, had they been reversed, must necessarily have altered so completely the whole constitution of human polity, society, and morals, that no sagacity can conjecture what, in that event, would have been the present aspect of Europe or America.

From the circumstances of other similarly situated regions we may however suppose, that had Greece succumbed before the countless myriads of Darius, Xerxes, and their successors, the civilization and society of Europe to-day would have nearly resembled those of Hindostan, before the erection of the Anglo-Indian empire; and that had Carthage prevailed over the Eagles of the Republic, a bloody superstition, a corrupt commercial tyranny, an illiterate, voluptuous, unenlightened society, such as we know to have existed in Tyre and Sidon, would have stood in stead of the pure religion, the liberal polity, and the elevated social condition which have gradually eliminated themselves from the institutions of Rome, and through her of the elder Hellas.

That the question, determined by the Saracenic and European strife, is simply whether the faith of the world should ultimately be that of Mahomet or Christ, it requires no sagacity or acumen to discover; and I, for one, certainly, shall not descend to argue whether event were for the greatest good of humanity at large.

Of these three great wars, by which, as I have, I think, shown, the fate of the human race has been thrice severally decided, the first two were won for posterity by the valor and virtue, the arms and the military arts, of the Greeks, and of the Romans, and it is thence especially that the histories of these two great nations are so full to us of interest, and that they can never be examined without entertainment and advantage.

That Greece—when her mission of checking the irruption and bridling the power of the eastern hordes, of giving a form and body to imaginative beauty, of creating the magic of letters, and making for the dreams of genius a real and immortal presence in the birth of art—should be accomplished, must succumb to the more vital and durable energies of Rome, was clearly in the design of Providence; for she lacked in herself the practical and legislative wisdom, which born in the Latin republic has in its maturity filled the world, and formed in a greater or less degree the base of every modern constitution. The means by which she overcame the barbarian myriads, and by which she was herself overcome in turn, were purely natural and physical; and the results were such as must, to an almost mathematical certainty, have followed from the employment of those means.

What these were, and wherefore and how successful, it is my purpose now to investigate. Nor will it be unimportant or uninstructive to see how little the real principles of strategy and tactics have been altered from the earliest ages to the latest times; and how continually, in spite of all the changes and improvements in the methods and instruments of warfare, in spite of the invention of gunpowder and the consequent substitution of scientific combinations for individual prowess, the same military principles have been attended with the same success; the same exercises and manœuvres have been crowned with the same victory; whether the arms of the combatants were the pike and shield of the Hellenic phalanx, the sword and buckler of the Roman legion, the bows and bills of the English foot, the lance and battle-axe of the Norman chivalry resistless in the thundering charge of their barbed horse, or the death-dealing musketry and ordnance, almost annihilating distance, of the men of the nineteenth century.

For the rest, we must believe that, in despite of all the efforts of peace societies and peace lecturers, wars will continue so long as the human race shall endure; and we know, that—inasmuch as war and its attendant circumstances, while they display humanity in many of its worst and most repulsive lights, at the same time call forth many of its noblest and grandest characteristics; give occasions for its most heroic efforts both of doing and suffering; and present its most touching sacrifices, its most admirable exemplars—the history and the romance of warfare will never grow dull to the ear, or dead to the heart of auditors, who must from the very nature of their constitutions glow with admiration and thrill with sympathy for the glorious and the good; must exult at the virtues and triumph at the victories, as they must mourn over the weaknesses and weep at the downfall, of the virtuous and the valiant of humanity; for though triumph and defeat are but things of the hour, and the man but the sport of the moment, still the pains and the passions of the heart are immortal, and its sympathies with the noble, and its hatred of the base, the same, yesterday and to-day and to-morrow and forever.

And now, without further apology or preamble, coming at once to the armature and array of the Greeks, we shall find that from the earliest period of recorded historic warfare, the mode of arming and arraying the masses was identical, or nearly so, with all the Hellenic tribes or nations. These, although using different dialects, affecting different customs and forms of polity, often at war with each other, and claiming various descents from divers demigods, were still of common origin and language, and in truth, howsoever subdivided, still constituted one homogeneous population, actuated for the most part by a common spirit of independence and liberty, of dislike to personal and hereditary dominion; imbued with a common love of arms and admiration of heroism and individual prowess and adventure, and capable at times of great common efforts against a common enemy. That this love of arms and adventure, at a later period of Grecian history, led to *condottierism*, and the formation of mercenary bands of Greek adventurers, serving under almost every banner in the known world, must not be ascribed to any defect in the Greek character, or want of patriotism in individuals, but to the subdivision of the whole country into numerous small hostile communities; and to the multiplication of political offences, in their turbulent and fierce democracies or persecuting oligarchies, which rendered the expatriation of the best statesmen and bravest leaders rather the rule than the exception, and annually cast out hundreds of valiant and adventurous soldiers on the world with no other resource than the employment of their swords in foreign service. Indeed it is greatly to the credit of the Greek mercenaries, or political exiles, for the terms are nearly synonymous, that they rarely if ever were induced to bear arms against their native states, or to serve the barbarian, who was their usual employer, against the Grecian name.

A similar state of things in the later Italian Republics of the middle ages led to a similar growth and diffusion of mercenary Italian forces serving under every standard, and with far less of honorable scruples than their Hellenic prototypes; since they rarely hesitated to lead or follow either against Italy in general or their own states in particular, and that even in behalf of the Turk or the Algerine.

That examples of common efforts of combined Hellenic states against homogeneous foreign enemies are less frequent, must be ascribed to the sectional and individual jealousies, ambitions, and divided interests which will arise between petty independent states, united by no common league or constitution, and existing under every different shade of government, from the wildest pantisocracy, through the intermediate forms of representative federacy, to the closest oligarchical corporation, as of Lacedæmon; and to autocratic monarchy, as of Sicily and Macedon. What would be the consequence of such a state of things, one may conjecture, by imagining the United States, as connected by no constitutional bonds, and linked together by no prevailing tie of general republicanism; but each several state self-governed as it might be, one with the limited monarchy and powerful aristocracy of England, another with the autocracy and serfdom of Russia; a third with the imbecile legitimacy of Spain or Naples; a fourth with the insane and visionary socialism of France; a fifth under the existing system of New York or Massachusetts—then throw in, apart from sectional interests and monetary jealousies, jarring national religions, conflicting social prejudices and distinctions, and the absence of one general national language; and it would soon appear how difficult of creation, and how short of duration, would be any alliance for common purposes, of states or nations having in truth no common cause. It is probable that nothing short of the invasion of foreign hosts bent on the general extermination or subjugation of the race could unite such nations even for a time, and that the defeat of those hosts would be the disruption of the union.

To the Athenian Attica was Greece, as to the Laconian Sparta, or to the Bœotian Thebes; and it was only when in reference to the Barbarian, meaning almost invariably the Persian king, that Hellas was considered as a whole, even by the purest of the Hellenes. In latter days even the imminence of Roman conquest could not subsist national combination; and the Achaian league was dissolved through intestine divisions, before the stranger had become the master of their fortunes and their land; for it must be remembered that the Roman came not as an exterminator to abolish, but rather as a colonist to adopt, the arts, the literature, nay but the very Gods, of Greece. Themselves half of a kindred race they differed less from many of the Greeks, than did the Greeks from one another, and therefore terror of their arms could lead to no strenuous or durable federation.

Still, although in a national sense there never was any such actual or acknowledged existence as Greece, there was a most distinct and real existence in the shape of Greek strategy, which word I now use in its broadest sense as embracing the whole theory and practice of the art military, from the smallest detail of individual armature and discipline, to the largest combination of men and measures. For throughout all the states of Greece, though this or that might excel in one or another arm of the service, the system was identical, and the force of the Greeks—τὸ ἑλληνικὸν—an unity.

The force and system we first find described, in its rude and unimproved form, before the invention of the trumpet or any other martial music, and previous to the use of mounted cavalry in warfare, in the Iliad, as operating against Ilion, or Troy, a city of Asia Minor, apparently of Grecian origin. Without entering at all into the question of the truth or fallacy of the myth of Troy divine, or arguing on the probability or improbability of such a confederation of kings as Homer describes, it is desirable to point out that the personal equipment of the Greek warrior of the Iliad differs but slightly from that of the *Hoplites*, or heavy-armed foot-soldiers of the authentic historical period; and that—although the maintenance of the battle, and the ultimate successes are invariably attributed to the individual prowess of the hero kings who fought, before the battles, hurling their spears, javelin-like, from two-horse chariots, or leaping down to engage in single combat with antagonists of equal rank and daring—the peculiar serried order of the Greek phalanx even then prevailed; and that the determination of the fight, when came the tug of war, was owing to the sturdy charge of the ponderous infantry, and to the push of the formidable pike.

The following lines, which are a very literal rendering of one of Homer's most spirited battles, would, with the substitution of true historic names, furnish as accurate a picture of the Macedonian army at "that dishonest fight of Chaironeia fatal to liberty," or of the deep Bæotian column that broke sheer through the Spartan centre at Mantineia, as of any fabulous encounter before the fated walls of Ilion the divine.

"Thus speaking the earth-shaker lent the Achaians better cheer,
And made the bands to rally, that were scattered far and near.
About the two Ajaces right steady with the spear;

That neither mighty Mars could blame their order, as they stood,
Nor Pallas queen of hosts. For all, that gallant were and good,
Stood steadfastly the Trojan shock and Hector's might divine.
Spear clashed with spear, and shield with shield, in stiff and stubborn line;
Targe beat on targe, rang helm with helm, met hero hero then,
And nodding crests right rankly pressed above the press of men.
So closely were the hosts arrayed with lances brandished high,
By gallant hands, by noble hearts, that each would each outvie
Right forward charging manfully. But first with onset dread
The Trojans charged the serried mass, great Hector at their head.
E'en as a block of massy stone leaps down, with reeling crash,
When wintry floods have mined its base, and rains with ceaseless plash
Its earthfast hold have loosened on the mountain's summit hoar.
Down thunders it; the tortured woods resound its mighty roar;
But unsubdued, with speed renewed, from each succeeding steep
Into the plain it rolls amain, and there forgets to leap.
Thus Hector, who so lately swore, with high and haughty boast,
Into the sea victoriously to drive the Achaian host,
Thus far drave furiously; but now was stopped in mid career,
Where that great band, so firmly manned, stood fast with shield and spear.
For sturdily with sword and pike the Achaians smote and slew,
And bore him back in his bloody track for all that he could do."

Thus it would appear that, from the first, the main trust of the Greek armies was in the heavy infantry clad in complete panoply, armed as the principal instrument of offence with the long pike, the sarissa of the Macedonians, by whose warlike kings the phalanx was undoubtedly carried to its perfection; and depending on the single steady and sustained charge of the deep solid column, which, in most cases, especially on smooth and level ground, carried all before it. At first this phalanx was probably little more than a dense body of soldiers, with a tolerably regular front, and a depth varying according to circumstances, the best and bravest men voluntarily pressing to the van, leaving the weaker and lower spirited to form the mass behind, lending the impetus of their forward pressure to the advance, and opposing the vis inertiæ of their dead weight to the retrogression of the front. In after ages it had its regular divisions and subdivisions, with duly constituted numbers of rank and file, and officers with their appointed places on the march and in action, and orderly appropriate manœuvres, by the tact and timing of which the action was very often decided. In all ages, however, from the times of the Homeric myth to the defeat of Perseus at Cynocephalœ, the individual dress and equipment of the men was nearly identical.

This dress, or uniform, consisted, at the period of which Xenophon writes, when the Greek army was in its most perfect and elaborate efficiency, both as regards armature and tactics, of a chiton, or shirt of woollen stuff without sleeves, and reaching barely to the knee. This was invariably of a bright crimson color, and the writer, whom I have last named, frequently alludes to the splendor of its contrast with the helmets, breastplates, and greaves of polished bronze in strong and vivid language; for he states, in one place, of the army of Agesilaus that "it appeared all bronze and scarlet;" and in another passage, speaking of the ten thousand, whose retreat he himself conducted with such admirable skill, he says that, "when they all wore casques of bronze and blood-red chitons, with brightly burnished greaves and shields, the whole plain bloomed with crimson, and lightened with bronze." The shield, which was the peculiar and characteristic arm of the Greek hoplites, as was the oblong buckler that of the Roman legionary, was, like the casque, of bronze, ponderous and unwieldy, of a perfectly circular form, with a boss in the centre, covering the whole body of the soldier, from above the shoulder to below the knee, and was certainly not less than three and a half or four feet in diameter. Indeed, so great was the incumbrance of this great piece of defensive armor, that every heavy-armed soldier was allowed a servant to carry it on the march, and take care of it when not in action; who, when the army was engaged, served either with the baggage-guard, or as a skirmisher. The technical name of this shield was *Aspis;* and by the number of these the effective force of the heavy Greek foot present under arms, was estimated, the men being reckoned by shields, as in modern warfare by bayonets and sabres. In addition to this, which was, however, his principal defence, the Greek soldier wore a breast-plate, or cuirass, likewise of bronze, reaching to the hips, sometimes above a buff coat, *stolas;* and greaves of the same metal, protecting the forepart of his legs, from the instep to a short distance above the knee. His offensive weapons were the formidable pike, or Macedonian Sarissa, which was twenty feet in length, and when levelled to the charge, projected fourteen feet in front of the line; so that, when the phalanx was engaged, the spear points of the five foremost ranks, at least, were directly serviceable, and were actually opposed to every front-rank man of the enemy. Besides the pike, he also carried a short stabbing sword, scarcely superior in length to a large knife or dagger, a most ineffective weapon; and perhaps left as such, not unintentionally; since upon reliance on the pike, and on the tactic consequent on its use, the whole efficiency of the phalanx depended; if it should once disclose its serried order, it was necessarily at the mercy of any assailant, and the hand to hand single-combat fighting of the Romans was as abhorrent to its system, as it was congenial to that of the legion. The order of the phalanx was invariably a close column varying in depth from twelve to fifty men, according to the nature of the ground and pleasure of the leader. Its smallest subdivision of men was the Enomoty, or as the name implies, *sworn-band*, which seems to have consisted originally and properly of twenty-four men beside the enomotarck, or leader of the band; yet Thucydides states distinctly that, in the first battle of Mantineia, fought between the Lacedæmonians and Argives, the enomoty* of the former was drawn up four front and eight deep, making it contain thirty-two men beside the leader, instead of twenty-four; while we have the authority of Xenophon† that at the battle of Leuctra the Spartan enomoty of Cleombrotus fought in three files which he says gave them a depth of twelve, while the Theban files opposed to them contained not less than fifty shields. From this it is obvious that the number of men in the enomoty, as indeed the number of enomoties in the next larger division, was variable; though from the name of this division, which was *pentecostys*, signifying a company of fifty men, led by a pentecoster or captain of fifty, we arrive at the regularly estimated number of men in the original enomoty; two of which formed a pentecostys, two of these again forming a lochus, and four of the latter a mora, or division. So that the mora with its polemarch or general, and all its subordinate officers must, as originally constituted, have consisted of 429 men of all ranks. The number of men, however, in the divisions is unimportant, unless where it is desirable to calculate the numerical force of antagonistic armies; for the modes of manœuvring and fighting are all clearly laid down and comprehensible enough, apart from the consideration of numbers, although I should be inclined to set down sixteen ranks as the ordinary depth of the latter, or Macedonian, phalanx.

It must not be, however, by any means supposed that, because the main dependence of the Greek armies was placed in the phalanx of their heavy infantry, they lacked the other arms of service. Light infantry, or skirmishers, and horse in a smaller proportion, but of excellent quality, they seem to have possessed from an early period; and after the peace of Antalcidas,‡ Iphicrates introduced a new species of force, intermediate between

* Thucydides, 416, IV. c. 68.

† Xenophon Hellenics, Lib. VI. c. 4. Xen. Rep. Lac. XI. 4

‡ Olymp. 98. II. BC. 387. Polybius 16. Diodorus XV. 51.

the heavy foot and mere skirmishers, which afterward became of very great importance under the name of *Peltastæ*, which is well rendered as Targeteers. The arms of this new force, which appears never to have been composed of citizens of any of the elder Greek republics, but of Thessalians, Œtolians, Acarnanians, Epirots, and perhaps at first of barbarian prisoners and manumitted slaves,* wore a brazen casque, and a target, *Pelta*, usually of a crescent or semilunar shape, much smaller and lighter than the great shield of the *Hoplites*, together with a quilted linen jacket instead of the bronze cuirass. The offensive weapons† of the targeteer, as improved by Iphicrates, were a sword double the length of that of the heavy foot and adapted for cutting as well as stabbing, together with a spear lengthened nearly in the same proportion. On this latter point all the authorities agree, but it is evident to me, as the targeteers are generally described as javelineers and not pikemen, that the spear alluded to must have been the *akontion* or light dart of the skirmishers, and not the *sarissa* of the phalanx, which being already twenty feet‡ long and stout in proportion could not have been used in its existing state as a missile, and if increased to forty feet must have been utterly unmanageable. We shall hear much of these targeteers in Xenophon's masterly retreat, and in the fine battles of Pyrrhus and Epaminondas.

The light-armed troops were variously equipped as archers, slingers, and javelineers, wearing merely a helmet and light shield; but as the continental Greeks never excelled either in archery or the use of the sling, and as the javelin which was their usual weapon was at best a very inferior missile, as deficient both in range and certainty, they were soon found to be so much inferior to the oriental skirmishers, that they appear to have been discarded so soon as warfare became a science, and armies were

* Xen. Anab. IV. 8. † Diodorus XV. 44. ‡ Some say twenty-four.

composed of regulars, and no longer of mere armed levies of citizens. After this period, we find Rhodian slingers, Cretan and even Scythian bowmen, and horse-archery from Thrace, employed in the Greek armies, as were the natives of the Balearic Isles, and the Numidians in those of Carthage.

The face of the country throughout Greece proper, especially the Peloponnesus and Attica, being of an exceedingly rough and craggy if not mountainous character, was of course very ill adapted for equestrian exercise or for the use of cavalry; and we find, of consequence, that, although horsemanship was much encouraged, and a valuable breed of animals maintained at a great expense, particularly for the Olympic contests, the cavalry of the original Greek cities was weak in numbers; and that of Sparta in particular singularly inefficient. The Thebans were the first power which attained to any great proficiency in this arm of the service, in consequence of their finding the want of it in their wars with their neighbors, the people of Orchomenos and Thespis; but afterward as the more northern nations of Greece gradually rose in the scale of ascendency, and the plains of Thessaly, Thrace, and Macedonia began to furnish their contingents, the cavalry became a favorite arm, the rather that it was much called for in the contests with the kings of Persia, which were now transferred from the broken country, hills and defiles, of Greece to the vast open plains and champaigns, swarming with admirable native horse, on the banks of the Euphrates, the Tigris and the Indus. On the proper armament and service of the horse we have a very fine and elaborate treatise from the pen of Xenophon the Athenian, by which we learn that the Greek cavalry were the most completely equipped with defensive armor of any branch of the service. The men wore, above a coat of buff, a heavy cuirass of bronze, fitted above with a sort of rim or frill of the same metal, which was at once, according to the author,* an ornament, and a

* Xenophon de re equestri XIII—Anabasis III. 3.

perfect protection to the neck and face of the rider so far as to the nose. It must have resembled, in a considerable degree, that singular piece of defensive armor known in the reign of Edward IV. of England as the volant piece, which may be seen to this day in the suit attributed to that prince in the Horse-armory of the Tower of London. The head of the rider was protected by a Bœotian casque, covering the whole face down to the tips of the ears and the nostrils, but leaving apertures by which to see and breathe without difficulty. On the left arm was worn no shield, but a complicated piece of armor, known by a word answering to our gauntlet, but in reality corresponding to the whole defence of the arm as worn by a knight of the fourteenth century; for it is said to have protected the shoulder, the elbow, the forearm, and the hand while grasping the reins, as well as the armpit, which was justly regarded as one of the most vital parts, and the most exposed in a horseman. As the right arm must frequently be raised whether in the act of striking, or of casting the spear, it was necessary that the corslet should be cut away above and below in order to give full sway to the muscles, and the defence was therefore made good by side-plates hinged on to the breastplate so as to give and return again with every motion of the wearer, the fore arm being guarded by plates of metal strapped upon the limb, but not attached to the panoply. The loins, flanks and abdomen were in like manner protected by jointed plates accommodating themselves to the movement of the body, the thighs by cuishes, and the feet and shins by boots of heavy leather. The horses moreover were fully caparisoned with frontlets on the head, poitrels on the chest, and bardings protecting the loins, croupe, and thighs; so that in fact the Greek cavalry were completely harnessed cuirassiers, as fully accoutred as the steel-clad chivalry of the middle ages, and as impenetrable to the weapons of ordinary assailants.

The offensive instruments of these ponderous cavaliers were

two spears of cornel wood, or wild cherry, which was esteemed the best adapted to that purpose by the ancients, and is especially recommended as superior to all others and especially to the reed, which was generally used for lance shafts, by the writer so often named above. One of these spears was to be hurled at the enemy while advancing, in order to check his onset and disarrange his charging line; the other was to be couched, as the knightly lance, and charged in close encounter. Besides this a sabre, or cutting sword, of Greek manufacture, and probably of a crooked form, was carried in lieu of the short stabbing blade carried by the infantry, which was from its very form inefficient for mounted men.

Of artillery for the casting of darts of vast size, sometimes wrapped with tow and kindled with Greek fire, and for hurling stones, whether into the walls of beleaguered cities, or from the walls into the lines of the besiegers, the Hellenic nations had long been in possession; but it was not until above a century after the death of Alexander the Great, that any thing like the use of artillery is mentioned as opposed to movable bodies of men in the field;* when Machanidas the tyrant of the Lacedæmonians endeavored to break the order of Philopœmen's Achaian phalanx by discharges of heavy missiles.

Having now described the armature of a whole Greek army, in its several arms of service, I shall proceed briefly to point out what was its ordinary mode, what the defects, and what the advantages of its array; and how it is that, invariably victorious as opposed to the orientals, even when overmatched in the ratio of ten to one, the whole system was found utterly defective when opposed to an enemy equally brave and strong, but using a different tactic.

The phalanx, being the nucleus of every Hellenic force, and the key of its tactic, was generally thus manœuvred. Drawn up in

* Polybius, XI., Frag. III. XI. 3. XII. 4.

files varying from eight to fifty shields in depth, the average and usual mode being sixteen, with the best man, and officer of the smallest subdivision, in front as file leader, and a good veteran as rear rank man, it formed a great oblong column, serried so closely, when in battle order, that the shields of the men touched. Accord ing to its numbers it was formed in one or more sections ; but, if the full force of a Macedonian phalanx was in the field, sixteen thousand strong, it usually formed three divisions, one in the centre of eight thousand, and one on either hand of four thousand, with intervals between for the convenience of manœuvring.

The skirmishers were thrown forward in front, at first; but as their weapons were exhausted and the enemy drove them in, they fell back as best they might, either by the flanks, or by the intervals between the sections of the phalanx, where and in the rear they rallied, until they should be wanted to pursue and cut up a defeated and flying enemy. The cavalry was always on the flanks, and it was with this arm usually that the action commenced.

Then came the formidable charge of the phalanx, not rapid or dashing, but steady, solid, and, as long as it kept its order and was assailed in front only, almost irresistible. Against the weaker orientals, as in the battles of Marathon,* Platæa,† Mycale,‡ Cynaxa,§ and the victories of Alexander, it was clearly demonstrated, that the shock of the Macedonian Sarissa was surely and necessarily victorious, since the weaker frame and feebler *morale* of the Asiatic was never able to encounter the European hand to hand with a chance of success, nor was the rush of that solid body less formidable, so long as its flanks were protected, to any troops armed only with short weapons or missiles; as the Romans found to their cost in their first battles with Pyrrhus the Epirot at the fords of the Siris,‖ and again on the field of Ascu-

* Herod. VI. 109. † Herod. IX. 102. ‡ Herod. IX. 62. 63

§ Xenoph. Anab. I. 8. 18. ‖ Plutarch. Vit. Pyrrhi, XVI.

lum,* in both of which encounters, long and desperately contested as they were by Roman valor, the hedge of spears presented by the phalanx could be no more hewed down by the swords of the legionaries, than they could be wrested at Platæa from the hands of the Hoplites by the naked grasp of the Persian infantry. "When Greek met Greek, then came the tug of war," and then so often as phalanx charged phalanx, front to front, accident or individual prowess decided the strife, if it were decided; and this unquestionably led to the improvements in tactics, and the strategetical inventions, for which the Hellenic leaders soon became famous. For finding that direct onslaughts were of little avail, on bodies nearly equal in physical force, and physical courage, and exactly equal in arms and organization, they early had recourse to flank attacks, oblique movements, and withdrawals of one or the other wing, long before any form of battle was thought of by the Italian captains, beyond that of setting their armies face to face with the foe, and then fighting it out to the last manfully.

These then, which have been thus slightly touched upon, were the advantages of the Greek formation and tactic; the force of their charge directly forward, like that of a bull, or, to which Xenophon likens Epaminondas' onset at Mantinea, of a galley under full headway, was hard to resist, if not irresistible. But once their flanks uncovered by the defeat of their horse, the absence of their skirmishers, the accidents of the ground, or the like, the whole mass was vulnerable to the very heart; and if once disordered the length and unwieldiness of their weapon, and the desuetude of the men to any thing like single combat rendered them an easy prey to any active and movable assailant. They were moreover the most inert and immovable column that can be conceived; for their system of manœuvring entirely on the single file, so as to bring the same file-leader

* Plutarch. Ibid. XXI.

always in the front of the battle, and the same rear rank man always in the rear, compelled every moment to be performed by a countermarching of all the files; so that if the phalanx were surprised or menaced with a sudden attack on the rear or either flank, instead of simply facing the men right, left, or about, as the necessity of the case might indicate, it was necessary to countermarch every file down the interval between itself and its next neighboring file, including the expansion of the front to nearly or quite double its original extent, in order to allow space for the passage of the men, and the corresponding contraction, so soon as the front rank should have reached the rear, and so have inverted their order of battle—a slow and perilous manœuvre to execute under the eyes of a vigilant and active enemy, eager to strike a blow and knowing where to plant it.

This was its grand and sovereign defect, and consequently we find that, when the phalanx was once formed to act in any one direction, any movement of the enemy, compelling a rapid change of disposition, while in action, was almost necessarily victorious. Such was the result of the masterly movement of Epaninondas at Leuctra,* when by the withdrawal of his own left wing, he induced the Lacedæmonians to extend their right, and charging their centre while in confusion, first with the sacred band of Pelopidas, and then with the force of his own right wing, fifty shields in file, cut them in two and annihilated them with such slaughter as had never before fallen upon a Spartan army. Such again was the oblique charge upon the centre of Agesilaus, by the same great captain, at Mantineia†; by which in like manner he broke through the whole Spartan phalanx, and would have unquestionably slaughtered them as at Leuctra, had he not himself fallen in the arms of victory, leaving no officer in his army of sufficient ability to finish the work which he had so gloriously commenced.

* Diod. XV. 55 Xen. Hell. VI. 4. † Diod. XV. 86. Xen. Hell. VII. 5.

Of the like nature again was the victory by Flaminius over the Macedonian phalanx of Philip at Cynoscephalæ;* where the Macedonian king, having beaten the Roman left with his own right on the level ground, and finding his own left somewhat shaken by the broken surface of the knolls among which it was engaged, endeavored to double the depth of his files while actively engaged with the legionaries in front; and thus disordered them so much that the Romans broke up their front, and getting within the points of their long pikes slaughtered them at pleasure with their stout stabbing swords. Again, at the final overthrow of the Greek power under Perseus by the legions of Æmilius Paulus† at Pydna, the battle was all but won by the charge of the phalanx, whose spears, locked in the shields of the hastati and principes of the Romans, bristled like an unbroken row of palisades, keeping an even front, and bearing down all before them; when a happy inspiration, or instinct, suggested to the consul the idea of withdrawing his alternate maniples and charging home with his reserves at different intervals, so as to render the pressure on the great column irregular and uneven. The consequence was as sudden as the idea; the even front of Macedonian pikes was bent into a sinuous line, the unopposed portions of the phalanx pressing forward into the intervals between the maniples, while the ranks which were attacked, either retrograded, or, at best, were held stationary; so that the Roman swordsmen found gaps, and exposed flanks, into which they broke with their short weapons, and decided the fate of Greece at a blow, when scarce an hour before their leader held himself already half defeated.

This then was the great and principal objection to the Greek Tactic; and this was the principal cause of its defeat, so soon as they came in contact with men neither personally braver, nor physically stronger than themselves, but differently armed, and more effectively arrayed. There was, however, another defect inherent

* Plut. Flamin. VIII. † Plut. Æmil. c. XX.

to the very nature and composition of this force; and this was its incapacity to cover its own retreat, or do any thing for its own defence if once broken; and its equal and similar incapacity to destroy, or even follow up with any adequate or close pursuit, a disordered and flying enemy.

According to the composition of Greek armies, in which the heavy armed foot consisted of the flower of the middle classes, while the light troops were of the lowest order of citizens, too poor to be able to arm themselves efficiently, and serving in some sort as the varlets or servants of the *Hoplites*—in the Spartan armies, being Helots, they were literally their slaves—very little dependence could be placed on the *Gymnetes*, as they were termed from their want of defensive armor, in case of the ranks being once broken; nor were they likely to risk themselves very far from the support of their solid columns in pursuing an enemy, especially if there were any likelihood of his rallying to resist. The cavalry were again such mere handfuls of men that no real or efficient service could be expected of them.

It is mentioned that the victory of Marathon* was admired of all men, and regarded as especially wonderful and distinguished, from the fact that the Athenians, without either horse or archery, should have charged, routed, and destroyed a host so greatly superior to themselves in numbers as the Persian army, and that they should have driven the fugitives quite to the ships and captured some of these also. This I think, however, proves little or nothing, more than that the distance was short; the Medes and Persians, accustomed to conquer the inferior races of barbarians, were utterly astounded by the fierce Greek onset; while the king's army, from some unknown reason, made no use of the cavalry in which arm it was so superior.

What is much more to the point is the opinion of Xenophon himself, as given at the council of war subsequent to the death

* Herod. VI. 109, 116.

of Cyrus, and the commencement of the retreat of the ten thousand, with regard to the inefficiency of the unsupported phalanx.

On the evening of the first day of their retreat, when being hard beset by the Persian Archery, Xenophon had charged and pursued the enemy with the Hoplites and targeteers of the rear guard, at some risk of being cut off from the main body, Cheirisophus and some of the elder leaders blamed Xenophon for incurring such risk, to whom that leader, frankly admitting his error, and acknowledging the danger he had run, gave the following statement as his defence, and as cause for different future arrangements. "As it now is, the enemy outshoot and outsling us so far that the Cretan archers and our javelineers cannot reach them. But in case we pursue, it is not safe to do so, to any distance from the supporting columns; and in a short distance even swift footmen cannot overtake footmen with a bowshot start. If, therefore, we would prevent their harassing attacks, we must fit ourselves immediately with cavalry and slingers; and, in fact, I understand that we have in our army Rhodian slingers who can send their shot to twice the distance of the Persians, since the latter cast stones large enough to fill the hand from their slings, while the Rhodians use leaden bullets, the range of which is infinitely greater."*

In consequence of this recommendation, it appears that measures were taken, and light troops created, by whom the Persian skirmishers were ultimately defeated and kept at a distance; so that the leaders were at length relieved from the apprehension, which they had at first with so much reason entertained; namely that, "since they were now left to themselves without either horse or allies, they must evidently be cut off to the last man if worsted in action; while, if victorious, it was impossible for them to do execution on the routed enemy."†

* Xenoph. Anab. III. 4. 13. † Ibid. Lib. III. 11.

Such and so great were the errors and defects of that system, which, in spite of all, produced effects so permanent and important, when directed by such heads and hearts as those of Miltiades, Epaminondas, Philip, Alexander the Great, and last, not least, Pyrrhus the Epirot; and which was destined only to be overthrown, and proved useless, when brought into contact with the improved Roman strategy; which is that shown by all experience, up to the present day, to be founded on the true scientific principle, and whenever put into practice under like circumstances of equality between the opposing masses, to be certain of success.

The principle is this, that whenever great solid columns with long vulnerable flanks, are launched against troops in line, the column must necessarily be enveloped, overlapped by the converging wings of the enemy; overwhelmed with missiles to which they can make no reply, whether the missiles be javelins, arrows, and bullets from the Rhodian and Balearic sling, or musketry and grape, rockets and shells and shrapnels, and all the terrible devices of modern European warfare; and finally ravaged and torn asunder by the hand-to-hand encounter with short weapons, and trampled underfoot by the thundering charge of the exterminating horse.

Such has been ever, and such will be ever, the final fate of every army which ventures to rush, blind and headlong as the charging bison, in close and solid column into the centre of lines which do not lack the courage to receive, and the obstinate steadiness to sustain, the impetus of its first onset. With effeminate dastards, or unskilled barbarians, the method may succeed; but when men are met by men, in any degree their equals, it must be fatal to the assailants.

All nations, in all ages, have at some time or other attempted this form of strategy; all have at some time or other, it is probable, succeeded with it; all when matched by their equals in determination have succumbed, through no want of valor, but through the viciousness of the very principle itself.

That the Greeks so long succeeded with it, is owing to the fact that they were opposed always, either to effeminate orientals who could not endure their steady charge, nor face the triumphant pœans and the clash and clang of the spearpoints on the brazen shields, which formed the prelude to their formidable onset; or to their own countrymen, who met them with equal arms and the same manœuvres, and left it, therefore, to valor, or the devices of individual genius, to decide the fate of battles.

The Romans charged in column at Cannæ into the centre of the Carthaginian lines, bore all before them for a while, and were annihilated by the convergence of the lines—the same fate had previously befallen the Epirot Pyrrhus at Beneventum, though his charge had been previously checked by his own elephants, which, maddened by the missiles of the enemy, rushed into his own lines scattering dismay and death. Similar were the routes of Philip at Cynoscephalæ, and of Perseus at Pydna, by enemies to whom the phalanx had at first seemed so terrible.

Precisely similar the route of the confederate peers by Philip-Augustus at Bovines; of the French chivalry at Cressy and Poitiers; and in more modern days, and with weapons and warfare far different, precisely similar the discomfiture of the great English square at Fontenoy, of the invincible column of Lannes at Aspern, and, last and most memorable of all, of Napoleon's young guard at Waterloo.

And now we arrive in due course at the formation, armature, and tactic of the Roman legion, which succeeding to and prevailing over the columnar tactic of the phalanx, conquered in point of fact the whole ancient world, and so long as Romans continued to be Romans was never excelled or equalled by infantry. As the Western empire gradually decayed, and the manners of the Eastern became more and more orientalized, mercenary troops supplied the place of the indomitable Romans, and cavalry became in consequence the great arm of the service, and the great engine of mediæval warfare; and so indeed, until the invention of gunpowder, and its first thoroughly victorious application, on the field of Pavia, when the gallant Francis lost to his imperial rival "all save honor," it continued to be. Nor can it be said that, between the extinction of the Roman legionary tactic and the commencement of the modern strategy with musketry and ordnance, with the exception of the Swiss confederates at Granson, Nanci, and Morat, victorious over the mailclad lancers of Burgundy, and the English bills and bows fatal to France's noble chivalry at Cressy and Poictiers and Agincourt, there was anything worthy of the name of infantry in Europe, or anything that could pretend to brook the levelled lances and barded destriers of the feudal cavalry.

With these, however, we have at present nothing to do, beyond the passing remark, that as a general rule the tactic of these bodies, the Swiss halberdiers and English bill-men, was akin to that of the Romans, as using short against long weapons, and affecting the formation of long ranks with shallow files, as opposed to columns of comparatively small front compensated by depth giving weight and impetus to the forward onset.

To resume, however, it would appear that the constitution of the ancient and original Roman legion, as regulated, it is said, by Servius Tullius, was framed in accordance to the means of the citizens who composed the various classes, from which the forces of the year were raised. The wealthier and better armed, for the terms were synonymous, forming the heavy armed infantry, fighting in the front and bearing the brunt of battle, the poorer and more feebly equipped bringing up the rear, and those who possessed nothing skirmishing in front with light and slender javelins until the shock of real war began, and then retreating by the flanks to rally in the rear of the battalia.

At this period, it is on many accounts evident that the early Roman battle, so long as the Servian constitution was in existence, coincided with that of the Greeks; that their formation was the column, the better armed burghers in the front, and the lighter and feebler, down to the naked supernumeraries, intended to assume the arms and fill the places of the fallen, holding themselves aloof from the shock of spears, and adding only the impetus of their dead weight in the rear to the force of the attack. At this time also the arms of the Hastati and Principes were the round shield, the long pike, and short stabbing sword, and their order of fighting, as is expressly stated by Livy, that of the Macedonian phalanx, while those of the second class, answering to the triarii, were the oblong shield, the heavy javelin, and larger sword: and at this period the front ranks of the legion were known as antepilani, or ranks before the javelineers.

The formation of the legion under the Servian constitution, which seems to have prevailed until nearly the termination of the Latin wars, was of this nature. All those citizens who possessed a capital of one hundred thousand asses, or pounds, of brass money and upward, formed the first class, divided into eighty centuries, forty of young, forty of elder men, who were appointed to bear as their arms defensive, the helmet, circular shield, greaves and breastplate, all of bronze, and as weapons the pike and sword. These two divisions of the first class corresponding to the divisions known later as the hastati and principes. To this class were added two centuries of mechanics, who bore no arms, but served at working the military engines. The second class consisted of those citizens possessing above seventy-five, and below a hundred, thousand asses, and they bore helmet and greaves without breastplate, the square buckler instead of the shield, the spear and sword. The third class rating at fifty thousand and upward were armed as the last, with the exception of the greaves which in their case were laid aside. The fourth, who were held at five and twenty thousand, wore no defensive armor and carried only a pike and javelin, acting as mere skirmishers; together with the fifth class of proletarians, who were destitute of property, subsisted by their own labor, and fought merely with slings and stones, hovering on the outskirts of the action and never coming up to the close encounter. To these were added a cavalry composed of six centuries of equites, a sort of half nobility, to whom horses were provided at the public expense; and this was the composition of the original Roman army, and in many points, even to the last when the arms of the classes and mode of fighting were altered, the foundation of the later system.

It is remarkable enough that, although we have Livy's express declaration that the original tactic of the Romans was the Macedonian phalanx, which is moreover self-evident from the nature of the weapons which they carried, and from the regular declension in the quality of their offensive arms in proportion as the ranks were farther removed from the front of battle, still all the actions which he has described so vividly and with such minute particulars, ascribe to the legions from the first the tactic of the manipule and the use of the sword and buckler. This discrepancy, however, only goes to show the imaginative character of the writer and his carelessness in adherence to facts, which he admitted, when not carried away by the enthusiasm and glow of composition.

It is, however, more singular that it is nowhere distinctly stated at what time the change of armature and tactic was adopted, nor why, nor from whom it was borrowed. Livy,* indeed, states generally, that the "Romans formerly used round shields, *clypei*, but that after they received regular pay, or became stipendiaries, they adopted oblong bucklers, *scuta*, in the place of shields"—and Sallust in his conspiracy of Catiline makes Julius Cæsar declare† that the Romans "borrowed their arms

* Liv. VIII. 8.

† Sallust, Catil. 51.

offensive and defensive of the Samnites, the insignia of their magistracies from the Tuscans"—and farther the account given by Livy of the splendid armor and weapons of the Samnite host, which was defeated by the Dictator Papirius Cursor beyond the Ciminian hills, corresponds very closely with what we know from contemporaneous authorities to have been the armature of the later legion. "There were two bands,"* says he, "the bucklers of the one were embossed with silver; the other with gold. The form was that of the buckler, *scutum*. But it was broader at the top, where the breast and shoulders were to be protected, with the top line level, or even, and wedge fashioned below, for the advantage which that form gave in handiness." It must have been fashioned therefore much like the heart-shaped, or as it is technically called *heater-shaped* shield, which was suspended round the necks of the knights and men-at-arms of the middle ages." "Their breasts were protected by sponge, and their left leg by a greave. Their casques were high-crested, which added to the appearance of the soldiers' stature." All that follows this lively picture shows that both armies fought in open order, and that a series of single combats with the buckler and stabbing sword prevailed along the whole front of the lines, proving that at this time the troops of the two nations were identical in weaponing and discipline, which of the two borrowed from the other, or whether either, not appearing.

On the contrary, Diodorus asserts, "that the Romans originally had quadrangular bucklers for warfare; but afterward, seeing that the Tyrrhenians made use of round brazen shields, conquered these by adopting the like armature."† In this statement, however, as the first assertion that the quadrangular buckler was laid aside for the round shield is manifestly incorrect, much stress I think need not be laid on the second, in relation to the suggestion being borrowed from the Tuscans. It is, even,

* Liv. IX. 40. † Diod. XXIII. Eclog. 3. 501.

doubtful in my opinion whether there was any direct borrowing in the case from any foreign country. All that we know, for certain, is that at the commencement of the Punic wars, throughout the terrible struggle on Italian soil, which shook Rome to her very foundations, with the unconquerable Hannibal; through the fierce civil wars of Sylla and Marius, Cæsar and Pompey, and that mad Triumvir who "lost a world for a woman," through all the series of years which led to the subjugation of the whole *terra cognita*—the weapons, the order of fighting, the castrametation, the field equipage and the discipline of the later Roman legion, was that which we have accurately and minutely laid down for us by the contemporaneous pen of Polybius, the friend and tent-companion of Lælius and the greater Scipio.

According to my judgment, the alterations and improvements in the art military, adopted by the Romans some time, more or less, previous to the commencement of the first Punic war, and in full practice at the time of the invasion of Pyrrhus, B.C. 280, are far more likely to have originated, as did the similar emendations of the Greek tactic and armature by Iphicrates at an earlier date, B.C. 387, in a perception of the defects of the columnar system of the phalanx, of its unwieldiness, and its liability to disarrangement and destruction by the flank attacks of a lighter and more active enemy. In the same manner we are told almost in the same breath that the Romans learned their method of castrametation from Pyrrhus of Epirus; and again, that, being out with a reconnoitring party on the eve of his first encounter with these very Romans, the same Pyrrhus exclaimed on seeing their encampment, "The tactic,* O Megacles, of these barbarians, is in no wise barbarical, and we shall learn their prowess." Two stories in themselves so discrepant, as, like the celebrated cats of Kilkenny, to annihilate one another nor leave a wreck behind.

But to come at once to the later legion, that I mean which we

* Plut. Vit. Pyr. 26.

find in full operation and efficiency in the fifth century of Rome and the third before the Christian era, we discover that of the legion according to the Servian constitution this much only has survived, namely—that the whole Roman cavalry were composed of a separate and superior order of the state, superior to the mere burghers but inferior to the great Patrician houses, for a portion of whom, at least, chargers and one mounted attendant to each were found at the expense of the republic; and that the heavy armed foot, that is to say the hastati, principes, and triarii, constituting the force of the legions, were levied from the wealthy middle classes, possessing the same original qualification of property, although there was, with one slight exception, no *pro rata* distinction in their armature, and none whatever in their place in the various divisions, which had reference solely to age, the younger men composing the ranks of the hastati, those in the flower of age the principes, while the triarii, who were differently equipped, were formed of the tried and experienced veterans of many wars, on whom it fell, if the day was going adversely, to restore the shaken ranks, and if it hung balanced to decide the victory by their fresh and formidable onset. The young men of the poorer classes were mustered as light-armed troops, not however acting as servants to the heavy foot, which was the practice in the Greek armies, but serving like them as independent citizens and soldiers. These are the men, known among the Romans as *velites*, *rorarii*, or *ferentarii*, names equivalent to the modern voltigeur or skirmisher, and to the Greek writers as *grosphomachi*, or javelineers, from the weapon which they used in action, the bow and sling being both ineffective if not unused by the Latin nations and the Greeks of Italy, although the natives of many neighboring isles were famous for their skill in archery and slinging.

These light-armed* troops wore plain casques on their heads,

* Polybius, Milit. Rom. VI. 22.

covered with wolf skins, or the spoils of other animals, both for defence and distinction, as between their several subdivisions. They had no cuirass or defence for the body or limbs beyond a light buckler, *parma*, of three feet in diameter, made of osier covered with leather. Their weapons were a cutlass, and several javelins, which appear to have been known as the *veru* or spit by the Romans, but which are accurately described as *grosphi* by Polybius. These were darts, the wood of which was about three feet in length by an inch in diameter, with a point of a span in length so tapering and sharp, whence its Latin name of spit, that it would bend and become useless after a single blow; and this was done intentionally, in order to prevent the same weapon from being returned with effect by the enemy.

Their duty was to skirmish in front, and cover the advance or conceal the manœuvres of the legions, until driven in by the approach or sustained resistance of heavier troops, when they fell back upon their supports, and ultimately retreated, through the intervals of the manipules, which have yet to be described, into the rear, whence as occasion offered they continued to annoy the enemy with their missiles. The light troops were divided into small bodies, each attached to a manipule of heavy foot of each of the three divisions, and could either act independently in force, or with the troops with whom they were brigaded and encamped.

The Hastati, Principes, and Triarii, forming the three divisions of heavy foot, wore the full panoply of the day,* consisting in the first place of the buckler, *scutum*, which was quadrangular and rectilinear, two feet and a half in width by four in height, not flat but curved on its shortest edge so as to assimilate to the shape of the body. It was composed of double plank, strongly glued together, lined with linen, covered on the exterior surface with calf-skin, bound with a strong iron verge, as a defence against

* Ibid, VI. 23.

sabre cuts, and provided with a strong iron boss in the centre, to ward off pike-thrusts or the blows of heavy stones. Together with this, and next in importance to it, was worn the short massive, two-edged, sharp-pointed, stabbing sword, the principal and most effective weapon of the legionary; it was hung on the right thigh and was known as the Iberian sword, whether that the blades were of Spanish temper which was then already famous, or that the weapon itself had been borrowed from the Spanish foot, who certainly in Hannibal's army did make use of the same deadly instrument. The legionary also carried two javelins, the well-known and formidable pila, one of which was essentially a javelin, being described as exactly similar to a slight well-balanced boar-spear; the other a ponderous and massive spear which could either be hurled at a short distance, from forty to sixty paces, with tremendous effect, or could be used in hand-to-hand encounter, especially to repel horse, as it was by Cæsar's veterans at Pharsalia with decided advantage against the high-born equites of Pompey's patrician army. The formation of these weapons is so singular as to deserve a more minute notice, as it is not easy to comprehend how instruments so ponderous could be so efficient, as we know that they were, whether cast from the hand or charged as the modern bayonet. The shafts* were of wood, four and a half feet long, and either round or quadrangular in shape, in the former instance having the diameter, in the latter the flat side, of no less than a palm, or three Greek inches, being a fraction more than three of our measure—a thickness which it would not be easy, and certainly very far from convenient, to grasp. These ponderous shafts were again adapted to barbed steel heads of a length equal to themselves, the lower half of which formed a hollow socket into which one half of the shaft was received and fastened with many clasps or bands, so that the weapon could not be rendered useless except by the breaking

* Polyb. VI. 23.

the steel, which was half an inch thick at the point of junction with the wood. The whole weapon was therefore six foot three inches in length, about eighteen of which was a strong triangular steel head. Their farther defensive weapons were an open helmet of bronze, with a projecting peak and cheekpieces, decked with a crest of plumes, and three upright feathers of black or crimson about two feet and a half in height, adding greatly to the splendor and apparent size of the soldier, and a plate of brass about a span in breadth both ways, attached upon the breast and called a heart-defender. Instead of this defence, those who were rated at above ten thousand drachmæ wore shirts of chain-mail, The Triarii, or reserve, who were all chosen veterans, were armed and weaponed exactly as the hastati and principes, except that in lieu of the pila they carried pikes fitted for charging hand-to-hand, although these were not so ponderous but that they could on occasion be hurled as javelins. Indeed, after the account given of the pila, it would be difficult to imagine what should be too ponderous for that purpose.

To complete the Roman force, we must not pass the equites, or cavalry, three hundred of whom were attached to every legion, four of which, two forming a regular consular army, constituted the regular peace establishment, as we may call it, of the Roman republic. The armature of these high-born horsemen, although they often did good service when matched against the similarly armed Latin or Samnite horse, and although they fought with stubborn gallantry when fearfully overmatched by the Greek cuirassiers of Pyrrhus, was ludicrously inefficient; and they proved wholly unable to sustain the shock of the Greek or Carthaginian horse, or even the impetuous onset of the wild Numidians, with their unbridled horses, long lances, and wild desert horsemanship.

They wore casques indeed, of bronze ornate of crest and plumes, but they had neither corslet, thigh-pieces, nor greaves, under the idea that such would impede their agility in leaping on their horses or dismounting. Their shields were of simple ox-hide, with neither boss nor binding; their spears were of brittle reeds, which shivered to the grasp at the first thrust; and their short Iberian swords, the same as those so deadly in the hands of the foot soldier, were as useless in those of the mounted cavalier, who requires, if any one, a long sabre, capable of dealing sweeping blows and doing service with either edge or point, against an enemy without arm's length.

The legionaries being thus armed and thus divided, their array and order of battle were as follows. Of each division, *hastati*, *principes*, and *triarii*, there were ten manipules, consisting each of two centuries under their proper centurions, subordinate again to a tribune, who led the manipule. Of the two first divisions, however, the hastati and principes, each manipule contained one hundred and twenty men, while each of the triarii contained but sixty. Of the skirmishers, an equal proportion was attached man for man to every manipule, forty-eight to each of the hastati and principes, twenty-four to each of the triarii. The legion consisted, therefore, of three thousand heavy armed, and twelve hundred light-armed infantry, with a detachment of three hundred horse belonging to it, the whole under the order of an officer termed legatus in the Roman, præfectus in the allied Latin legions, which were similar in all respects to them except that they had double the number of horse. A regular consular army consisted of two Roman and two allied legions, making an aggregate of sixteen thousand eight hundred foot and eighteen hundred horse. At a subsequent period the rank and file of the legion were increased from four thousand two hundred, to five thousand two hundred, raising the whole force to twenty-two thousand six hundred men. Upon the whole, about twenty thousand men may be generally computed as the effective force of the consular army, though according to circumstances it might exceed or fall short of that complement.

This force, when the day of battle came, was drawn up in three lines of alternate squares; for each manipule in itself, when in battle order, formed a sort of loose square, although the whole of each division was a long line pierced with equal gaps at equal distances.

Each manipule, as I have said, contained one hundred and twenty men, I speak of the two first divisions, and these were drawn up ten deep, consequently with a front of twelve soldiers, to every one of whom a space of five feet was allowed for freedom of play with the sword and buckler, and hurling the heavy pilum. Thus every manipule would occupy a space of sixty feet rank and fifty feet file, and, the intervals between each manipule being equal to the whole front of the manipule, each division of a Roman legion would form a line of eleven hundred and forty feet front, really occupied by only one hundred and twenty men. It must be observed, again, that in each manipule the men did not cover their file-leaders, but the intervals between them, and in like manner the several manipules of the principes did not cover the manipules of the hastati, but their intervals, and so again the triarii of the principes. So that in fact the whole Roman legion, when in battle order, exactly resembled the arrangement of three lines of a chess board, each containing ten squares of men, and nine square intervals.

There was, however, a longitudinal lane between each of the three divisions, equal in width to the transverse lanes between the manipules. So that the depth of the whole legion would be two hundred and fifteen feet, since the manipules of the triarii preserving the same front or nearly so with those of the other divisions, would be necessarily but three deep; and a whole consular army of four legions would form a treble line, independent of the cavalry who were stationed on the wings, of four thousand seven hundred and ten feet front, by one hundred and fifteen feet depth.

The consequence is, that when in action with an equal force of men drawn up in the Greek phalanx, directed against their centre, the Roman legionary army would overflank them at each extremity of the line by at least a thousand feet, so that by retiring its own centre manipules, or advancing those of its own wings, it must necessarily envelope and overlap them, finally involving them in such and so fatal a catastrophe as those of Cannæ, Fontenoy, Aspern, and Waterloo.

It must at once be apparent that the individual fighting of a Roman legion, dependent as it was on the personal prowess, strength, and skill with his weapons of the individual soldier, must have been singularly fine, manful, and exciting.

We will suppose the red flag hoisted on the Prætorium, or great pavilion of the general, being the signal for delivering battle, the three divisions of the heavy infantry, steady as insulated towers, mutually supporting one another, with their glittering brazen casques and erect black and crimson plumes, their long shields advancing all in line, their tremendous pila brandished in the air. The trumpet gives the signal and out flies a cloud of nimble skirmishers, covering the onset of the manipules and disturbing the approach of the enemy, by the arrowy hail of their keen javelins. Meanwhile the tramp of charging horse and the clang of close battle peal from either wing, showing that the cavalry are at work already, and now the skirmishers, driven in by the solid advance of heavy troops, fall back by the intervals and rally, each squad in the rear of its own particular manipule. Then with their well-known shout and the long stern trumpet blast, "which bids the Romans close," in rush the stout nastati, sending their fearful pila hurtling through the air, rending the strongest shields, piercing the best made corslets as though they were but paper, and then, before they have recovered from

CHARGE OF THE ROMAN LEGION.

p 48.

that deadly volley, upon them with the sword and buckler—'till the whole front is one series of hand-to-hand encounters. If the hastati overmatched retire before the weight of the enemy, the principes receive them in the intervals between their fresh manipules, the line is restored and is now solid and continuous, and if it be a phalanx which they are engaging, the onset of the triarii, with their long pikes wheeling in upon either flank, decides the victory, and almost before it is a victory, lo! it is a rout, an extermination.

Such for the most part was the Roman tactic; at times it was altered in adaptation to circumstances, as at Zama, where Scipio covered the manipules of his hastati by those of his principes, and those again by his triarii, purposely leaving avenues directly through his lines, down which his skirmishers were instructed to provoke the formidable elephants to pursue them. The manœuvre was successful, the terrible monsters were disposed of, and the long contested battle was determined, the hastati and principes having been both successively driven in, by the decisive and overwhelming charge of the reserved triarii. But of this more anon.

Sometimes the tactic was abandoned, and always fatally; as at Thrasymene where Flaminius blindly rushed in column into the broken defiles, where his flank was exposed to the terrible claymores of the Gauls, and the mad charge of the wild Numidian lances, while his van was fighting stubbornly against the African and Spanish foot, who barred their onward way. The result was that of an army, at night-fall not a man lived, save as a captive to the merciless Carthaginian. As again at Cannæ, where for some inconceivable reason the Romans fought without intervals between their manipules or between their three several divisions, but rushed in one vast wedge-like column into the centre of the enemy, carrying all bodily before them, until the Punic wings, strengthened by their great leader to that very end, broke in on both their naked flanks, while Maharbal, with his victorious horse, thundered upon their rear, and the carnage of Waterloo was anticipated by above two thousand years.

And now I have briefly, and I hope clearly sketched out, the precise nature of the tactics of these two great powers ; I have endeavored to show that the success of the one and defeats of the other system were the consequence of necessary causes, still existing unaltered even by the alterations of modern warfare, and proving I hope to the satisfaction of my readers that of troops equal in courage and manhood, equal or nearly equal in numerical force, and equally well led, the direct attack in column upon line must to an almost mathematical certainty prove destructive, even to extermination, to the assailing column. A truth which is, I think, beginning to be generally perceived and admitted, whether in terrestrial or naval warfare; so much so that I believe the famous manœuvre of breaking the line at sea by a perpendicular attack, will never again be resorted to by any officer, and that if it be, it will be to his ruin. There can be little doubt that, if the circumstances of Trafalgar had been reversed, so that the French had borne down in double column of perpendicular attack into the midst of an English receiving semicircle, the action would have been decided in a quarter of the time, and would have been guiltless of the blood of Nelson. Nor is there much more doubt, that if—which heaven forefend—an English and American fleet should come into action together, and one or the other should attack a line on a perpendicular, as that great seaman did at Trafalgar, the attacking fleet would never open its fire, but be annihilated, or ere it should come along side, while its leader would lose together his fleet, his life and his reputation.

Hereafter, a review of the lives of the great captains of old will give space for a fuller examination, and more interesting and graphic description of their great actions; and will, I think, establish the fact that strategy has been, and will be, in all ages, one and the same; that we are but fighting in these latter days the very battles that were fought ages before the Christian era, and winning them by the self-same manœuvres that won them for the nations, to whom, if we were known at all, we were known but as the most remote and barbarous of barbarians—that strategy, in a word, is a direct and simple science, and therefore like truth must be the same for ever, and all its principles immortal.

II.

MILTIADES,

THE SON OF CIMON.

HIS BATTLE OF MARATHON, CAMPAIGNS, CHARACTER, AND CONDUCT.

A tyrant! But our tyrants then
Were still, at least, our countrymen.
The tyrant of the Chersonese
Was freedom's best and dearest friend;
That tyrant was Miltiades.—THE ISLES OF GREECE.

THUS sang, in his resonant and harmonious verse, and in the fulness of his enthusiasm for that fair land of Hellas, in whose behalf it was his lot to die, " as those whom the gods love die," young, Lord Byron, first martyr for her new-born freedom. But so assuredly, had not his eyes, dazzled by the splendor of his great fame whom he celebrates, refused to look into the obscurer portions of his career, would he not have sung. Nor does he so sing truly. For whatsoever else of greatness or of grandeur may be ascribed to the life of Miltiades, it certainly is not as to a fast and consistent friend of freedom, that his altar will be erected in the shrine of national honor; and, though he did fight once the good fight in her cause, it was as a Hellene earnest to die for Hellas, an Athenian careless to survive Athens, not as a freeman sincere in his love of liberty, not as a man devoted to the emancipation of mankind. Indeed, it would be scarcely less absurd to heap praises on the Emperor of Russia, and the Austrian Cæsar, as sure friends of freedom, because they broke the chains of Europe under the walls of Leipsic and on the heights of Montmartre, than to do the like of Miltiades, because he preserved the liberty of Greece upon the plain of Marathon. Not to desire to be a slave himself, and to be a friend of freedom, are in a man, as it were, moral antipodes. And so it was with Miltiades. But of this anon; inasmuch as my first concern is with his military genius, not with his moral character; and it comes as much within my plan to commemorate the strategetic skill of "a Borgia or a Catiline," as of a Tell or an Epaminondas.

It will be necessary, however, before coming direct to the campaigns and career of my hero, with his one almost inimitable battle, to take a brief glance at the position of affairs, and the state of nations in Europe at the period of the Persian wars, as well as at the parentage and condition of Miltiades himself, in order to avoid interruptions of the narrative when once begun, and those retrospective episodes, which are so annoying to the reader.

At the commencement of these celebrated wars, which was in fact the commencement of the long struggle for existence and supremacy between the religion and polity of the Eastern and Western races, scarcely terminated until within two centuries of the present day, the kingdom of Persia was the most extensive, the most wealthy, the most powerful, and, probably as a whole, the most civilized empire in the world. It comprehended all the countries between the Indus and the Mediterranean, between the Euxine and Caspian Seas and the Indian Ocean; and of all these countries the population were the subjects, the hereditary or appointed princes the slaves, of the great king. From the Punjaub and the banks of the Scinde to the Levantine Sea and the broad rush of the fertilizing Nile; from the pearl-freighted waters of the Persian Gulf to the wild and inhospitable waves of the Black Sea, every tribe and nation, every nomad horde and civilized kingdom, poured lavish tribute of its wealth into his central treasuries, sent myriads and tens of myriads to perish under the banners, and at the slightest nod of that most sovereign monarch.

Tyre and Sidon were his marts and naval depots, Egypt his granary, and the wild steppes of Northern Asia his horse pastures, and nurseries for innumerable cavalries, indomitable hordes of archery. And, at that moment, the throne of this gigantic kingdom was occupied by a prince, the greatest of his race, capable of developing and employing his vast resources to their fullest extent, eager in ambition, fierce lover of glory, covetous to enlarge dominions, which already embraced seven-tenths of the known world. This was the first Darius, son of Hystaspes; who, having already added the Punjaub to the dominions of the Persian, which Hardinge and Gough have the other day attached to those of the British crown—and having previously met with his first reverse in his remarkable Scythian campaign, wherein, after crossing the Danube and penetrating so far, according to some geographers, as the Volga, without bringing his nomadic and active enemy to action, he lost nearly all his host by thirst, fatigue and famine, and felt himself thrice happy to find the bridge of boats, whereby he might recross the Hellespont, unbroken—now determined on reducing all Greece, but Attica especially, into a Persian province. At this period, then—with the exception of Persia—Greece, Sicily, Italy, and Carthage were the only free and civilized states of Europe; for the Greek cities of Asia Minor and of Eastern Europe, along the borders of the Hellespont, and most of the Eastern isles of the Archipelago, though highly refined, flourishing, and wealthy, were, like Tyre and Sidon, Egypt, and even Ethiopia, dependents on the Persian empire, and as such bound to pay their tributes in peace, and to furnish their contingents in time of war. Greece, in the prime of her literary splendor, and wanting but a few years of the era of her greatest artistic glory, consisted of a few antagonistic and jealous republics, rich in arts, in valor, and in glory, but poor in the numbers of her men, poorer yet in moneys; and relied only on the patriotism, the heroism, the inimitable discipline, and unlimited resources of the Hellenic mind. She extended no farther north than Mount Olympus and the mouth of the river Peneus, had no states of any great importance, with the exception of Thebes and Athens—for Thessaly and Macedonia were still but barbarous regions—beyond the Peloponnesus, or as we should say north of the isthmus of Corinth, and could not compare in magnitude with the smallest Asiatic province, or in united opulence with several of the tributary cities of the Persian empire.

Sicily, which was rich and powerful, was too much occupied in contesting the commercial enterprise and wealth of the Italian cities of Magna Græcia, as the south-eastern extremity of Italy was then called, and with the territorial and maritime encroachments of Carthage, to intermeddle at all in the affairs of the East, or of Eastern Europe. The eyes of Carthage, selfish and undeviating worshipper of Mammon and of Moloch, capable of no generous sentiment, no intellectual impulse, were turned already westward; westward, beyond Abyla and Calpe, pillars of Hercules, far into the great unknown ocean, southward to the fortunate isles, the soft Canaries and the Cape di Verds, and northward to the stormy Cassiterides, the wave-lashed crags of Cornwall. No thought had she, at the farthest, to carry her arms eastward of the Adriatic, and little cared she what fell out, so long as her galleys might sweep the Mediterranean unmolested, rich with the gold and silver of the Spanish Tarshish, rich with the tin and copper of the barbarous Britons. Rome, to complete the tale, can scarcely as yet be said to have fallen within the pale of civilization. Her history, so far as this, is still purely fabulous, though no longer wholly mythical. She counted two hundred and sixty-three years of existence from her foundation by the sons of Mars Quirinus and the Latin priestess Ilia; nineteen of liberty, from the expulsion of the Tarquins by Brutus, the son of Marcus Junius. Her consuls* were Marcus Minucius Ligurinus, and Aulus Sempronius Atratinus. Thus far the annalists. The facts, however, show that, although in Italy proper Rome was beginning to make herself known and in some sort respected, though she had even, nineteen years before this date, ratified a treaty† relative to navigation and commerce with the Carthaginians, she was utterly unknown, as a power, to the world at large; and was sufficiently engaged at home in struggling for national existence, with her neighbors the Etruscans and the Latins, to be utterly unwilling to take any share in foreign affairs; even if, by what would have been scarce less than a miracle, any rumor of the great armament of the Persian king against the liberties of Greece should have penetrated through the morasses and forests of central Italy, to the ears of the Quirites, busy as they were, establishing on sure foundations, their own new-conquered freedom.

It is true, that some time before the planning of this invasion, the Athenians had afforded a pretext to Darius for interfering with them; when, Miletus having revolted from the Persian rule, and Aristagoras, its tyrant, having required their aid, they lent twenty of their own galleys, to which the Eretrians added five more; and, not content with succoring Miletus, invaded Asia, and burned Sardis, an important city of Lydia, and seat of the Satrap's government. This, it is true, was an unprovoked breach of a treaty, and was in itself a very sufficient cause of war. It cannot, however, I think, be doubted, that, between the lust of territorial aggrandizement on the part of the Oriental

* Dionysius Kal., VII. 20. † Polybius III., 22.

monarchs, and the sturdy love of liberty, and determination to assist freemen when fighting for freedom at all hazards, on that of the Athenians, the war must have come on sooner or later, and the invasion, which might have been delayed awhile, was but precipitated by this act of imprudent interference.

Such, then, was the state of the world, in general, at this eventful moment; and such that of Greece, Athens, and Sparta, with Thebes, as an inferior third, being greatly, in all respects, the superior powers of Hellas, and each, singly, superior to several of the smaller, but still independent states, which lent manful contribution to the general cause. Nor, if Attica was thus, in some sort, already mixed up in the desultory hostilities which had been going on, almost from time immemorial, between some of the Hellenic tribes, the Ionians more especially, and the Oriental empire, was Miltiades, to whom her fate or her fortune gave the leading of her phalanx on the eventful day of Marathon, less remarkably involved in almost personal, although hereditary hostilities with the king of Persia.

It fell out in this wise, and that not many years previous to the occurrences which are to be related hereafter. The tale in itself is somewhat singular and romantic; and, as it explains how a man could be at one time tyrant of the Thracian Chersonese—as was then called the narrow peninsula lying between the gulf of Saros and the Dardanelles, or Hellespont, of which it forms the northern or European shore—and a citizen of Athens, besides throwing some light on the character of "freedom's best and dearest friend," I shall not pause, but introduce it, no less, I hope, for the instruction, than for the amusement of my readers.

Nor will it be absurd in this place to say a few words on the meaning of the term tyrant, as one which will occur frequently throughout this volume, and which has, with the Greeks, an absolute and positive meaning, from which it never wanders, bearing no relation whatever to the moral qualities of the man, or the manner in which he administered his authority, but to the means only by which he attained it. The mildest and most moderate, the wisest and most beneficent of men, might easily bear, under the Greek interpretation of the term, the name of tyrant; and such was actually the case of Gelo, and the second Hiero of Syracuse, as of many others, on whom we need not dwell. Again, it is not true, as some have asserted, that the Greeks held the office and very name of king in such abhorrence, that they gave to all kings the opprobrious name of tyrant. So far from this, to the end of their polity the Spartan republic was administered by two kings, *basileis*, hereditary, from two royal houses, though their power was restricted by the privileges and authority of the *ephori* and senate; while the Epirots, Macedonians and other northern nations, were governed by hereditary princes, who ruled with sovereignty and state not less than that of Louis the Fourteenth of France. Lastly, in no one instance is the king of Persia, whom they did most detest, as they had the most reason to detest him, styled tyrant but invariably king, with the emphatic accent preceding it, so as to signify *the* king, as equivalent to the great king. The fact is, that the Greek Tyrant, τύραννος, signifies one who raised himself, or was raised by others, even the people themselves, to a power which did not belong to him, or which was not recognized by the state in which it existed. Our term usurper is the nearest to it, but is scarcely so extended in its sense. For if a democratic state became weary of its own democracy, and elected a man as its sovereign, he would be a tyrant; and so also, if in a country ruled by a dynasty of kings, a foreign and victorious power should overthrow one line, and erect another in its stead, the princes of the intrusive line would be tyrants. The latter was a common case; as the Spartans, themselves strictly oligarchical, were constantly setting up in conquered cities individual rulers, as in the case of the thirty tyrants at Athens; and the king of Persia did little more, in the subject Ionian cities, than set individual Greek rulers over them, abolishing republican forms, and imposing a moderate tribute. Sometimes the aristocratic and democratic tendencies of a state were so nearly balanced, that it were difficult to say which form the people really preferred. Still the prince was a tyrant. Sometimes the prince revolted, on behalf of his own people, against the power which had made him their lord, and was sustained by them. Still he was a tyrant.

The more general meaning of the term, however, is one who holds regal office, where such does not legally exist, or where it belongs to another, supporting himself, contrary to the will of the citizens, by aid of foreign mercenary forces; and such a tyrant was Miltiades.

How he became so, as I have observed above, is a curious story, and singularly characteristic of those wild early times, in which the highest refinement in literature and the arts was blended with simplicity of manners almost patriarchal; and thus it runs.

In the latter part of the reign of Cyrus, the Dolonci, a Thracian tribe, who occupied the Thracian Chersonese, being hard pressed by their mainland neighbors, the Apsinthians, sent their *kings** to consult the oracle at Delphi, by what means they should sustain themselves. To them the oracle made answer: "Who first shall receive you as his guests into his house, returning homeward from this temple, him take along with you, to be your general." So they turned home again, and they traversed Phocis, traversed Bœotia, and none offered them hospitality, none received them. And, late on an evening, they entered Athens travel-stained and weary. Now, at this time, Pisistratus held rule in Attica, not of right, nor of the popular choice, but

* Herodotus, Erato, VI., 32.

self-imposed, a tyrant; and of the first citizens in the state, was Miltiades, the son of Cypselus, of noble race, descended from Æacus and Ægina, of a house famous for its chariot victories at Olympia, and himself a four-horse victor; and he was ill disposed towards the ruler of the state. But he, happening to sit in the portico of his house as the ambassadors of the Dolonci passed, observing their outlandish dresses and the strange fashion of their spear-heads, shouted after them, and, when they returned, proffered them lodging and guest-rites; and they, mindful of the oracle, accepting, entered in; and, choosing their time, told him all their errand, and begged him to go with them and be their general. And he, in no wise indisposed, inclined to their will; and, after consulting the oracle upon it, sailed with them, accompanied by many Athenian volunteers; and so, by the choice of the people, became the tyrant of the Chersonese. How he conquered their old enemies, the Apsinthians, and how, warring against Lampsacus, he fell into an ambush and was captured, and how he owed his release to the good offices of his friend Cræsus, king of Lydia, may be read elsewhere; for it is not with him that I have to do, but with his nephew, Miltiades the son of Cimon.

Being rescued thus, Miltiades returned again to his Chersonese, and died there soon after, much beloved of his Dolonci, childless, leaving his place and power to his brother Cimon's son, Stesagoras. Miltiades, the son of Cypselus, might be termed friend of freedom, since freely chosen by a free people, he ruled them by their own laws, and freed them from their enemies.

Stesagoras in his own turn died also, knocked on the head with an axe by a man of Lampsacus, in seeming a deserter, but indeed a most active enemy, he too childless, and intestate. There was no tyrant now of the Dolonci. But the sons of Pisistratus, Hippias and Hipparchus, who now held, not filled, their father's place in Athens, partly, it may be thought, from a desire of supporting tyrannies in the abstract, more from the wish to get rid of a dangerous citizen, lent a trireme with its crew to Stesagoras' brother, Miltiades the son of Cimon, and sent him to try his fortune with the Dolonci. He, by a rare mixture of force and fraud, succeeded, and became tyrant of the Chersonese, holding it with a force of five hundred foreign mercenaries, and marrying a daughter of Olorus, king of the Thracians, thereby strengthening himself in his usurped authority. Assuredly a deep and crafty statesman, as he afterward approved himself a brave and able soldier, but, to my mind, in no respect a friend of freedom.

Thereafter his career was adventurous and full of vicissitudes. For, since the arrival of the Dolonci, seeking a general in Athens, great changes had occurred the world over. Not only Miltiades, the son of Cypselus, was dead, and Stesagoras his nephew and successor, but his friend Cræsus, no longer king of Lydia, conquered of Cyrus, and Cyrus too his conqueror, and Cambyses son of Cyrus, and Smerdis the Magian, who usurped the throne of Persia; and now Darius, son of Hystaspes, had become THE KING, and, being set to conquer the European Scythians, who were in all probability the Huns of later ages, he summoned the contingents of all the Greek cities, and of the Chersonese among the rest; and then passing over the Bosphorus into Europe, by a bridge of boats, marched onward into the Northern deserts with a host of seven hundred thousand Asiatics. The guardianship of the second bridge of boats, on which he crossed the Danube, between Ismail, it is said, and the Pruth, he entrusted to the Ionian leaders of the fleet by which it was composed, and among them to Miltiades the son of Cimon, and Histiæus, tyrant of Miletus. But the march of Darius and his seven hundred thousand was the very prototype of the march of a far greater than Darius, into the same inhospitable regions, though from a different quarter. The Scythians would not fight him, or fought him only, Parthian-like, retreating; until the country and the climate, and disease and weariness and want had conquered the great host, that it turned, desperate, to retreat. Then Cossack-like they hung upon his rear, never seen till they were felt, invisible, yet ever present, and slaughtered the weary Asiatics, unresisted and unsparing. And they sent secret word to the Ionians, who had guard of the bridge, that they should break it and get them home; and, had they done the bidding of the Scythians, the Danube had been an earlier Beresina; and there had been no Marathon nor Salamis, nor perhaps any wars for ever more of Greece and Persia. And Miltiades was very urgent with the confederates, that they should break the bridge, for that the Persian was the natural enemy of all Greeks, and that the Ionians owed him neither fealty nor faith, but followed him as tributaries only on compulsion. But Histiæus of Miletus, and the tyrants of the other Ionian cities, declared against Miltiades; saying that if Darius were the enemy of Greeks, he was the friend of tyrants; and that, he dead, all they should lose their cities and hold tyrannies no longer. And they prevailed over Miltiades, and the bridge was maintained. So Darius returned to Asia to execute conquest of the Punjaub, to meditate conquest of Greece. Nor had not Miltiades, thereafter, his reward at the king's hands for his treason; for, in the third year of his sovereignty, the Nomadic Scythians, at instigation of Darius, broke into the Chersonese and over-ran it, hoping to take him for the king, who had him at feud on account of the bridge over the Danube. But he escaped and absented himself from his dominions until, the Scythians retiring, the Dolonci brought him back again, showing thereby that although an usurper, he was by no means, in our sense of the word, a tyrant, but had in some sort gained the good will of his subjects. Not now, however, was it his fate long to reign over them; for learning that a Phœnician fleet was stationed at Tenedos, and hovering off his coasts, with what intent he knew but too well, he put his property on board five triremes, and setting sail from the city of Kardia on the gulf of Melas, now the gulf of Saros, took leave of the Chersonese for ever, and steered for Athens, whence his enemies Hippias and Hipparchus had been expelled by Harmodius and Aristogeiton. Meanwhile his ill-fortune followed him. The Phœnicians, whom he had hoped to elude, gave chase, and took one of his ships, commanded by his eldest son, Metiochus, born of a previous marriage, not of the Thracian princess. Him, the Phœnicians handed over to Darius, that he might work his will on him in revenge for the treason of the bridge. But Darius did him no ill, but good; and gave him a house and lands and a Persian woman to his wife, of whom he had children that were altogether Persians.

With the four other ships, hard pressed, Miltiades got into port, at Imbros, and difficultly thence to Athens. Nor here did the spite of fortune leave him; for the laws of Attica were so strenuous against tyrants, that, although he had been sent out in an Athenian vessel, under Athenian orders, to do precisely as he did, he was put on his trial for his life, and was acquitted by popular favor, not because he had not made himself tyrant of the Dolonci, but because when their tyrant he had not, like the other Ionian princes, made common cause with Darius, but had remained a Greek at heart, although a tyrant, and had even preferred the common good of Greece, to the maintenance of his usurped authority.

Heartily sick was he probably, of his tyranny of the Chersonese, and heartily glad to escape its consequences, for in truth he had played but a poor figure in the part; and, had his career ended with it little would the world have ever heard of Miltiades the tyrant of the Chersonese.

But now a greater contest was at hand, a wider field was open for the display of military genius, for the gratification of "vaulting ambition that overleaps itself and falls on the other side," and of all others Miltiades was the man to grasp the golden opportunity.

I have stated above, that there had been a deep-set animosity long kindled in the heart of Darius against the Athenians, who had presumed, daring and insolent republicans, to assist his rebels of Miletus, and burn his royal city of Sardis. And now, his time was fully come; his own dominions were composed in the deep tranquillity of servitude, the vast conquests of Cyrus and Cambyses thoroughly consolidated, and, by his own late victories in the Punjaub, the utmost portions of his enormous empire were guaranteed from the incursions, for a while at least, of the fierce and unruly Indians.

There was now no need any longer, that, as the king sat down to meat with his assembled nobles, his criers should make proclamation thrice, as had been the usage ever since the conflagration of Sardis, "Master, remember the Athenians"—for already he had remembered them.

The conduct of the war was entrusted to Mardonius, the son of Gobryas, who had lately espoused the king's daughter Artozostra, and the preparations were made on the scale in which oriental warfare has in all ages been conducted. I am aware that it has been the fashion to doubt and deny the numbers of the Persian armies, as related by the Greek authors; but when we look to the facts, which have been clearly ascertained within the last half century, concerning the enormous numerical force which Eastern armies, and even European armies fighting in the East, are compelled by the necessities of the climate to bring into the field, counting the mere camp followers and baggage drivers by hundreds, the elephants and camels by tens, of thousands, till the united numbers nearly swell to millions, I see no cause to doubt the accounts given to us of the hordes urged forward by the will of a despot, unlimited in resources either of men or moneys, for the accomplishment of the dearest object of his ambition.

A fleet sailed from the Hellespont, with orders to reduce the Ionian cities of the coast and the Greek islands, and thereafter to rendezvous at the isle of Thasos, where it would meet, and act in communication with the land forces of five hundred thousand men, which crossing the Dardanelles, should march through Thrace upon Macedonia; nor until reaching its frontiers did they look to encounter enemies. In the first instance, the movements of the fleet were entirely successful, the Ionian cities submitting to receive tyrants in lieu of their own democratic governments, and the islands of the Archipelago surrendering without a blow. The fleet reached Thasos, loaded with booty, flushed with success, and confident of future victory—confidence soon to be changed to despair. For as they attempted to round Mount Athos, now the Monte Santo, the huge and towering head land of the easternmost of those three long protruding promontories which formed the Macedonian district of Chalcidice, separated from the mainland of Greece by the Thermaic Bay, now the Gulf of Salonica, a violent north wind, with a heavy broken sea, drove them upon the craggy shores of the promontory, where above three hundred war-ships were wrecked and twenty thousand men perished. On a first glance at the map, this account would appear preposterous, and the catastrophe impossible, as connected with a north wind blowing at the time; since the true course which to steer from Thasos to clear the headland is south, about three points westerly; so that a north wind instead of setting them upon Athos would have carried them clear off it, and the first land they would have made, running dead before it, would have been the isle of Scyros, about two degrees distant. As is, however, in such instances very often the case, the very discrepancy, as it seems, proves the fact; for if, instead of steering broad out into the open sea and stretching away straight for the headland, they had crept close in shore, following all the sinuosities of the coast, round the Gulf of Contessa, *Sinus Strymonicus*, they would ultimately find themselves embayed directly to the northward of the stern and rock-bound coast; and that they did so is certain, as it is stated by Herodotus,* that they anchored for the night at *Akanthos*, the modern Hieriso, which is situated at the southern extremity of such a bay, and weighing thence encountered the gale which destroyed them, as it necessarily must do, since to work out thence and round the headland they must needs lay a northeast course.

The fleet being destroyed thus and its crews lost, some dashed upon the rocks, some perishing of cold, and some devoured, as Herodotus informs us, by the monsters which abound in those most prolific seas, scarcely a relique was saved to tell of the disaster. Nor was Mardonius much more successful with his land forces than he had been by sea; for having reached the confines of Macedonia, the Brygian tribe of Scythians beat up his quarters at night, and, forcing his defences, handled him so severely that, although he was subsequently able to chastise them, and even to reduce them to permanent subjection, he was so much weakened by their first onslaught and by the subsequent operations, that he perceived the utter hopelessness of prosecuting any schemes of conquest, when unsupported by a fleet, drew off his shattered forces and returned home, disgracefully beaten, even to humiliation.

For two or three years subsequent to this disaster, Darius employed himself in humbling his own immediate tributaries, especially the Thasians, in whose island there were exceeding rich gold mines, of which he made himself master; not neglecting, however, to make preparations for a fresh attack on Greece, which to subdue, his very reverses had but the more obstinately determined him. In the opening of the third season, he sent

* Herod. Erato. VI., 44.

ambassadors to demand earth and water, implying unconditional surrender, by land and sea, of all the Hellenic states. On the main land this concession was made by all the semi-barbarous kingdoms of Thessaly, Macedonia, and Epirus, and even by the civilized and powerful confederacy of Bœotia—in the islands it was denied by none of whom it was demanded; and thence arose a fierce naval warfare between Athens and the Æginetans, who had submitted, inhabiting an island almost within bowshot of the coasts of Attica. This war was strenuously insisted on by Themistocles, the wisest of Greek statesmen, and undeniably a great commander; who, foreseeing the tempest which was about to break over Athens, from a point far remote and unsuspected by the many, and knowing the restless impatience of his countrymen under taxation, except when under the impulse of any immediate excitement, made use of this trivial quarrel as a pretext for an increase of the navy wholly disproportionate to the present object, to which in the end the preservation of Greece itself from the barbarian yoke has been ascribed, and not I think without sufficient reason.*

But now the decisive moment had arrived. In the beginning of the year 490, before the Christian era, being the 19th of the Roman republic, and the 4th of the 72d Olympiad, Darius, constantly whetted to action by the instigation of Hippias—the fugitive tyrant of Athens, who, disappointed of Spartan aid to avenge him on his native land, had fled to Persia—and smarting under his late defeat, raised a new force under Datis, the Mede, and his brother's son, Artaphernes. To these he gave six hundred triremes, each carrying two hundred men, besides horse-transports, with orders to destroy Athens and Eretria, that not one stone should stand upon other, and to bring away all the population in chains, to be sold as bond-slaves; and sent the

* Plutarch. Themist. 5.

traitor Hippias, to whom, of all infamies, this last was only wanting, to guide them and reveal the weak points of his country.

These leaders justly dreading the stormy cape of Athos, marched down their forces by land, through Asia Minor, embarked them at the isle of Samos, and steered their course through the islands of the Archipelago, taking Naxos which had not surrendered the previous year, right upon Eubœa, the Negropont, there to obey their master's commands, in reference to the city of Eretria. There the inhabitants were panic-stricken, and wavering between three minds, whether to desert the city and take refuge among the craggy fortresses of the island, whether to accept the assistance of four thousand Hoplitai from the colonists of Chalcidice, or lastly whether to submit themselves to the mercy of the Persians. Naturally, as ever is the case with waverers, they determined on nothing; some fled to the hills for shelter from the tempest, and escaped it; some took refuge in Oropus, on the mainland of Bœotia; and a few made fruitless resistance on the walls, which were stormed after an assault of six days, when four hundred prisoners only, ten of the number being women, were taken and transported to Asia, according to Darius' orders; where they were entreated kindly and settled in the district of Crissa.

In the meantime, the Athenians, not unmindful of their peril, nor unmindful either of their past deeds and present glory, made preparation for a stern resistance, being resolved as gallant men, and who can resolve more, to deserve at least, if they might not command, success.

They raised men, heavy-armed foot all, the prime of their best citizens, to the number of nine thousand, for so many, only in such an emergency, could the first city of Hellas muster, to defend her national existence; and to command this handful, for such it was as compared to the vast array of the orientals, which embraced the contingents of no less than six and forty nations, they elected ten generals, the last chosen of whom was Miltiades the son of Cimon, who should command on alternate days, in addition to the Polemarch, or second Archon of the year, whose office it was at this time, although at a later period he seems to have performed the duties rather of war-minister than warrior, to command the right wing of the army. A disposition more subversive of all true military principles cannot possibly be imagined than this; for, however well it might succeed, as regards the mere tactics on the day of action in the face of the enemy, it must of course prevent and nullify any long series of combined strategetical movements, unless in the case of unanimity, a thing hardly to be expected; since a single malcontent could, on the return of his day for commanding, disarrange and frustrate all the movements of the past nine days, and bring on or decline action on his own individual responsibility. It is singular enough, considering that in strategy, above all other sciences, promptitude in determining, decision in acting, and pertinacity in adhering to a course of action once taken, are emphatically the qualities most essential, and that these can only be attained by unity of counsel, combined with unity of command, how many nations have erred by insisting, almost unto their own destruction, on this subdivision of responsibility, and partition of command. It would seem to have been, in most cases, prompted by a jealousy of entrusting too much power to the hands of a single individual; since it is always in the most ultra republics that we observe this strange fallacy most predominant. By the Athenians, it was far more consistently acted upon, than by any other nation; yet we find it showing itself, at times, even among the wise and politic Romans; as in the case of Terentius Varro, and Æmilius Paullus, whose alternate command led to the fatal defeat of Cannæ; and again in that of Fabius and Minucius, where a similar result was prevented only by the celerity, most unusual in him, and genius of the old dictator. It was a regular principle with the Venetians, to send with every fleet and army, a citizen *proveditore*, or overlooker, whose province it was to command the commander, hamper him in all his movements, and dictate to him in his own profession. The detestable demagogues of the French directory introduced the same invention, attaching to all their expeditions a representative, as he was called, of the French people. The object of the directory was, however, different, being in fact the procuring of fresh and illustrious victims for the guillotine; as the duty of the representative was merely that of spy and informer. These gentlemen did, however, less harm than would have been expected, as they invariably ran away at the first shot; like citizen Jean Bon St. André, representative on board the French flag ship, on the fourth of June, who at the first broadside of the Queen Charlotte, dived into the cockpit, and was seen no more until the firing ceased. It is more remarkable than this, that the cold autocratic Austria, so lately as the last great European war, should have hampered the movements, and frustrated the successes of her greatest leader, the Arch-duke Charles, by the slow and stupid intervention of her Aulic council. In all ages, by whatever polity or form of government it has been adopted, it has been, and it ever will be, impolitic, disastrous, and well if it be not fatal. Better two pilots in a ship, battling with the tempest amid reefs and breakers, than two leaders, equal in authority, upon a day of battle.

Such had well nigh been the case at Marathon, and such it would have been, but for the prudence, wisdom, and moderation of one man—one man very great, because he was so very good; for beyond this, the closest examination of history shows us nothing conspicuously striking in the character or conduct of Aristides. Nowhere do we discover any brilliant talents, much less any genius, in his serene and even course of action. He was no orator, he was not a great strategist; but he was something better, he was a man of such sterling probity, such unquestionable truth, candor, justice, and integrity, that men greater and abler, and far more brilliant in themselves than he, submitted themselves to his guidance, and surrendered even their own convictions to the certainty that his judgment, founded on his integrity, must needs be sound and solid; and so indeed it was.

But I must not anticipate, nor indeed is there occasion, for the crisis is even now at hand, and the struggle imminent. The first question which arose between the numerous commanders turned on the method of defence to be adopted; a majority in the first instance wishing to remain within the city, and risk an assault; the insanity of such a plan being obvious on its face, when the overwhelming numbers of the Persian would enable them to attack on all points at the same moment, or if they should prefer blockading, to carry out lines of circumvallation in the least given space of time. On this Miltiades insisting strenuously, and defending his insistency by good and soldierly reasons, for it was founded on a true principle of warfare, that to stand a siege when there is no hope of relief from without is an absurdity, he prevailed so far that his colleagues consented to march out, and fortify a camp at a few miles distance from the city. Before leaving the walls, however, a herald, of that class called ἡμεροδρόμοι, men who can run through an entire day, was despatched to Sparta, to inform the Lacedæmonians, how Eretria was taken and all its inhabitants carried into bondage, in what present peril Athens stood, and to implore their present aid and succor. The name of this runner was Phidippides. Now as this runner, full of enthusiasm and of high thoughts concerning his country, and her ancient glories, and her ancient gods, sped onward, having long passed the Corinthian isthmus, and entered the mountainous and forest-mantled country of Arkadia, and passed beneath the dark and solemn heights of Mount Parthenios, near the city of Tegea, he imagined—for imagination it must have been, unless we are prepared to believe that evil spirits actually were the gods of the old time, which I at least am not—that a strange voice, greater than human, shouted to him from the hill-side, "Phidippides, Phidippides"—and that as he turned him round, the wood god Pan stood manifest before him, and bade him tell the Athenians "that they should take no fear of him, since he was friendly to the Athenians, and oftentimes had aided them before, and so would now, and again in the times to come."

Such tales as these are curious; not that we must do aught but discard them altogether as matters of every day fact; and yet they were indeed the cause of facts and great ones. There was a freshness in the world in those days, a freshness and sincerity and youth in the heart of man such as we find rarely now-a-days; and then only in some earnest, shy, and world-secluded student; in some half precocious, half dull-witted child; or perhaps in some remote mountaineer, from the wildest and most solitary district.

The earth, with all its unshorn garniture of woodlands, its sacred fountains, its mysterious tarns and umbrageous mountains; was full of poetry; and from it poetry had welled up into the heart of every man, in a greater or less degree; and whether the poetry had engendered the religion, or the religion created the poetry, there they were, two in one, self-existent in every heart; so that to dream and muse, until the mortal senses became conscious as it were of their real presence, of white nymphs sporting round their crystal waterfalls, or wood-gods waking wild melodies from reedy pipes, or huge heroic shades brooding in giant majesty over their lonely barrows, was a thing usual and common; and neither the seer nor the hearer doubted, for an instant, the absolute reality of such creations of the fantastical and teeming brain, or hesitated to place implicit confidence in their reported revelations. For I dismiss, at once, as mere pedantic efforts to explain away, in a matter of fact counting-house style, things which cannot be explained at all, the attempts of a certain school of would-be classical authorities and expositors, who are, however, daily becoming rarer and less intrusively absurd, to represent such messages and apparitions, as this, as being devices and inventions of this or that leader, for the encouragement of his own people or the discomfiture of his enemy. Indeed it is as plain as anything can be, that the leaders believed themselves—believed, and often trembled, as much as the meanest of their people. It is a well-known fact, that of uncultivated men, the inhabitants of forest and mountain lands are far more imaginative and even superstitious, if you will, than those of the broad valley or the open plain. The inexplicable phenomena of light and shade, of atmospheric and perhaps subterranean, even volcanic, influences, producing sounds and sights for which no science of theirs can account, are to them voices from the past or tidings of the future, manifestations of demigods and demons, perhaps revelations from the great gods themselves. Just such a land was Greece, so framed, so modelled, with unseen subterranean torrents, whose murmurs struggled upward oppressed to the doubting ear, and twilight passes through the crags, and glades and gorges full of strange accidents of light, suggesting strange imaginations. And when to this the bent and inclination of the national mind, the almost universal prevalence of poetry, and the direct tendency of the national religion were added, strengthening every half-doubted fancy, and giving ear to every wildest mythos, how shall we doubt—we who know that even to this day of Christian illumination and mid-day blaze of almost skeptical science, doubting all things, denying all things, that are not mathematically proven, the Scottish belief in the *Taishatr* or second sight is absolute in many a highland glen and corrie—how shall we doubt, I say, that the intellectual, dreaming, sensuous Greek, five hundred years before the birth of Christ, nourished the conviction of his real intercourse with

Dryad and Nereid, Pan and Sylvan, as we cherish the most lovely doctrines of our own pure religion.

Therefore, I say that to Phidippides the god Pan did appear, and that he did speak thus—for to Phidippides and to the auditors of Phidippides, whether it was a scathed pine tree blackening in the forest amid the silver moonlight, or a mist wreath glittering through the shadows, it was the great god Pan. And it was the voice of that god Pan, whether that voice were the night wind howling through the pine-tops, or the torrent bellowing through the ravine, which bade them be of good cheer and conquer; and they were of good cheer, and they did conquer.

The power of faith, as stated in holy writ, even if applied to mortal matters and to mere physical efforts, is scarcely overrated. He who has faith that he can accomplish anything rarely fails, even if he task his strength almost beyond the utmost, to accomplish it. He, who doubts his own powers, surely fails to execute that which he could have performed with ease, had his heart been high of cheer and courage.

Therefore, to the Athenians, to those who fought at Marathon, Pan, who appeared to Phidippides on Mount Parthenios, near Tegea, was a fact, and a true fact. And it helped the runner on his way doubtless, for on the second day from Athens he stood before the Ephori in Sparta, and said what the time required. And the Spartans were much moved, and eager to rush to the rescue; and they promised speedy reinforcement, but not yet; for it was now the ninth day of the month, and between the ninth day and the full of the moon it was forbidden to the Spartans to set on foot any expedition, to go forth in arms beyond the city gates. And this they said, not seeking pretexts, nor wishing to defer their succor until they might withhold it altogether; for they perceived the urgency of the common peril, and perceived, too, that should Athens perish, the brunt must fall on themselves the next, with none at hand to succor them. But it was their religion and their law that they must await the full of the moon. And the religion must not be despised, nor the law broken. So they awaited the full of the moon; and Phidippides returned home, full of the vision which he had seen, and elated by the thought that instead of mortal aid, he brought back to his countrymen the tidings of an immortal alliance.

When he returned, the Athenians—having been joined by the little city of Plataia, their subordinate ally, which with a rare fidelity had turned out, in this desperate emergency, mindful of past benefits, not of present peril, with every man that she could muster capable of bearing arms, to the number of a thousand shields all of Hoplitai—had marched out and sat down in a fortified camp at the opening of the valley of Marathon, now Vrana, where its torrent issues from the hills to discharge itself across the plain into the Gulf of Eghina.

The mountains look on Marathon,
And Marathon looks on the sea—

says Byron—than whom there are few more accurate observers or vivid describers of natural scenery; and accordingly we find from other authorities that the scene of this celebrated battle is an elevated plain of about two miles and a half in width, hemmed in at either extremity by difficult craggy heights, and bounded to the southeast by the sea. At the northwestern extremity of the plain a deep gorge-like valley, in the upper part of which the village of Vrana is situated, opens into the plain, discharging across it a torrent which falls into the middle of the Bay of Marathon by three shallow channels. The northern boundary of the bay is a narrow rocky point, close to which is a salt stream connected with a shallow lake and a large extent of marsh land. Such to this day are the features of this great natural battle-field, with scarce an exception, the only ground in Attica fit for a charge of cavalry, and, as such, selected for his place of debarkation by the traitor renegado Hippias. To complete the picture, as it meets the modern eye, towards the middle of the plain stands a large tumulus or barrow, about twenty-five feet high, resembling those on the plain of Troy, says the traveller whom I quote, and I will add closely resembling those scattered through many of the western states, beneath which sleeps undisturbed all that is mortal of those high spirits, whom Demosthenes was wont to adjure—swearing "By those who died at Marathon!" It is said, also, that the remains of marble monuments and trophies may be seen still on the salt marsh. But on that day there was no mound, no monument, no trophies; only the long, dry, bent grass, tossing in the gentle sea-breeze over the smooth plain, and the broom and heather waving upon the craggy sides of the gray hills, whither the bees came often from Hymetos to recruit their stores.

In the mouth of the glen, between the village and the sea, lay the Athenian army in its lines, ten thousand shields of heavy infantry, full armed, without taking into account their servants, who are not indeed numbered in any of the accounts of the battle extant, but whom I confidently set down at ten thousand more; since it was the invariable practice with Hellenic armies, and expressly so stated by Herodotus* of the battle of Plataia, that every heavy armed soldier had one citizen of a lower class to carry his shield on the march, and otherwise attend on his person—these men forming the light troops in action, and generally known as *gymnetes*, or naked men, from their carrying no offensive armor beyond a light casque and buckler. The Spartans proper, when in the field, were attended each by no less than seven helots; so that the Spartan shield represented eight fighting men, as the term lance in the middle ages was understood to embrace five persons, the man-at-arms himself and four var-

* Herod. IX. 29.

lets. The whole fighting force of the Athenians at Marathon may therefore be set down, unhesitatingly, at twenty thousand men; only ten thousand of whom, however, were capable of breasting the brunt of battle; although the rest might do good service with their javelins, skirmishing in the van until driven in, and in cutting up and routing a beaten enemy. To this last employment their duties on this occasion must have been limited, since the circumstances of the action, to which I shall come forthwith, precluded the possibility of skirmishing. Among other great deficiencies of the Athenians, the greatest of which was being inferior to their enemy in the ratio of something more than one to five, was their total lack of either horse or archers, in the presence of an army which was incomparably the best in the world in those services. With none of the continental Greeks was the bow a favorite weapon, but with the Athenians it was regarded as slavish and degrading to the hands of a freeman. The absence of their cavalry at Marathon must be ascribed, I suppose, to their prudently holding it back as utterly useless, consisting at this time of not above two hundred young men of the noblest families, who could only have been literally trampled under foot by the overwhelming charge of ten thousand Oriental horse.

In the mean time, while the Athenian force lay encamped near to the mouth of the valley of Marathon, within the consecrated ground and grove of the *Herakleion*, or temple of Herakles, at the distance of about fifteen English miles from the Acropolis, Hippias, who appears from the arrival of the armament upon the shores of Greece to have succeeded to the chief command, landed the captives whom they had secured at Eretria, on the small island of Ægileia; and then bringing to his vessels in the bay of Marathon, disembarked all his power, and arrayed it, as for battle, in the plain, between the sea and the Athenian encampment.

On that night, a council of war was held in the camp of the Greeks; and, as invariably is the case with councils of war, even when composed of men individually the most daring and even rash, the decision was *not* to fight; for where there can be no individual censure or responsibility, every one shelters himself under the impunity of the whole, and easily admits or advises actions, which if personally and solely accountable, he would be ashamed to adopt, much more to recommend. Indeed, as it has become a proverb everywhere that corporations have no conscience, so might it be urged, and with even more justice, that councils of war have no courage. Another palpable argument against the subdivision of military command.

The ten generals were divided; five voted to give battle, five insisted that their numbers were so desperately inadequate, until the Spartans should arrive, that to fight was merely to die without aiding their country or advancing the cause of freedom. The names of the voters are not given by Herodotus, who merely states the fact that Miltiades urgently but vainly insisted on delivering battle, the ten generals being divided; and that he prevailed by inducing Callimachus the Polemarch, who, according to the Athenian law, had an equal vote with each of the generals, to throw his casting vote in favor of fighting. Plutarch asserts, however, that the change in the ultimate decision of the council was greatly attributable to the efforts of that noble man Aristides, who, as well as Themistocles, was a general on that occasion, and with him commanded the centre, in the action which ensued.

The arguments produced by Miltiades can easily be imagined. If not to fight for what were they sent thither? for what purpose, indeed, had an army been raised at all? The ground, if favorable to the Persian horse, was no less favorable to the phalanx, which could not manœuvre with effect in broken ground, and required a level and unbroken surface to make its charge effective. If not there—there, at Marathon, where were they to give battle? In broken ground and among craggy eminences the missiles and short weapons of the Orientals would be superior to their long and unwieldy pikes. Lastly—this he urged on Callimachus, it is said, in private—it could not be doubted, if the army lay in the presence of the enemy long inactive, that a revolution would take place in the minds of the Athenian democracy, and that the state would in all probability surrender, and accept Median usages, and a Median governor. Besides this, he expressed a full conviction in their power of winning the battle, in spite of all the superiority of the enemy in numbers, horse, and archery; a conviction arising doubtless from his long acquaintance with oriental armies—having seen them in the field, and having learned how, by fighting on their side, to fight against them with effect; a conviction, which proved, as it is by the event, to have been founded on no vainglorious over-estimate of himself, or of the men under his command, on no weak and unsoldierly contempt of his antagonist, is in itself an evidence of his possessing the genius of a great and veritable captain. All his decisions—so far as we know them—were correct; all his perceptions lucid; all his conclusions just. His first determination to leave the walls and deliver battle in the field, was soldierly; and not soldierly only, but politically sound and wise. Soldierly, for he knew, that men will fight better always, as the black Douglas wont to say, where they can hear the lark sing than the mouse squeak—that to give men courage and confidence before the enemy, their general must show that he has confidence in them—politically wise, because to show Hellas that Athens despaired neither of Athens nor of Hellas, was the only hope to kindle anything of general or impulsive ardor in the hearts of Greeks; was the surest mode of bringing Sparta in arms to the rescue. His second, to deliver battle then and there, was no less sound and masterly judgment; since he had nothing on which to retreat except the city, from which he had just marched out; when to retreat on that would have crowned the spirits of the Persian hordes, and their traitor general Hippias, with the certainty of triumph, and depressed those of his countrymen, it is most like, as he predicted, even to the point of instant submission.

Fortunately Kallimachos the Polemarch, on whom, as having the casting vote, something of personal responsibility now rested, was a man both of nerve and judgment, and he decided instantly for battle. And thereupon arose one of those strange and sudden conversions, which are not, after all, so unnatural as they at first appear, among the very men who had so strenuously opposed Miltiades but a moment, as it were, before. They now, on the motion of Aristides, determined, each one on the day when his turn of command should come about, to resign it to Miltiades, virtually constituting him sole general and commander in chief, as his right, in behalf of superior military genius.

I have said that this was not so wonderful as it would seem at first sight—for it was not that those generals lacked patriotism, or judgment, or perception of what was right, or generosity, or, least of all, courage. It was that they shunned—as ninety-nine men in a hundred do and ever will shun—responsibility, when it may be shuffled off without disgrace; and, although they were defeated in their argument, and the counter opinion had prevailed, it was, not improbably, with something of gratitude, that they regarded the man who had relieved them of that onerous burthen.

Nor, be it observed, was it an unnatural thing for the bravest to shrink from assuming, or even from involuntarily incurring, responsibility to the people of Athens—for with all their splendid intellectual capacities, all their brilliancy and wit, all their fiery courage, and impulsive appreciation of the good and great, there was nothing in them of that stern and perdurable resolution, that constancy not elevated by success nor prostrated by reverse, which in truth belongs not to democracies—such as that I mean which prompted the Roman Senate to thank the fugitive Varro, escaped with a mere handful from the field of Cannæ, all but fatal to the state, "for that he had not despaired of the republic."

With the Athenians, to be entrusted with command, and to bring home defeat instead of victory, ruin instead of glory, was in nine cases out of ten, to die a criminal. As to defeated general of the French Republic was the guillotine, so to the Attic captain, unsuccessful, was the draught of hemlock; and such it may be held, with little doubt, would have been the fate of Miltiades, if, having overborne the scruples of his colleagues, fighting, he had lost his army, and so returned to the Acropolis.

But of such things, it is clear, he never thought; never, probably, contemplated the possibility of defeat. He knew, what probably no other man upon the field, of either army, knew, the men of whom he was himself the leader, and the men against whom he was about to lead them. A soldier almost by profession; a soldier, almost an adventurer; the wearer of a sword prompt to leap from its scabbard—not literally for hire, but in any cause where renown and riches were to win—a soldier as opposed to an armed citizen, Miltiades had of course studied strategy as a science; and, as a most important part of that science, had observed the characters of men and nations. He was acquainted with the arms, the mode of fighting, the tactics, the very mental characteristics of every different nation, tribe, or nomad horde, which was to be marshalled against him under the banners of the Persian monarch. He had partaken their war against the Scythians, and seen its miserable and disgraceful termination. He knew, too, his countrymen, their perfect discipline, their fiery yet manageable valor, the compact array of their impenetrable phalanx, and the effect of its tremendous onset.

he knew all this, and, knowing it, was serene in the security of his conviction.

Fifty years afterwards, what Miltiades did, winning thereby renown immortal, would have been done by any leader whom chance placed at the head of a Greek phalanx; for it was then an established fact that the bravest of the orientals could not stand for an instant the pæans and the pikes of the Hellenic column, which cut through them as the war-ship cuts the billows, and scarce feels that they resist her passage.

But now, this was not so; the trial had not yet been made, much less decision had; and so far as the *prestige* went, it was in favor of the Medes and Persians, and against the Europeans. Within a few years the former, from being a small inland state of Asia, had raised themselves under three successive monarchs —I say successive, for the reign of Smerdis the Magian was a mere interlude—Cyrus, Cambyses, and the present king, to the mastery of the whole Eastern continent, and that by mere force of arms and courage. No enemy had yet been found to oppose them with equality, much less with success. For if Cambyses lost a host in the Egyptian deserts, it was the fatal simoom, and the shifting sand-pillars, not the hand of man that smote him. And if Darius left the bones of nations to whiten on the steppes of Scythia, it was that the roving tribes let the elements and the country do their battle for them, not that they met the invaders beard to beard, and beat them back by valiant opposition. And of this very battle, Herodotus observes,* that "the Athenians at Marathon, were the first men who endured the sight of the Median garb, and resisted men so clad, for that at this time it was a terror to the Greeks, only to hear the name of the Medians."

The greatness of Miltiades' genius, therefore, is evident in this; that he, from observation, drew a conclusion directly opposite to that of all the men of his day, amounting to a perfect conviction

* Herod. VI. 112.

of success; which conviction, success proved sound and true. That, from theory and principle, he himself devised and invented a mode of attack on these dreaded antagonistics, which was not only overwhelmingly successful, but which was ever after the mode of Greek attack on orientals, by the best generals, never improved upon, and invariably crowned with complete triumph, even in the days of Alexander, who found nothing to innovate on the charge of Marathon.

Being thus appointed commander-in-chief, and that too by the voluntary cession of his colleagues, and having accepted the appointment, it is somewhat remarkable that Miltiades did not at once put his own plans in force, and give battle on the instant. For some reason, however, which we cannot now fully ascertain, he did not do so until his own proper day of command came round. That he was not waiting the arrival of Lacedæmonian succors is certain; for the day on which they would leave Sparta, was accurately known, and the time which it would require to bring them on the field, could be judged to a nicety; yet he did deliver battle before their arrival, and that only by a single day. That he could be actuated by any mere vanity as to fighting on his own proper day of command, is out of the question; and, although it is possible that he might have been deterred from using a day ceded to him by some other leader, through the apprehension that he might attempt to interfere, or re-assume the chief command; there are yet strong reasons for believing that there was a deeper cause, for his not delivering battle until the moment when he did so. Marathon, as I have stated, lies on the eastern coast upon the straits of Egripo, *Euripus*, at about fifteen miles distance from Athens, midway between that city and Carystus now Castel Rosso, in Bœotia, something to the southward of Eretria, which had just been captured. It had been selected probably by the Athenian commander, as his post, from the facilities of observation it gave him; since, at whatever point of

Attica, the enemy might land, he must be within striking distance, while in those narrow seas, the fleet could not make a movement without being seen by a thousand eyes; while Hippias had chosen it as his point of debarcation, from its being the spot of all Attica, most adapted to the manœuvres of his numerous and powerful cavalry. The Athenians, as we have seen, were encamped in the gorge of a valley, opening from the northwest upon this plain, which runs from northeast along the coast, southwesterly. They were, therefore, interposed directly between the Persians and the city. Now, it is clear that it was in the power of the Persians, either to attack Miltiades in his lines, or to turn either of his flanks by the rough ground, and march upon the city. The first of these, Hippias probably dared not do, on account of the strength of the position, and of the lines themselves, which were fortified, according to Cornelius Nepos,* by an abattis of felled timber—although he ascribes a purpose to it, which the circumstances of the battle by no means bear out. The second, which would unquestionably have been the true movement, especially against such a force as the phalanx, unable either to manœuvre or fight advantageously in uneven ground, and still more so when he could have observed them, and masked his own operations, by his clouds of horse, he was probably deterred from doing by the peril of leaving such a force in his rear, as that under Miltiades.

For several days, therefore, and it would seem to have been ten, from the fact that Miltiades is stated to have been tenth chosen, the two armies lay face to face, with about one mile intervening; Hippias not daring to attack the Athenian camp, Miltiades not choosing, although eager to deliver battle on the first chance, for some unknown reason, to attack the Persians. Now there is an obscure story or tradition, connected, by some persons, with the account of the abattis of trees described by

* Miltiades, Chap. V.

Nepos, which appears to me to explain the whole. "In the explanation of the proverb χωρὶς ἱππεῖς"*—I quote from Professor Anthon's classical dictionary, not having an opportunity of referring to the original—" we read that when Datis invaded Attica, the Ionians got upon the trees (?) and made signals to the Athenians, that the cavalry had gone away, ὡς ἐιεν χωρὶς ὁι ἵππεις, and that Miltiades upon learning its retreat, joined battle and gained the victory."

The Ionians alluded to, are of course the Asiatic or Island Greeks, in the host of Datis and Artaphernes; the trees Professor Anthon conceives to be an allusion to the abattis named above. This does not however appear to me probable or requisite to the solution of the case.

The Asiatic army consisted, according to Nepos, of one hundred thousand foot and ten thousand horse, present under arms, besides a hundred thousand camp followers and non-combatants; and this number agrees consistently and well with the numerical force of the fleet, six hundred galleys, beside horse transports, as stated by Herodotus, who elsewhere assigns two hundred fighting men to each Persian trireme.

Now it is self-evident that the daily consumption of food by such a host, in an enemy's country, unprovided with magazines, and compelled to make war support war, must be enormous; and that in a poor and sterile country like Attica supplies could only have been procured, even for a few days, by sweeping the country to a very considerable distance; for which purpose horse would of necessity be employed. Again, although we are distinctly informed that Hippias selected Marathon as his point of debarcation for the sake of employing his horse, yet in the battle itself not only are no horse mentioned, but it is pretty clear that none could have been there; since such a pursuit and slaughter as occurred could not have taken place in the teeth of cavalry over an open plain.

* Suidas, Ant. 14, 73.—Scholt.

All this would necessarily be seen and anticipated by such a general as Miltiades approved himself to be; and I cannot doubt that, perceiving the unwillingness of Hippias to attempt his lines, and foreseeing the time when he must send off his horse to forage at a distance, he waited patiently until the moment should arrive, as it did on his own proper day of command; when he at once gave the signal and joined battle.

The plain of Marathon must have presented a singular and gorgeous sight upon that summer morning. The magnificent array of the Cyprian and Phœnician galleys, drawn upon along the beach, and covering the narrow straits of the Euripus; the gorgeous tents of the Asiatics, glittering in barbaric splendor, of gold and purple and embroidery, toward the green marge of the salt marsh; and all along the plain, between the mountains and the sea, the countless multitudes of the barbarian army. It was the boast of the Athenians, when ten years later, on the field of Platæa, they contended with the Tegeatans of Arcadia for the leading of the right wing of the combined Hellenic forces, that they had conquered forty-six nations at Marathon; and it is not a little remarkable that this is the precise number of tribes whose names and arms are given by Herodotus, in his description of the muster made by Xerxes of his army before crossing the Hellespont, on his most calamitous expedition. Moreover, to this day flint-headed Æthiopian arrows are found on Marathon, proving that one at least of the tribes enumerated, and that tribe the most remote of the Persian empire, was present in that bloody battle.

In the centre, therefore, of the barbarian lines might be seen the Persians, with their high straight tiaras, their many-colored tunics of gay needlework, their brigantines glittering with fish-like scales of steel, their quivers swinging at their left sides, their long bows and straight daggers on the right; and next to these the Medes, in similar array; Assyrians, with brazen casques and steel-shod war clubs and Egyptian daggers; Sacians, with lofty caps recurved, trowsers, and brazen shields and battle-axes; Indians, in dresses wrought of palm leaves, with bows and steel-tipped shafts of reeds, from the Oxus or the Ganges; Bactrians, Chorasmians, Parthians, each in their native garb, with bows and javelins; Caspians, in shaggy goat skins; Sarangians, in long many-colored garments, flowing to their heels; Arabians, with high-turbaned brows and doubly-bended bows; Æthiopians, wrapped in panther skins and lion hides, with bows and obsidian-headed arrows, and spears pointed with staghorn, and huge war-clubs, black as night, some of them woolly-headed—the woolliest-headed of mankind*—their bodies painted, half white with gypsum, half red with vermillion; the first negroes probably who ever trod on European soil. Then, there were Libyans, clad in leather, with spears fire-hardened; and Paphlagonians, with chain-mail hoods of brass, small bucklers, and high buskins, armed with spears, javelins and daggers; Bithynians, with their foxskin casques, and variegated robes and buckskin leggins; Thracians, with shields of raw bull-hides, and each two wolf-spears in his hand, and helmets on their heads, with horns and ears of oxen wrought in brass, and towering crests over all; there were Moschians and Mosynæcians, Tibarenians, and Macrones with little bucklers and long pikes; Colchians, in wooden head-pieces, with shields of bull-hide and long-crooked scymetars; and Alarodians and Saspærians, armed like the Colchians; and Lydians, clad like the Greeks in panoply—and twice as many more, wild strangers from the utmost ends of the earth, staring with eyes of savage wonder on the new world that met their gaze for the first time, in Europe.

And to confront this army and armament of nations, Miltiades drew out his handful, his ten tribes of Attica, his brave Platæans, and, as light troops, the slaves†—on that day, for the

* Herod. VII., 70. † Pausan. Attic. 1, 32,

first time, trusted with arms in Attica. Steadily, but without delay, he formed his army, which he was compelled to extend, even to the weakening of his centre—where fought Themistocles and Aristides, with the tribes Leontis and Antiochis—in order to avoid being surrounded by the enemy, who overflanked him on both sides; to counteract which peril he had reinforced his wings with double files. Kallimachos, by virtue of his office, led the right wing; the brave Platæans held the next post of honor, in acknowledgment of their prompt rescue, on the left. His little band thus marshalled, the sacrifices proved propitious; and, in a few brief words, he spoke to them as soldiers should be spoken to. His words are not recorded, nor, were they, should I quote them; for it is well known that in ancient history the speeches introduced embody only the author's understanding of the leader's motives—but we may confidently feel how an Athenian must have spoken, when the sacred earth of his country was polluted by such a scum of all barbarous nations; when he was leading forth from the consecrated grove of Herakles; when he was almost under the eyes of Athene on the Acropolis. Nor could he have failed to point out to the sensuous and superstitious Greeks, that, within sight of the battle-field selected by the enemy himself, was the cave of the god Pan, a little higher up the plain, and his baths, and the scattered stones, goat-shaped, which had from immemorial time been known and honored as his flock—the god Pan, who had announced himself their sure ally, and promised them his succor.

Then, without further pause, he gave the word, and contrary to all previous usage, led them at a run against the enemy, although the distance intervening was eight stadia, a little short of an English mile. The pace could not, of course, have been rapid; since it was absolutely necessary to the very existence of the phalanx that it should come in with all its large round shields close serried, and all its pike points in a row; neither could the men, after running a mile at speed, have been in breath to maintain a close struggle. The δρόμος of the Greeks, which is rendered run, was probably somewhat analogous to the French *pas de charge*, or our double quick time, hurried undoubtedly, within the last few yards, to a headlong and overwhelming rush.

The object of this movement was threefold; first to precipitate the Athenians into action as rapidly as possible, without giving them time to consider the numbers, or calculate the odds against them; second, to dismay and surprise the barbarians by attacking, instead of waiting to be attacked; lastly, to get hand-to-hand at the earliest, and to avoid the storm of javelins and arrows, which must have been shot and hurled into their ranks like hail; since they had neither horse to make a diversion in their favor, nor archery to cover their advance.

Down they came, closing their ranks still as they rushed on, and quickening their pace at every stride, "a long array of helmets bright, a long array of spears," shouting their pæans, and hymning Enyalios, the war god—for to the Greeks, as to our Anglo-Norman race, the same shout was the charging cry of battle, and the cheer for victory—shouting their pæans, till the craggy heights of Brilessos sent back the prophetic clamor; and clashing their spear-heads against their shields of bronze, till the whole air was alive with the brazen clangor.

The Persians saw them come, and joyously stood forth to meet them. For, as they saw them charging, as men never charged before, with flanks unguarded either by archery or horse, they believed that some madness, and most destructive madness too, had fallen upon the Greeks, and that the gods had given them into their hands. Thus thought the barbarians, and shot, and slung, and darted, and received them front to front, manfully.

What Hippias, the renegado and ex-tyrant, thought, what felt, when he heard those pealing pæans, prophetical of triumph, and saw those serried shields come down abreast, with the bright

5

spear points all advanced, in swift unbroken order, history has not told us, could not tell us—but he well knew what was that madness, which swelled the Attic war note.

"When the Athenians broke down upon the barbarians, in close order," says Herodotus, "they fought worthily of mention. But a long time elapsed while they were engaged hand-to-hand." There is no greater error than to fancy, because they were perpetually beaten by numbers so far inferior, that the Asiatics were pusillanimous or dastards. Inferior in physical strength to the Europeans, to the Greeks, trained athletes all, they were undoubtedly; and in arms, weapons, discipline, most hopelessly behind them. But, in all instances, they fought worthily of their ancient renown, even to striving to break with their bare hands, or wrest from the grasp of the Greek Hoplitai, the formidable pikes, whose bristling lines they could not penetrate, and now, in the centre, where fought the Persians proper, and the Sacians, they actually forced back the weak lines of the attenuated phalanx, and drove them in confusion toward the upland, broken but still resisting and retreating with their faces to the foe. In the meantime, however, on both wings, where the files were doubled, the Attic charge had been irresistible; and, though the enemy fought well, falling where they stood, rank after rank, and giving way only when bodily borne down by the brunt of the unbroken spears, they were now routed utterly and fled toward the sea. Such a resistance only can account for the length of time consumed in an action, which was decided by one charge, without much subsequent manœuvring.

Still at this moment, the battle so far from being won, might, like Marengo by the Austrians, have been lost right easily by a single error. Had Miltiades chased with his wings, as was Rupert's wont, his centre would have been annihilated before his return; the barbarians would have renewed the battle on the following day; and, the Greeks disheartened, numbers would probably have carried it. But the Greek captain was too able so to err. Halting both wings simultaneously, and wheeling both inward, this to the spear, that to the shield, he closed them both into a compact body, in an inverse direction to that in which they fought before, with their backs now to the sea, and their faces to the mountains.

One charge more full on the rear of the victorious Persian centre, Themistokles and Aristides, rallying their men stoutly in their front, and the last enemy was broken; and, all but the after slaughter, the day won.

The Persians fled, not to their camp—that they left with all its pomp and treasures, striking no blow to defend it—but to their ships, slaughtered mercilessly now, not by the phalanx only, but by the light-armed slaves, who butchered them at pleasure. About the ships the fight again waxed hot and furious; and here it was a melée, each man fighting for himself, so that the Greeks had less advantage either of discipline or weapons. And here was slain the Polemarch Kallimachos, a man of great note on that day; and here, Stesileos, son of Thrasyleos, one of the ten generals; and here, with many other notable Athenians, Kynegeiros, son of Euphorion, but more remarkable as brother of the poet Aischylos, his arm lopped off with a battle-axe, as he grasped the stern-decoration of a Phœnician galley.

The Greeks took seven triremes, and won gold and silver in heaps,* and wealth, in plate and garments, unspeakable. But they won more than this—they won their liberty, and fame immortal, fame, even to this time unforgotten; that men who fight to-day for freedom,

> "Still point to Greece, and turn to tread,
> So sanctioned, on the tyrant's head."

Of the barbarians there had fallen about six thousand and

* Plutarch, Aristides, V.

four hundred men; of the Athenians one hundred and ninety-two. But severe as had been the defeat, and total the discomfiture of the Oriental army, still the actual loss of six thousand, out of one hundred and twenty thousand men, was a mere nothing toward crippling them or putting an end to farther operations; unless so far as the moral effect of the rout is to be considered.

Accordingly, so soon as the fleet was under way, it steered straight for the headland of Sunion, now known as Cape Colonna, with wind and tide both favoring it, and, some of the ships pausing to take on board the Eretrian captives from the isle of Ægileia, doubled the promontory, and made all sail for Athens, hoping to surprise it, empty of its defenders; it is said, also, having secret information from the Alkmaionidai; which last is not credible, since it was they who expelled Hippias. Nor can it be doubted, that the appearance of the fleet at that juncture, before the arrival of news from the army, might have produced a fatal result, as the Athenians would naturally have supposed their forces to be annihilated, and, if they had not surrendered, would have probably made but a weak defence. Miltiades, however, and the noble troops he commanded were equal to the emergency; as they stood, reeking from that wonderful and glorious battle, without staying to rest themselves, or to break bread, with their heavy panoply and great shields, they made a forced march, with nine tribes of the ten, and the Plataians, at their utmost speed—for with tide and wind favoring, plying sail and oar, the fleet might reasonably be off the Phalerum, then the port of Athens,* in six hours, and they had more than fifteen miles to march ere they could reach it—and arrived there that same evening,† and encamped on the hill of Kynosarges, without the city, and, what was remarked at the time as

* Herod. VI., 116. † Plutarch, Aristides, V.

singular, again in a Herakleion, consecrated ground of Herakles. The Persians made land shortly after their arrival, and cast anchor in the roadstead, but, seeing themselves anticipated, weighed again and made sail for Asia. One tribe alone, the tribe Antiochis, was left to guard the ground, the captives, and the treasure. If Athens had but one captain who could deliver such a battle as that of Marathon, she had but one man who could guard such a booty, and that was Aristides.

On the following day, true to their word, for they had marched so soon as the moon was full, and with such speed that they performed within three days a distance of a hundred and fifty miles, came the Lacedæmonians, with two thousand shields, to the rescue; and, though they came too late, wishing to see the Medes, they marched to Marathon. One can conceive the joy, the pride, the pomp of that procession—all Athens pouring forth her youth, her manhood, and her beauty, to escort those brave auxiliaries, to that field of unexampled glory. One can imagine how they were entranced by the barbaric splendor of the camp, the tents, the spoils, the captured galleys; with what wonder, blended with disgust, they surveyed, now for the first time, the flat faces, and thick lips, and woolly heads, of the black Æthiopians, cold and stark in their lion hides and war paint; with what curiosity they turned over the ox-eared and ox-horned helmets of the Asiatic Thracians; how they proved the gleaming scale armor of the Persians; how they balanced the battle-axes of the Sacians, and tried the edges of the Colchian scymetars. One cannot doubt how they were feasted in the Akropolis, how the temples rang with triumphant Pæans, how the city smoked with incense. Then greatly praising the Athenians, and giving them great glory for that which they had done, they returned home secure and rejoicing.

Here ended Marathon; and would that here had ended, also, the career of its conqueror.

Miltiades was now the first man in Athens; his influence was immense, his popularity unbounded. Athens was, in those days, poor and incorrupt; barbaric wealth had not yet invaded, barbaric luxury not vitiated, Hellas; so for his great reward the Athenians, in the picture, which they caused to be painted of Marathon and suspended in the portico called Poikile, the beauteously adorned, he and Kallimachos were depicted, apart from the rest, in the foreground. Pausanias saw that very picture, in the days probably of the Antonines, with the battle shown there, as it raged hand to hand, the Plataians and Athenians, side by side; and a little farther off the Persians flying and entangled in the salt marsh, and the Greeks slaying them; and conspicuous above all the combatants Kallimachos and Miltiades, and the hero Echetlos, whose terrible eidolon the soldiers saw in the thickest of the fray, with his beard overshadowing all his buckler; and in the distance the Phœnician galleys.

But to return to the hero of this wonderful day, who should either have reposed here on his glory, or gone on to things yet greater, if greater there might be—for there is no battle known which in every point reflects more credit on its winner, than this of Marathon on Miltiades.

But history must be written, if history it is to be, truly; no place for partiality, no room for prejudice.

Availing himself of his unbounded popularity and weight, he now asked the Athenians for seventy galleys, with a land force to correspond, and a military chest proportionate; telling them nothing of his intents, but that he would enrich them beyond all their hopes, by this expedition. And they, confiding in him absolutely, and supposing that he was about to foray on the maritime cities of the king, granted him all he asked, unquestioning. Then he sailed straight to Paros, under the pretext of exacting punishment or ransom from them, because they had served the Persians against Greece; but in reality to avenge a private injury done to him by one of their citizens, Tisagoras, who had accused him to Hydarnes the Persian, in the original matter, it is to be supposed, of the bridge over the Danube. Be that as it may, he demanded of them a hundred talents, equal to about twenty-five thousand pounds sterling, which they refnsed to pay, and thereafter resisted him so strenuously, that, after being himself severely wounded, he was obliged to draw off his army, and return to Athens, disgraced and defeated.

Here he was at once impeached for malversation, and tried for his life. Making no defence himself, on the plea of illness, he was brought into court, wounded, in his litter, and his brother being present pled his cause strenuously with the people—so strenuously, that, although he was convicted, in pity for his fallen greatness, and in gratitude for the great deeds he had wrought in the deliverance of Athens, the capital condemnation was remitted; and he was only cast, as in a civil suit, for the expenses of the expedition, which he had diverted from the public service to the prosecution of his own private animosities, and the furtherance of his own individual interests. As great a crime, certainly, as any of which the public servant, however high in station or renown, of a free state, can well be guilty, and meriting as severe and ignominious punishment.

Those expenses, amounting to some fifty talents, half the sum which he had endeavored unjustly to extort from the Parians, he was unable to pay on the moment; and, being thrown into prison, he chanced there to die of his wound, which probably would have proved fatal anywhere.

It was a sad fate, truly, for such a man, for such a captain. But it is far sadder, that a man who was capable of exploits so noble, should also be capable of crimes so base, as to render such a fate less, not greater, than his desert.

Much obloquy has been heaped on Athens on his account; much ink has been spilt; and much fine writing wasted thereanent, concerning the ingratitude of that state in particular, and of democracies in general. Myself, I have little faith in the gratitude of governments at all; unless gratitude be, as defined by the witty Frenchman, a keen sense of benefits to come; and I believe that democracies are more liable to vehement and strenuous impulses, than to persistency in anything, whether good or evil; but all the outcry in this case is futile, unjust, and absurd. Miltiades was a successful and victorious soldier; he was rewarded, according to the laws of his state, to the utmost—he was the first man in Athens. He was a bad citizen, almost a traitor, and all the severity and disgrace of his punishment was remitted in memory of his great deeds past. Is this ingratitude?

His character is summed up in ten lines.

As a captain, in genius, resource, conception, execution, soundness of principle, rapidity of coup d'œil, brilliancy and suddenness of action, he never had a superior; perhaps, as an originator, never an equal. So long as the Greek tactic endured, his system was never improved, never altered—it was invariably used; invariably victorious.

As a man—it must be said—he was flawed. Wholly unfitted to be a citizen of a free state, he might command others, but he could not command himself.

It is not a little strange, though true, that the man who fought perhaps the best fight the world ever saw for freedom, should be in his heart a tyrant. But so it was; and gallant soldier as he was, I cannot doubt that the tyrant of the Chersonese would have been no wise loth, had occasion offered, to write himself tyrant of Hellas also.

III.

THEMISTOKLES,

HIS SEA-FIGHT OFF SALAMIS, HIS CAMPAIGNS, CHARACTER, AND CONDUCT.

A king sat on the rocky brow,
That looks o'er sea-born Salamis;
And ships by thousands lay below,
And men by nations—all were his.
He counted them at break of day,
And when the sun set, where were they?—THE ISLES OF GREECE.

It cannot, one would imagine, have failed to strike every thoughtful reader of the history of Greece, that there is something entirely peculiar, original, and different from the ordinary stamp of human nature, in the character of almost every one of the distinguished citizens of Athens—that marvellous state and city which, with a territory inferior* in dimensions to a modern county of America or England, and within a period of a century and a half,† performed more extraordinary actions, gave birth to

* The territory of Attica extends from N. E. to S.W., about 80 miles, with an average breadth of 40.

† The battle of Marathon, whence dates Athens' greatness, was fought B.C. 490. That of Chaironeia, which destroyed her independence, B.C. 338.

more extraordinary men, and produced more extraordinary impressions on moral and intellectual humanity, than any other nation of the universe, in as many generations as she counted years of existence.

Think of her citizens. What men! Generals, statesmen, orators, historians, buffoons, tragedians, sculptors, rhetoricians, pedants, philosophers, patriots, incendiaries, all in their line, the greatest; unequalled in the splendor of their genius and their virtues, inimitable in the depth of their infamy and baseness; various, as nature herself, in genius, character, conduct, conception, principle, it yet seems to me that in one point only all were closely similar; that in them, the seeds of vice and virtue, nobleness and dishonor, innocence and infamy, patriotism and disloyalty were sown more rankly intermingled, and shot up more inextricably blended, than in any other race of men who ever lived; unless it be the French, whom they most resemble, during the brief fury of the first revolution.

Where else, in the history of the whole world, shall we look for such prodigies, for instance, of versatility and genius, of public capacity and domestic worthlessness, of political wisdom and private folly, of honor and disgrace, as Miltiades, as Themistokles, as Kimon, as Alkibiades, as any one of half a dozen others who successively, and more or less successfully also, swayed the fortunes of this strange republic. England, in her whole long career of centuries, has produced one Sheridan; but these Athenians, in wit and wildness, in eloquence and eccentricity, in the glory of their genius and the grossness of their debaucheries, were all Sheridans. France—nay, but the world! since Athens ceased to be—has given birth to but a single Mirabeau; and it is to be hoped that, when she generated him, she destroyed the monster-making matrix; but what were all these, in the versatility both of their vices and their virtues, in the pollution of their lives and the perfection of their policy, in the facility and indifference with which they could soar into the empyrean of glory, or sink into the abyss of infamy—what were all these, but so many earlier Mirabeaus?

In that singular and splendid state, we can discern everything, save, with a single exception, one—for Aristides *was* a consistent, single-minded, honest, rational, straightforward man and citizen; and it is for this reason that he stands out in such bold and positive relief, from the glittering back-ground of splendid Charlatans and glorious Mountebanks, by whom he was surrounded. Aristides might, in strength, solidity, steadiness, and sincerity of mind, judgment, purpose and performance, have been an Englishman or an American—he alone of all his people. And I know scarce another of the age, for I do not regard the immortal Demosthenes as belonging to that period, though his career actually commenced within it; I know scarce, I say, another of the age, however brilliant his exploits, however splendid the services rendered to his country, who did not taint those exploits, and tarnish those services, by some trickiness and indirection of his whole career, by some crowning act of political baseness and tergiversation, or by some habit of daily and familiar infamy, which in any other country would have consigned him to utter exclusion from society, much more from the head of affairs, if indeed it had not subjected him to the direct censure and judgment of the laws.

To this fact, indeed, far more than to the generally alleged levity, inconsistency and ingratitude of the Athenian democracy, is it to be attributed that so many of the leading generals and statesmen, so many of what are generally regarded as the greatest benefactors of Athens, died in exile, died as suicides, died by the hands of the common executioner; and that so few escaped, at some period of their career, the penalties of criminal jurisdiction. I do not write thus from any prejudice in favor either of the people or the policy of Attica; since I regard the former, as in the main, a turbulent, instable, and impulsive rabble; and the latter as the worst form of government ever devised by the human mind, and scarcely worthy even to be called a government; but simply because I believe that there was a distinct peculiarity in the Attic mind, from the highest to the lowest order, both of the rulers and the ruled, which rendered them all indisposed to take, if not incapable of taking, the direct road to any object; which led them to prefer and select, as if of set purpose, the most tortuous and intricate paths of intrigue, where the beaten highroad of common sense and honesty would have led them to the very point they desired to gain, with no sacrifice of character or credit.

Treachery and chicanery appear, in a word, to have been two requisites almost indispensable to the composition of an Athenian statesman, and although Kimon and Perikles are clearer than most others on this point, though both deeply tainted in their private lives with that moral filth in which even the philosophers of Athens were not ashamed to wallow, still there is enough of obliquity and corruption in the methods which they adopted to conciliate or secure popularity and public favor, to justify the generalness of the charge.

And this appears to have been peculiarly an Attic characteristic; for, although we find traitors in other Hellenic states, and unscrupulousness of various kinds and degrees prevailing in the policy of each and all, we no where else find the same systematic hypocrisy, duplicity and falsehood, as in the conduct of Athenian generals and ministers; and that too recorded by their own writers, without a blush, as traits of laudable finesse and statesmanship, worthy of invitation.

Nor of any one is this more true than of Themistokles; who but for this almost inexplicable passion for the indirect, must have ranked as one of the greatest men, not merely generals or politicians, of the world.

Every thing was in his favor, nothing was adverse to his ambition, wild as it might be. Although not properly a full freeborn Athenian citizen—for although Neokles, his father, was of the tribe of Leontis and the demus Phrearion, yet he not a man of much distinction, his mother was an alien, some say from Thraké, others from Akarnania, and others yet again a Lydian from Halikarnassos—he began at a very early age to intermingle in public affairs, constantly frequenting the forum and the courts, and, applying himself with the most remarkable diligence to all sorts of practical science and civil knowledge, while he wholly discarded the lighter arts and accomplishments then generally studied, displayed so much ability and earnestness, that he speedily drew on himself general attention, the first step toward notoriety and celebrity.

The rivalry which existed throughout life between himself and Aristides, had commenced already, sharpened, it is said, while they were yet mere youths, into something partaking strongly of personal animosity by antagonism in love affairs, and still more, it is not to be doubted, by the contempt which a man of Aristides' solid and sterling character must naturally feel for the tortuous trickery of Themistokles' entire career, and which his candor as certainly would not permit him to conceal.

So early as the first invasion of Greece by Datis and Artaphernes for Darios, the two rivals were of the number of the ten generals who fought at Marathon; and they two had command of the Athenian centre, which was very severely handled, and indeed broken, by the Persians after a stubborn resistance, each at the head of his own tribe.

Both, of course, shared the credit and the honors of the victory, and obtained a degree of favor with their citizens; but so far was this from satisfying the fierce and ardent ambition of the young politician, that he is reported to have exclaimed constantly, "that the trophies of Miltiades would not suffer him to sleep of nights ;* and foreseeing fresh troubles and wars with the Asiatics, he kept himself, as it were, constantly anointed and in training for the contest, in which he already anticipated that he should occupy the prominent position.

At this period, we have the first instance of that peculiar obliquity of dealing to the charge of which his whole career is obnoxious. Previous to the invasion of Darios and the battle of Marathon, a war already existed between the Athenians and the people of Aigina, the former desirous of inflicting punishment on these for submitting to the Persian by the rendition of earth and water to his ambassadors. The rapid and disastrous termination of that formidable invasion, and the immense influence and authority, as well as fame, which it gave to the Athenians throughout Hellas, by no means induced them to seek for reconciliation, or to discontinue the war. On the contrary, they felt better disposed than ever, to take ample vengeance of all who had been untrue to the general cause of Greece.

And to this Themistokles urged and incited them with all his exquisite plausibility, all his shrewd, pointed and persuasive eloquence. Not that he valued Aigina, her alliance, or her disaffection, at a pin's fee, but that he saw in her, as being then the most powerful state of Greece in maritime force, and in fact the mistress of the seas, an instrument for the exciting and maintaining a war spirit among the Athenians, for compelling them to establish and keep up a sufficient navy, and to support a large force, at all times in readiness against any emergency.

It seems, that he had already determined it to be the true policy of Athens to constitute herself a maritime power—which was in all probability the case, as the extent of her territory and the character and avocations of her inhabitants were not such as to enable her to cope either with her Peloponnesian or continental neighbors, in the number and efficiency of her land ser-

* Plutarch. Themist. 4.

vice, which was defective in material, both for light troops, archers more especially, and cavalry; notwithstanding that the quality of her heavy foot was not to be surpassed by any, as had been proved already on the glorious plain of Marathon, and as was shown thereafter in many a sanguinary conflict both on European and Asiatic soil.

All other politicians at this period, it would seem, considered that the danger of Oriental invasion was completely at an end—the courage of the Persians having, as they argued, been thoroughly broken, and their hopes of success permanently overthrown, by the check they had encountered from Miltiades. Not so Themistokles. He was by far too good a judge of human nature in general, and of the vainglorious, heaven-reaching ambition of the Persian kings in particular, to believe that the defeat of Marathon would have any other effect than to convert what had been, in the first instance, but a passing scheme of ambition and aggrandizement, into a settled purpose of hatred and revenge.

It would not, however, have been Themistokles to stand forth manfully and boldly on the turret-top, like the mariner, who, from the mast-head, peers with eager eyes into the gathering gloom of the horizon, where his experienced eye can presage, and his alone, the brooding of the tempest that shall burst anon in wreck and devastation, and cry to all the city, "Sleep no more! Gird up your loins, and belt your swords upon your thighs, and keep your watch fires burning; for lo! in the hour that you think not the Persian cometh." No! had he been certain that his words would have found ears to hear him and hearts to leap at his warning, that course he would not have taken. To convince men to their good, seemed to his acute, subtle, and casuistical intellect a poor, homely, and unscientific way of coming to his end. In order to be satisfactory to him, the result, whatever it was, at issue, must be gained by skill, by craft, by playing a deep artificial game. All men, whether friends or foes, must be tricked and cheated—his friends and countrymen cheated to their own good; his antagonists and enemies cheated to their ruin.

And thus it was, throughout his whole career; he was perpetually playing games of political chess with whomsoever he came in contact; and it was his highest satisfaction, his most exquisite delight, when he could see them squirming and writhing impotently to avoid his imminent checkmate.

Thus he induced the impulsive and improvident populace to raise their navy to two hundred admirable triremes, which were the finest class of war-ships then in use, thoroughly manned, in the most effective state of equipment, and with crews in rigid discipline through constant practice. Nay! he even obtained a decree, setting aside the whole revenue of the silver mines on the promontory of Laurion for the expenses of the navy, and for the annual building of twenty new galleys. And all this, without one word concerning Asia, one hint at the danger approaching from Persia, Darios, or Xerxes. There was the crowning rapture! One can fancy, when the Persian actually came, and instead of empty dockyards, an impoverished treasury, a navy to be hastily knocked together and manned with slaves and merchant sailors, the wily statesman found himself with the finest and best manned fleet on earth in his command, with ample supplies, and with all the sinews of war strung, and as it were case-hardened—one can fancy, not how he rejoiced with a noble and statesmanlike exultation—this is my doing; I it was who forewarned my people of this peril, when it was yet afar off and invisible, and they believed me, and lo! here we are prepared to beat the peril back—oh no! But how he grinned, and chuckled, and crowed in the secret places of his cunning heart, that he had checkmated his rash and headstrong fellow-citizens—tricked them, sorely against their own will, to their own advantage.

And so it was. And so he played many political chess-games in his life; and checkmated all who played against him. But, like all men of his stamp, he played one game too many, and checkmated himself at last. For when all was done, there was no man living who could cheat Themistokles, except Themistokles.

It was precisely ten years after the first unfortunate invasion of Darios, and the decisive battle of Marathon, that Xerxes, who had succeeded his father on the Persian throne, though without either the fortune or ability of his father—after spending four whole years in the collection of forces and preparation for their armature and commissariat, as well as in cutting a navigable canal across the isthmus of Mount Athos, by means of which to avoid the peril of doubling that formidable headland, and the chance of such a disaster as had befallen the great fleet of Darios—set on foot the gigantic expedition, which must have appeared even to minds less arrogant and sanguine than his own, sufficient to overrun every territory and overturn every government of Hellas, almost without an effort.

His fleet consisted of twelve hundred* and seven galleys, manned by above five hundred thousand souls; his land array, according to Herodotos,† amounted to one million seven hundred thousand fighting men—camp-followers, and non-combatants, who were equal probably in numbers to the whole force enumerated, not included; and added to these eighty thousand admirable horse, exclusive of Sagartian and Arabian camel-squadrons, and charioteers from Libya and India, rated at twenty thousand more. With such a multitude of combatants, both by land and sea, the Persian king set forth, in the early spring of the fifth year of his reign, which corresponds, according to the synchronism of Diodorus Siculus,‡ to the first year of the seventy-fifth Olym-

* Herod. VII., 89. Aischylos, Persæ, 34.

† Herod. VII., 60. ‡ Diod. XI. I.

piad, archonship at Athens of Kalliades; to the two hundred and seventy-third year of Rome, twenty-ninth year of the republic, consulship of Spurius Cassius, and Proculus Virginius; and to the year four hundred and eighty before the Christian era.

Thus prepared, he marched boldly and successfully onward; and, with no losses beyond the ordinary casualties of so great a multitude of men and so long a route, traversed the wide regions of Thrace, and entered the territories of Continental Greece, receiving on his way southward the submission, and in most instances the alliances of the Thessalians, Dolopians, Ainianians, Perrhabians—these being at this period hardly considered Greeks—and of the Lokrians, Magnesians, Melians, Achaians of Phthiotis, Thebans, and indeed all the Boiotians with the exception of the Thespians and Plataians, who were held firm in their allegiance to the cause of Hellas, by their gratitude to Athens, their protectress, and their inveterate hatred of the Thebans.

To meet this very deluge of war-ships and warriors, the Greeks, divided among themselves by selfishness, jealousy, and something of feudal animosity, had none on whom they could rely but the kingdoms within the Peloponnesos, or *Morea;* and, without, Athens, with her allies of Thespiai and Plataia, and two or three small communities on the western side of the continent, bordering on the Adriatic. Nor, even among these, the only staunch defenders of liberty, was there that perfect unanimity and mutual confidence, which is the only safe and effectual bond of strength and security between allied bodies*—*idem velle atque idem nolle, ea demum firma amicitia est*—for the Athenians and other Greeks to the northward of the Isthmus of Corinth, which was in process of fortification, suspected, and as the event showed, not wholly without reason, that the Peloponnesians felt little inclination to risk the delivering battle without their own guarded confines, and might easily be determined, if they were

* Sallust. Catilina, 20.

not so already, to abandon them and their countries to the first furious irruption of the barbaric hordes, whose brunt, at all events, they must encounter foremost. Indeed, so well satisfied was Themistocles, even earlier than this, of the impossibility of defending Attika, or even the city of Athens, by land, that, taking advantage of two oracles rendered from Delphi—the one foretelling the capture and conflagration of the city, the other declaring that, when all their other strongholds should be taken, their wooden walls would hold out, to the preservation of their children and themselves—he persuaded the people, with great difficulty, to abandon their fortifications, desert their homes, remove their seat of government to the isle of Salamis, entrust their women, children, and non-combatants to the kind offices and good faith of the Troizenians and their Peloponnesian neighbors, and embark all their fighting men on board the two hundred excellent triremes, which he had induced them to build, on the pretext of the war with the Aiginetans.

The first movement of the combined Greek allies was to send an army of Lakedaimonian and Athenian heavy-infantry, ten thousand strong, respectively commanded by Evainetus, the son of Karenus and Themistokles, by sea to the city of Alos, in Thessaly, at the head of the Sinus Pagasæus, now the gulf of Volo, with instructions to march northward to the valley of Tempe, and the outlet of the river Peneios, now Salambria, and occupy the defiles through which the great road winds down from Makedonia, between the mountains of Olympus and Ossa, into the plains of Thessaly; where with the assistance of the Thessalian cavalry, then the best in Greece, it was expected that they would be able to make an effective stand against the Persian host. After remaining there encamped a few days, on receiving intelligence from Alexander, the son of Amyntas, advising them that the embouchure of the Peneios was not defensible, and farther that the position could be turned by the pass of Gonni, some ten or twelve miles to the southwestward, they broke up from their position, and returning to their ships, made the best of their way to the Hellenic head-quarters, on the Isthmus. And, thereupon, the Thessalians, having indeed no alternative, as thus abandoned by their allies, submitted to the Persians, and adopting their alliance, heartily and in good earnest, proved themselves right serviceable men in action.

Thereafter, it was determined by the Greeks to defend the narrow pass of Thermopylai, lying between the precipitous crags of Mount Oita, on the left, and the waters to the right of the Sinus Maliacus, or Gulf of Zituni; a pass, which scarcely admitting the transit of a single chariot, at two different points of the defile, at that time—for the ground has been greatly altered in the lapse of ages, by the deposit of the river Spercheios, and the consequent encroachment of the land on the sea—was tenable by a mere handful against a host. Thither, then, an advanced-guard consisting of three hundred Spartans, a thousand Tegeatians and Mantineans, eleven hundred and twenty Arka dians, four hundred Korinthians, two hundred and eighty Mykenaians and Phliuntians, seven hundred Thespians and four hundred Thebans, the last unwilling as secretly friends to the Persians and under compulsion; in all four thousand four hundred hoplitai of Peloponnesians, with a thousand Lokrians, Opuntians, and Phokians, inhabitants of that district, were thrown forward to hold the enemy in check, and to give courage to the allies by demonstrating the good faith of the Greeks within the Isthmus.

It appears that the Persian armament had even outstripped the anticipation of the Hellenes, for it was by no means intended that this small band should be opposed to the vast hordes of Xerxes; on the contrary the whole Peloponnesian force was destined to support them, so soon as the religious festival of the Karneia at Sparta and the Olympic games, then both in process of celebration, should permit the marching of the reinforcements. What is more singular than this miscalculation is, that to no one of all the assembled nations, gathered in council of war, at the Isthmus, was the existence known of a practicable route through an elevated valley to the west of Thermopylai, by which the position of the defenders might be easily turned by the left flank, and themselves attacked in the rear.

At the same time, with this advanced guard, the Hellenic fleet, consisting of one hundred and twenty-seven Attic triremes, manned by Athenian citizens, and twenty more with Chalcidean crews, with a hundred and twenty-four others furnished by the Peloponnesian confederates, forty of which were Korinthians, and the remainder made up by the small contingents of inferior states, amounting in all to two hundred and seventy-one sail of war-ships, besides twelve penteconters, or long single-banked vessels, pulled by fifty oars on one range, took post at Artemision, the northern promontory of the Island of Euboia, now Egripo, at the mouth of the strait dividing it from the mainland, lying over against the gulf of Volo, to the northward, and nearly opposite to the station of the land forces at Thermopylai, toward the southwest.

There, almost as soon as they arrived, they encountered Xerxes and his host, the land forces occupying the plains beyond the pass, about the rivers Melas and Asopos, and the fleet twelve hundred and seven galleys strong, anchored off Aphetai or Trikhiri, the eastern headland at the mouth of the gulf of Volo.

And, here, so strenuously and with such stern and steady resolution did Leonidas, the Spartan king, defend the defiles, that had the confederates from the Isthmus come up in time with reinforcements, enabling him to occupy the upper pass of Anopaia with a sufficient body of Peloponnesians, there can be little doubt that Xerxes would have been arrested at this point and have returned foiled and disappointed into Asia.

I am not writing the life of Leonidas, nor have I anything to do with the battle of Thermopylai, otherwise than as it is necessarily connected with the events which followed it; for, although as a soldier and a hero, the Spartan king is unsurpassed if not unequalled through all time, and as a display of valor and self-devotion the struggle in the pass is inimitable, yet neither had the chieftain an opportunity of exerting any strategetical talents which he might possess, nor was the action remarkable for any thing, but the immovable courage and constancy of the Greeks.

The result is known to the world. A Melian traitor, Ephialtes by name, betrayed the upper pass of Anopaia to Xerxes, and guided Hydarnes with the ten thousand Persian immortals by the ravines Oita, round their left flank to the rear of the Greeks; this movement being known to Leonidas, he dismissed all his forces, except his own three hundred Spartans, who had all devoted themselves with him to death, the four hundred Thebans whom he had detained unwilling hostages, and seven hundred Thespians, who refused to leave their captain, preferring such a death to ignoble safety. The Phokians, who had been detached to defend the upper pass, failed of their duty, the Immortals forced the defile, the Spartans and Thespians were slain to a man, the Thebans laying down their arms at the first onset, and the pass of Thermopylai was carried; but with such terrible carnage of the Orientals as rendered their success more similar to defeat than to victory. It were useless to debate the utility or moral propriety of such a sacrifice at the present day; inasmuch as modern ideas, both of expediency and duty, are utterly at variance with those of the ancients, and more especially with those of the Spartans. It cannot, however, be doubted, that in very many instances the desperate defence of untenable posts by self-devoted handfuls, has proved the preservation of armies, nay, even of nations, by giving time for the bringing up of reinforcements; for the maturing of plans, and for the organizing of large and general operations. These could not, however, have been the principles on which, in this case, Leonidas acted; for he well knew, before dismissing the main body of his forces, that no reinforcement was on the way, or could by any chance come up in season to make good or recover the disputed pass.

This notion of duty, then, was founded partly on the principle of obedience to the Spartan laws, which declared flight from the field to be the last disgrace, as death upon it was the highest glory, of the citizen; partly, on the necessity of setting a great example of constancy and devotedness to the hesitating and terror-stricken nations of Hellas; and partly, on the desire of winning immortal glory for himself and his companions in arms. And, if it were so, his object was gained from point to point—the obedience to the laws was granted, even by his rigid countrymen, to be perfect as it was marvellous; the example was followed implicitly so long as a Persian stood on the sacred soil of Greece; the glory has been so far immortal, that now, after the lapse of well nigh four and twenty centuries, the memory of Leonidas lives as freshly, and his bays flourish as greenly, the wide world over, as they did then through the brief confines of narrow Hellas.

Two monuments were erected over their ashes, buried on the spot where they fell—monuments nobler than trophies, even as their defeat and death were grander than any victory—one, to the memory of those who died fighting, their flank not yet turned, in the hope of victory; the other above those who remained to die, when not a hope was left save of an honorable death. Their epitaphs run thus,* preserved by Herodotus, who was himself almost their contemporary, rendered literally from the Greek Hexameter and Pentameter into the heroic couplet—of the first,

* Herod. II., 228.

" Here did we fight with Persian millions three,
Peloponnesians, twice two thousand, we."

And of the second, sacred to the three hundred only,

" Go tell the Spartans, friend, that here we lie,
Obedient to their laws, which bade us die."

And this latter one, it is to be presumed, gives us as nearly as possible, the true sentiment and spirit of those true self-sacrificing heroes. There is yet another splendid tribute to their memory, in the form of a brief elegy by the poet Simonides, so beautiful in phraseology, and withal so terse and pointed, that I would fain here embody it, but that my limits, as well as the strict observance of my proper subject, admonish me to abstain.

In the meantime, the Greek and Persian fleets had encountered thrice; and, after some hard fighting, had been thrice separated by nightfall, with no very decided advantage to either party. In the first place, indeed, beholding the Straits and the whole surface of the Gulf of Volo covered, so far as the eye could reach, with the tall and splendid triremes of the Phoinikians and Sidonians, crowded with fighting men, and bearing down on them to offer action, the Greeks, as was in no wise wonderful, were dismayed and confounded at sight of the desperate odds which they had to meet, in seas, too, so open in their idea, though the straits were not above ten miles in width; and had almost determined on retreating to the isthmus, where they might take advantage of narrower waters, in which they might better cope with the vast navy of the Asiatics. And, here, was first brought into play, during the actual imminence of warfare, the singular obliquity of mind, and proneness to deceit and stratagems of all kinds, which I have mentioned as the leading characteristic of the Athenian commander.

The Euboians, it seems, had discovered the purpose of the Greek captains to withdraw their fleet, from the waters of Euboia, within Cape Sunion and into the Saronic gulf; and, dreading the consequences of being thus abandoned to the fury of the Persian, besought Eurybiades the Lakedaimonian, who had been appointed commander-in-chief at the instance of the allies—who were from jealousy reluctant to serve under the Athenians—that he would at least tarry until they could place their children and families in security. On his refusal, they bribed Themistokles, the leader of the Athenians, with the great sum of thirty talents —in round numbers thirty-five thousand dollars—to await the enemy, and deliver battle off the coast of Euboia. He, receiving the money nothing loth, set himself forthwith to gratify the Euboians; for indeed he was from the first well inclined to fight, had he not been over-ruled; and this he effected by purchasing the opinion of Eurybiades at the price of five, and that of Adeimantos the Korinthian, of three talents, which he gave as presents on his own account, and which his colleagues believed to be furnished to that end by the Athenians. They tarried, therefore, and gave battle, Themistokles quietly pocketing the remainder of the enormous prize, and probably consoling himself in the idea that his conduct was unimpeachable, inasmuch as he had only accepted money for doing that which he had previously resolved to do, if possible, as most to the advantage of his own country; perhaps he went so far, in his self-justification, as to convince himself that it was by means of the bribe alone that he was enabled so to serve his country, and that the taking of it was, therefore, not excusable only, but highly virtuous and patriotic. Nor do I well know why he should not have succeeded in so convincing himself; since such is the argument, neither more nor less, which a brilliant and plausible historian* of our own day adduces in defence of Algernon Sidney; who took bribes from Louis the Fourteenth of France, in order to carry on

* Macaulay, Hist. of England. Charles II.

intrigues against the ministry, and to embarrass and frustrate the policy of his own government.

As afterwards at Salamis, so now, the Persians, seeing that the Greeks would abide them, and eager in their confidence of triumph near at hand, sent off two hundred triremes, with orders to round the island of Skiathos to the northward, to circumnavigate Euboia, and to interpose themselves between the Grecian fleet and its harbors, with a view of cutting it off in its anticipated flight—not intending themselves to fight until signals should be made them that their own galleys were in the enemy's rear. But in this they were frustrated, again, by the judgment of Themistokles; who had, not without difficulty, persuaded the Hellenic leaders, almost unanimous before to receive the enemy's onslaught, that it were wiser to sail out and assume the offensive without delay.

There is little doubt that this wily and accomplished leader was perfectly acquainted with the extraordinary and unaccountable changes and seasons of the tide—or current rather, since the Mediterranean is all but tideless—as they prevail in those narrow waters; and that he so chose his hour of attack that the rush of water "which changes its direction many times a day like the wind," as Livy expresses it, "from one point to another, and is hurried along like a torrent tumbling from a steep mountain," should be adverse to the manœuvres of the lofty and unmanageable vessels of the Persian. In the first onset, the Greeks took and sunk thirty sail of the enemy, and made prisoner Philaon the son of Chersis, nephew of Gorgos, king of the Kyprian Salamis—a man of considerable repute—but when the fleets joined in close action, and the encounter was hand to hand, both parties suffered heavy mutual loss, and fighting sturdily, with no thought of flight, were separated only by night, "that common comforter of weary and dismantled armies."

That live-long night, the thunder roared over the whole vault of heaven, which was alive with lightnings flashing from the top of Pelion; and the rains descended insatiate, and the winds lashed the sea into fury, fighting for the Athenians, even as the tempest and the ocean fought for England, on that Christmas night when Hoche's armament was dispersed, never to be combined again, which had anchored at sunset in Bantry bay, already in their hopes victorious. The triremes, which had been sent round on the outside of Euboia, were caught helpless by the tempest, hard-jammed upon a lee-shore, were driven in upon the breakers and the craggy coast, where they perished with their crews, almost to a man; while the corpses and the fragments of the wrecks were drifted into the Persian anchorage off Aphetai, where they whirled in the eddies about the prows, and hampered the oar-blades of the barbarians, filling their minds with present awe, and presages of future ruin. On the following day the Greeks were reinforced by fifty-three new Athenian galleys; and cheered by this accession to their strength, as well as encouraged by previous successes, they again stood out from Artemision, at the same season of the tide, and falling on the Kilikian squadron, which they handled pretty roughly, but still without accomplishing any thing decisive, fought until it was quite dark, when they returned once again to their moorings off the promontory. On the third day, indignant at finding themselves held in check so long, and by so mere a handful, and dreading the wrath of Xerxes, the Persians no longer awaited the attack of the Greeks, but weighing all at once, bore down on them in a vast semicircle, with its wings thrust forward so as to turn both their flanks and envelope them. But, at the same instant, the Athenians met them midway, and the battle waxed furious, and was maintained with dogged obstinacy until nightfall, the loss being very great and nearly equal on both sides; for the very size and numbers of the enemy embarrassed them, falling on board each other and giving rise to confusion worse confounded, so that they derived no advantage from their superiority.

On these three very days, the conflict was raging by land also in the defiles of Thermopylai, with the same object, and for a while with the same result; the Persians in either position striving to force the passes by dint of superior numbers, the Greeks resisting and debarring their further ingress, and at first with absolute success. But that same evening tidings were brought to the leaders of the fleet, how that the Persians had turned the position of Thermopylai, by the left, and how dismissing the allies, Leonidas had fallen worthily of his royal parentage, and of his warlike country; and, their own position being in like manner turned and rendered untenable by the advance of the barbarians, whom there was now no possibility of checking to the northward of the Isthmus, they fell back in good order to Salamis, where they were again in communication with their land-forces, and in readiness to act in concert with them for the defence of the Peloponnesos. Before he retreated, however, Themistokles, still as ever intent on stratagem, ran in with the best sailers of his squadron, to the mouths of the rivers in search of drinking water; and landing there, caused inscriptions to be carved on various stones, which were left scattered here and there for the purpose of being found by the enemy on their advance. These were addressed to the Ionians in the Persian service, exhorting them to remember their Hellenic parentage, and to make common cause with their natural friends and kinsmen, against the common enemy of Greeks and Ionians; or, should that prove impossible, at least to misconduct themselves in action, bearing it in mind that the Athenians had first incurred the resentment of the king, in consequence of their friendly aid, freely rendered to the Ionians of Miletos.

And in this stratagem there was a double craft, a sharpness cutting, as it were, on both edges; first. if it might be, and chiefly, to prevail upon the Karians and Ionians to revolt from the king, which he was well-assured they had good will to do, were they not enforced to obedience; secondly, if that device should be useless, to render them suspect to Xerxes, and so throw the germs of jealousy and discord into the camp of the enemy.

On this, finding himself master, both by sea and land, of the long contested straits, though at a fearful cost of life, for at Thermopylai, twenty thousand men lay dead in the bloody defiles, and between shipwreck and slaughter not less than fifty thousand more had fallen around Artemision, Xerxes prepared to advance into the interior. But first, after performing a deed so unworthy as the mutilation of the corpse of the hero Leonidas, by cutting of his right hand and head, as it was the Persian custom to do with rebels, he concealed the evidences of the heavy loss he had sustained, burying all his dead, with the exception of a thousand, whom he left on the plain, together with the bodies of the slaughtered Greeks, until they should be seen by the crews of the fleet, whom he caused to land and survey the scene of his recent triumph. Yet the stratagem availed him nothing; for, although he had ordered the earth from the pits and trenches to be cast into the sea, that their whereabouts should not be betrayed by the mounds above them, and the disturbance of the soil to be masked by heaps of dead leaves scattered on the surface, the deceit was too palpable even for oriental credulity; when they saw the thousand Persian corpses lying, as they had fallen, scattered here and there about the little plain of Anthela, just without the pass, while the Greeks,* to the number of four thousand, all lay piled together in one heap of carnage, for there were many helots among them, who were readily distinguished from the citizens of Thespia and Plataia, being in all but a thousand men. And this fact would seem to show that at

* Herod. VIII. 25.

Thermopylai, there was even a larger proportion of these light-armed slaves, than subsequently at Plataia, where seven were allotted to each Spartan; for it is probable that, in the three consecutive days of victory, the number slain of the Greek Hoplitai must have been entirely inconsiderable, not exceeding, to take the average of their losses as against the light-armed orientals, fifty or a hundred men; and this would require nearly three thousand helots to make up the tale of the Hellenic dead.

During that day the fleet was deserted, all crowding to glut their eyes with the bloody spectacle, but on the following morning, the mariners returned to Histaia, a city of Euboia, situate a little to the west of Artemision, where the Persian navy had fixed its head-quarters after the retreat of the Greeks to the Isthmus; and the land-forces broke up from their encampment, and poured down on the lower country, like a deluge, devastating and laying waste all the lands, and burning all the temples, villages, and cities, far and near, except within the territory of the Boiotians, who, from hatred to the Athenians, had joined the barbarian to a man. One division, conducted and urged on by the Thessalians, who had an old grudge against the Phokians, broke through the gorge of the Asopus, into the valley of the Kephisus, burning every town they entered, but finding no inhabitants, on whom to wreak their vengeance. All had fled, old and young, male and female, to the wild and cloud-capped summits of Parnassos. A second band marched direct on Delphi, with especial orders from the king to plunder the rich treasury of all its hoarded stores, its golden ingots, vases, statues, tripods, consecrated to the God through ages. But when these were involved in the dim and twilight passes of the mountain, among the solemn gloom of pine forests and thickets of wild bay, with the strange din of subterranean waters and headlong cataracts thundering around them, and the superstitious awe of the dreadful sanctity of the spot, the dark *religio loci*, overshadowing their souls, a fearful tempest burst above them with continuous bellowing of thunders, reverberated from the craggy summits, and vivid flashes, and fiery balls shooting above their heads; while, to complete their consternation, an earthquake—no rare occurrence in that limestone region, though now attributed to the immediate action of Apollo—shook the hills, that two mighty fragments, severed from the twin summits of Parnass s, came crashing down, among the riven and roaring forests, and plunged into their serried masses, crushing and maiming many, and turning all to panic-stricken and disordered flight. Then dreadful voices, and shouts mightier than human, pealed forth from the Korykian cave with a clang as of immortal arms—for in that haunted grotto, and the pathless woods and crags around it, the whole population of Delphi lay concealed, with the exception of sixty men who abided in the temple with the Prophet. And when these saw the terrified barbarians, into what an ecstacy of terror they had fallen, they rushed down upon them from the mountain, rolling great stones and trunks of trees from the precipices, and hurling shafts and javelins into their ranks, amid the storm and lightnings, until the Persians, in the abject terror of their hearts, swore that they saw two gigantic heroes, armed in proof, pursuing them with ruthless slaughter. And these the Delphians said were the phantasms of Autonoos and Phylakos, indigenous heroes of the place, who had their shrines, this by the Kastalian fountain under the summit Hyampeia of Parnassus, that by the roadside, above the temple of Athene Proneie. The third division, which was in truth the main body, under the command of Xerxes in person, passed through Boiotia, sparing the country as being received by the inhabitants with submission and proffered alliance, destroying only Thespia and Plataia, into Attika, which they devastated from end to end, cutting down the olive trees and vineyards, killing the cattle even to the smallest domestic animals, and burning all from the private villa, and the smallest hamlet, to the city itself, with the Acropolis, which he took by a coup-de-main, after a long siege, with the handful of men who defended it, the only citizens of Attika, who fell into his power. The rest, either before the battle of Artemision, or after the return of the fleet to Salamis, had taken refuge, some in the island of Aginæ, some in the smaller isle of Salamis, and some in Troizene of the Peloponnesos, where they were received hospitably, a daily allowance of provision-money being assigned to them with public lodgings, and permission to gather of the vintage at their pleasure.

Salamis is a small rocky island, now called Colouri, situate at the inmost extremity of the Saronic gulf, now the gulf of Eghina, which it nearly bars from each side, leaving only two narrow straits between either extremity and the main land of Attika and Megara, communicating with an interior bay, completely land-locked, about ten miles in breadth by half that length inland. The isle itself is rugged of surface, in the form of an irregular narrow horse-shoe, its outer circumference being about eighteen miles, and its width varying from three to five. It contained at this period three cities, the principal of which was of the same name with the island; and some of its ruins, with traces of walls four miles in circumference, and remains of a temple, supposed to be that of Aias, exist to the present day; but all the more elevated portions of it were clothed to the very top of its rugged and craggy hills, with a luxuriant growth of pine trees—whence its ancient name Pityusa. Thus shaped, it lay close off the coast of Attika, opposite to Eleusis, and due west from the triple harbor of Piræus, Munychia and Phaleron, at about six miles distant, and having Megara about equi-distant to the eastward. The isle of Aigina lay to the south, in the middle of the bay, within ten miles, its splendid temple of Jupiter Panhellenios and the towering cliffs of the tall mountain behind it, in view.

Here, then, in that small and sheltered bay the confederate

Greeks still lay, having put in thither on their return from Artemision, for the purpose of taking off those of the Athenians who had been left within the city; and here, it was at once clear to the mind of the Athenian leader, that battle could be delivered by the Greeks with the most advantage, since the advantage of numbers on the part of the Persians would be so far neutralized by the narrowness of the scene of action that they would be enabled to bring up no more ships in line at once than could be met prow to prow by the Hellenic fleet. Not such, however, was the opinion of the other leaders, especially of Eurybiades, the commander-in-chief, and Adeimantos the Corinthian captain. These argued that to give battle in the bay or the straits, Attika being already in the hands of the enemy, would be in the last degree impolitic, since, in the event of a defeat, they had no retreat except the isle of Salamis, on which they could be easily blockaded, and forced to unconditional surrender. They proposed, therefore, to remove to the Isthmus, on which their land forces were already collected, and which they were rapidly fortifying, and there to fight, having, in the worst view of affairs, the whole of the Peloponnesos on which to fall back.

Themistokles well knew, however, that if once they retired to the isthmus, the confederates would rapidly disperse to their respective cities, and that all regular and organized resistance to the Persian would at once be at an end. He argued, therefore, earnestly, vehemently, and eloquently—for he was a powerful speaker, and the best and strongest feelings of his nature were aroused. Delicacy was needful also, for he dared not allude to his distrust of the Peloponnesian confederates, and his argument was necessarily limited to the military advantages of the one station, and disadvantages of the other; since, by fighting at the Isthmus, they would be compelled to engage in the open sea, where they might be surrounded by the enemy's ships, and overwhelmed by numbers, the rather that they were duller sailers—**βαρυτέραι*—than the Phoinikian and Sidonian war-ships of the king.

Eurybiades appears to have been a cold, cautious, calculating leader, but top-full of that overweening pride and assumption, which was characteristic of the Lakedaimonians—to him, therefore, Themistokles was obliged to preserve an air of deference and almost of humility, by which he in a great degree conciliated his good will; but when Adeimantos the Corinthian taunted him, that "he, a man without a city, should presume to advise men of free states"—for Athens was in the hands of Xerxes, and the ruins of the Akropolis were still smoking in plain view of the fleet—his natural impetuosity burst out, and he exclaimed proudly and fiercely, that the Athenians had a city, and the best city of all Hellas, too, for the present service, their good two hundred galleys, with which they were present there, to fight the battle of all Greece; and in which, should the Greeks desert them, they would embark all the citizens, their families, and treasures, and sail away to Siris, in Italy, which had belonged to them of old, and where they would plant a colony that should be to them a new Athens. And this threat for a while decided them. But when the great armament of Xerxes came into view, augmented by the accession of the Malian, Dorian, Lokrian, and Boiotian contingents, and by reinforcements from Karystos, Andros, Tenos, and other of the Greek islands, so that it was more numerous than that which had fought at Artemision, consternation again fell upon the Greeks, and, after a long and stormy debate, they determined to weigh in the morning, and sail by the western strait along the coast of Megara for the Isthmus, leaving the Athenians only with the Megarenses and Aiginetans to defend Salamis and Megara. Then it was that Themistokles had recourse to his famous stratagem, by which, in the event, he saved Greece, though he might

* Herodotus VIII., 60.

almost as readily have lost it by the same device. He had a Persian in his service, by name Sikinnos, as tutor to his children, and as usual a slave. By this man he sent a message across the straits to Xerxes, who lay at the Phaleron, coming from himself, as if he were disaffected to his country, and desirous of serving the king—to the effect that the Greeks were about to fly to the Isthmus, and that if he desired to crush them at a blow, for they were all in a state of panic and confusion, and incapable of resistance, he would do well to surround the passes of the island, and prevent their egress. Xerxes believed, and so promptly did he act—for contrary to the prudent advice of Artemisia, he had determined to deliver battle—that he caused all his ships to put out at once, although it was already night, and blockaded both the straits, and landed a strong Persian force on the little islet of Psittaleia, on which he expected that many wrecks of the enemy would be driven. And all this was accomplished with such celerity, that, while the council was yet in session, news of the movement was brought to Themistokles by his personal and political enemy, Aristides, whose ostracism he had procured of old, but who had now returned to serve his ungrateful country in her extremity, and in the greatness of his noble nature set aside all individual feelings, and co-operated heart and hand with his gallant antagonist and rival. To him Themistokles communicated his stratagem, and on meeting his approbation, requested him to carry the intelligence to the assembled leaders, for that they would not believe himself, but would suppose it to be a ruse for the prevention of their departure, But still there was doubt and dismay among the Greeks—for the greater part of the leaders were incredulous, until a Tenian ship came in; a deserter from the Persian fleet, confirming the tidings which Aristides brought, he having only escaped capture with difficulty, as he came in a row-boat from Aigina.

It cannot well be doubted that this strange trick of Themistokles was played in good faith to his country, and this is established by his confession of it to Aristides; yet it is not easy to believe, especially when we consider the habitual double-dealing of the man, and the termination of his career, that it was not in some degree actuated by the desire of obtaining Xerxes' good will and favor, in the event of an unfavorable issue.

The next morning, however, terminated all discussion, for with the early dawn, the Persian navy sailed in through the straits, bore down upon the Greeks, who were drawn up in line to receive them, the Athenians on the right toward Eleusis, and the Peloponnesians on the left, towards Phaleron.

The number of the Greek triremes, according to Herodotus, amounted to three hundred and eighty, including the Tenian ship, and another a Samian, which had deserted at Artemision, although in his enumeration of the different nations who were engaged, he does not come up to that amount of galleys. Aischylos, on the other hand, who was himself present in the action, and who greatly distinguished himself, asserts that the whole force of the Hellenes was three hundred, with ten of superior swiftness added; while that of Xerxes was one thousand, with two hundred and seven of unusual speed, and selected for that quality from the rest, agreeing in this precisely with Herodotus, who states expressly that this was the number which sailed from Persia, in the first instance, and that after the shipwrecks and losses at Artemisium, it was furnished to the original number by the accession of the Greeks who had *medized*, as the phrase went, or those who had joined the party of the invaders. This coincidence on one point, renders the difference on the other more striking, and although Herodotus is a most correct and veracious historian, I incline in this instance to give more credit to the Tragedian, as having been present under arms on the occasion, and as giving all the details of the battle, modestly and truth-

* Herodotus, VII. 89. VIII. 46. † Æschylus Persæ, 340.

fully with no poetical inflation, or partizan exaggeration. The following are his words, which although attributed in the tragedy to a Persian messenger, seem to bear something of a personal character:

> This, then, know surely. The barbaric host
> In force of ships prevailed. For of the Greeks
> Ten thirties were the sum, and ten beside
> Select. But Xerxes, for I know it well,
> A thousand ships commanded, and yet more,
> In swiftness all surpassing, hundreds twain
> And seven. So runs the tale.

In any event, the superiority of the Persian in numbers was so extraordinary, that the boldest might well have despaired, and that every advantage of position became necessary to equalize the conflict. At the first, as the Persians entered the bay and bore down upon the Greeks, the latter retreated toward the shoal waters at the head of the bay, expecting to gain something by the change which is not easily discernible at present; but it may have been done in order to cause the Orientals, rowing rashly onward as if in triumphant pursuit, to break their order, if they had any, and to attack one by one in hurry and confusion. If this were the design it was decidedly successful, for the barbaric triremes kept no array or order of battle, nor sailed or fought, as Herodotus has it, on any principle, or with any show of intellect and reason; yet they fought better far and more stubbornly than on the three previous days at Artemisium, for shame and emulation spurred them on, and to these powerful incitements the fear of punishment was added, for upon a spur of the mountain Aigaleos, projecting into the sea opposite to Salamis, sat Xerxes on his golden throne, with a royal canopy above him, scribes crouching around him with their books wherein to inscribe the names, the countries and the cities of the trierarchs or captains of galleys who should distinguish themselves in the engagement, and if he were like to prove a munificent rewarder of merit and valor, it was no less certain that he would mercilessly visit on the heads of delinquents, the penalty of failure, as if it were necessarily the consequence of misconduct and poltroonery—and all along the mountain ridges of the mainland, spectators from the Akropolis, from the rocky brow of thePnyx, from the heights of the Areopagos, the far-famed hill of Mars, westward so far as to Eleusis, glittered the gorgeous masses of the army, with all their bravery of many colored banners fluttering in the sea-breeze, with the rich magnificence of oriental garments, and the gleam of gilded armature, beholding every incident of the encounter, as if from the rows of an amphitheatre, acknowledging every deed of valor by shouts that seemed to rend the very skies, and sympathising even to tears with the disasters of their countrymen.

It is stated by Plutarch, that Themistokles avoided engaging until the hour arrived when a brisk sea-breeze was always wont to blow, bringing in through the straits a heavy and broken surge, which embarrassed the tall Persian vessels, with their castellated sterns and elevated decks, driving them on board one and another, and drifting them so as to expose their defenceless sides and quarters to the beaks of the Hellenic triremes; and this may perhaps explain the temporary retreat of the Greek squadron. How the battle commenced is not perfectly clear, since the Aiginitans assert that one of their ships first turned upon the enemy; while the Athenians claim that honor in behalf of Ameinias, the brother of the poet Aischylos, who at the close of the day obtained the prize proclaimed for the most valiant; and this appears the more probable, as we find him repeatedly named by Herodotus and Plutarch; while his brother, in the Persians, ascribes the first attack to an Athenian ship on a Phoinikian, which coincides precisely with the account of Herodotus, who states that Ameinias, of the tribe of Pallene—Plutarch says of Dekeleia—went about, and, running on board an enemy's ship, got foul of her so that the rest of the fleet were compelled to bring to, and come to close action, in order to relieve him. It is certain that the Athenians and Aiginetans, on the extreme right of the Greek fleet, came into action first; which can only be explained by supposing the Phoinikian galleys opposed to them to have greatly outsailed the other Orientals; since the left wing, consisting of the Peloponnesians, extending eastward toward the Piraios and the strait between Salamis and Attika—by which it would seem probable that the Persians entered from the Phaleron—would have been much nearer to the enemy; unless, indeed, the Phoinikians had been detached to guard the bay of Megara, and so entered by the western strait, rounding the headland of Nisaia, and came at once in contact with the right wing and the Athenians. It was not long, however, before the Lakedaimonians were closely engaged, also, with the Ionians, who attacked on the side of the Piraios, and the action was carried on with the utmost spirit on both sides. It was then that Amenias and Sosides at the same moment ran into the opposite broadsides of the great ship of the Persian admiral, Ariamenes* or Ariabignes†—for authorities differ as to his name—the best and bravest of the brothers of Xerxes, from which the archers and javelineers shot and darted as from a lofty fortress; and these two driving their brazen beaks into its ribs, boarded it, fighting hand to hand with their long spears, and bore the admiral himself overboard into the sea, where he was drowned; so that his body was swept along with fragments of wreck, and being recognized by Artemisia, was carried to Xerxes, after the close of that bloody day.

This was not, however, the mode of fighting generally adopted by the Greeks, whose triremes for the most part were manned only with eighteen fighting men, four of whom were archers, and the rest hoplitai, so that it was not for their advantage to

* Phil. Themist. XIV. † Herod. VIII. 39.

come to close quarters. They depended, therefore, on their superior seamanship and the rapidity of their evolutions, shattering the unwieldy ships of the enemy with the violent onset of their sharp beaks, and throwing them into confusion and disorderly flight.

Some of the Peloponnesians, however, purposely behaved amiss from ill will to the Athenians and Themistokles, but not many; and not a few of the Persians conducted themselves with honorable spirit and valor, even to the capturing or sinking several of the Greek triremes, the crews of which for the most part, except those who were killed or wounded in the conflict, escaped, by swimming to the shores of Salamis. Among these Theomestor, son of Androdamas, and Phylakos, the son of Histiaios, Samians, both captured the ships opposed to them; the former of whom was made tyrant of Samos, for his deeds on that day, and the latter was entitled benefactor of the king, in the Persian tongue Orosanges, and endowed with large territories. Artemisia also, queen of Halikarnassos and the island of Kos, so conducted herself that she extorted from Xerxes the exclamation, that their women on that day were men, and their men, women; and this by a singular and somewhat treasonable stratagem; for being so closely pursued by Ameinias that she had no chance of escape, a reward of ten thousand drachmæ having been offered for her head by the Athenians, and so thickly crowded the fugitives ahead of her, she put up her helm and run her beak directly amidships into the trireme of Damasithumos, king of the Kalynaians, which went down at once with all its crew, not one of whom escaped to tell the tale. Ameinias seeing this, supposed her ship to be either a Greek or a deserter from the king, and so bore up and discontinued his pursuit; while Xerxes, on the other hand, believing the sunken vessel to be a Greek, gave her great praise and honor for the deed. In the midst of the conflict, again, a Samothrakian vessel ran down and sank an

Athenian ship, and was herself, iu turn, run down by an Aiginetan,—when the Samothrakian crew, being javelineers and bowmen, vastly superior in numbers to the Greek fighting men, overwhelmed them with missiles, and making themselves masters of the vessel which had destroyed their own, came off scatheless. The greater number, however, of the Greek ships, captured or disabled, were retaken by their countrymen; as was the case of the Aiginetan guardship of the isle of Skiathos, which being taken by a Sidonian vessel, was with her captor, jointly pursued by Themistokles, in his flag-ship, and by Polykritos, the son of Krios; and was recovered by the latter, who thus saved the life of Pytheas, the son of Ischenor, her commander, who was prisoner to the Persians, and by them condemned to a cruel death, in vengeance for his resolute resistance.

After a fierce conflict between the leading squadrons of the Asiatics and the Greek triremes, in which, though they fought long and stubbornly, the former were completely outmanœuvred, shattered, and dismantled by the sharp onslaughts of the brazen beaks, the Persians turned to fly; and from that instant all was lost, all was over, but the wild confusion and the ruthless carnage. For as the leading ranks of the van turned to fly, the rear had come rushing up through the narrow straits, before a fresh breeze and following sea, and in those narrow passes they fell prow to prow into their own retiring galleys; so that they shattered one another, and were ultimately wedged together into one helpless weltering mass, upon which their swift and active enemy did fearful execution. The vessels of the Aiginetans had, moreover, taken advantage of the blind and reeling fury of the tumult to get below the enemy, and taking post in the throat of the straits toward Phaleron, were ready to intercept them, when they should turn to flight; and thus the Athenians, shattering with their beaks, the prows of those who still resisted, and thundering down upon the sterns of those who fled, and the Aiginetans cutting them off as they strove to escape, the defeat and slaughter were signal and decisive.

How decisive, is evident from the fact, that Xerxes, although his land-forces were entire, unbroken, encouraged by victory, and fierce for renewed action; and his fleet, terribly beaten and shattered as it had been, still probably superior in numbers to the whole Hellenic power; perceiving how completely all his forces of both services were demoralized and spirit-broken by the result of that disastrous day, gave up all thoughts of proceeding with his design of conquest, and gave order for immediate retreat, fearing that the Greeks might anticipate him and break the bridges of the Hellespont, by which alone he could make good his escape into Asia. As it may be agreeable to my readers to compare the prose account of this remarkable and splendid sea-fight, which in its magnitude, completeness, and greatness of ulterior consequence, is in no respect inferior to Actium, Lepanto, or Trafalgar, with the poetical narrative of the great tragedian, who was an eye-witness and participator in the glories of the day, I have thought well to subjoin a translation of the following fine passage from the Persians of Aischylos.

What time the morning with her steeds of light
Had climbed the sky and filled with radiance clear
The universal earth, a cheering shout
Of bold defiance from the Greeks arose,
Hymning their battle anthems; and the voice
Of answering echo from the island rock
Sent back the thrilling clamor. Deep dismay
Fell on the Persians in their hopes deceived;
For not as flying did the Hellenes chaunt
Their solemn pæans, but with souls afire
Fierce rushing to the fight. The trumpets' breath
Inflamed all hearts to glory, and their oars
Cleft the rough billows with harmonious sweep.
Nor long the pause, 'ere seen distinct and clear

Their squadrons hove in view—the right wing first,
With serried ranks well marshalled, and hard after
On came the fleet. Then loud and long upwent
The mighty clamor, "Sons of the Greeks, arise!
"Strike for your country's freedom, for your wives,
"Your children, for the temples of your Gods,
"The graves of your forefathers! now strike home!
"The contest is for all." Nor pealed the while
In fainter accents from the Persian host
Their roar of battle. Doubt was not, nor fear.
But ship to ship with shock of brazen beaks
Was urged incessant—first a Greek trireme
Razed the tall bulwarks and the carven pride
Of a Phoinikian ship; then through the hosts
Each against other drave his trireme strong;
And first the mighty flood o' the Persian fleet
Sustained the onset, but anon the throng
Of their own numbers, in the strait confused,
Wrought tumult to themselves and disarray.
Nor each his neighbor aided; but the beaks
And arrowy prows of brass their groaning sides
Ungovernably smote, and brake their oars.
Meantime the Hellenic ships with constant charge
Thundered around them, that the foamy surge
Was covered by the broken hulls o'erset
Of sinking galleys, not a wave to see
For drifting wrack and weltering warriors slain.
The sea-beat shores, the reefs were piled aloft
With armed carcases. The barbarous host
No longer strove, but in disordered flight
Rowed wildly onward, while the avenging foe
Slew them, like tunnies in the meshy toils
Enveloped, and with broken oars and spars
Of shattered vessels, beat the flyers down,
And smote and slaughtered. Havoc, and despair,
And lamentation o'er the deep prevailed,
'Till night's dim eye closed o'er the glooming sea.

And this, I doubt not, is as true a picture of the scene as ever was drawn by the pen of poet. And yet it would seem, from other accounts, that the strife was over at an earlier hour. Since the Athenians had time to land a body of hoplitai, under Aristides, on the island of Psittaleia, and cut off to a man the Persians who had been landed on it, in view of a widely different termination; and after that, to secure such of the wrecks as floated toward Salamis, where they anchored and repaired damages, so that they were perfectly ready to renew the action, if as they hoped, the king would again offer battle.

Xerxes, moreover, even in the midst of his vexation and distress, found opportunity to make such demonstration of intending to prosecute the war, as prevented the Athenians from taking measures to intercept his escape, and actually began making preparations to throw a mole across the strait to Salamis, though he had indeed no thought but to fly on the instant, and that with all speed.

But when, at dawn of the following day, the Greeks saw that the army still held its ground about Athens, they rejoiced, as thinking to find the fleet off the Phaleron, and sailed out at once in order, eager to deliver battle. But the ships were gone, Xerxes having entrusted his children to the charge of the brave queen Artemisia; and though the Greeks chased so far as to the isle of Andros, they never got sight of a sail. And here, indeed, the campaign, and the military career also of Themistokles, terminated; for when he proposed that the confederates should at once sail to the Hellespont, and break the bridges, so that, as he expressed himself, they might capture Asia in Europe, the other Greeks overpowered his opinion, on the ground that it was dangerous to reduce an enemy yet so powerful to the necessity of finding valor in despair, and fighting not for conquest but existence. And he again had recourse to his characteristic trickery, sending Sikinnos once again to Xerxes, with a message to the effect that he, Themistokles, had prevailed with the Greeks not to break the bridges, as wishing well to the king, and advised him to make the best of his way back to Asia, or ere he should be pursued in force; and this, as he represented, to get rid of him the quicker.

After this, on the return of the fleet of the Isthmus, Xerxes having already fled with the bulk of his forces, nearly the whole of whom perished before reaching the Hellespont, of fatigue, pestilence and famine, leaving Mardonios only with three hundred thousand men, rather, as Herodotus conceives, to cover his retreat than to effect any thing real toward the subjugation of Greece; the prizes of valor were ascribed, among the states, to the Aiginetans; among the men to Polykritos of Ægina, and to Ameinias of Pallene, and Eumenes of Anagyrasis, both Athenians. But to Themistokles, of the leaders, the highest honors were assigned by general consent; and afterwards, on his visiting Sparta, by invitation, an olive wreath was presented to him as the wisest of captains; and, on his departure, he received a gift of the finest chariot in Lakedaimon, and was escorted over the frontiers by a guard of honor of three hundred Spartan nobles, mounted in war array—a tribute of merit never paid before or after to any citizen by that stern and rigid people.

It would be well, if the life of Themistokles had terminated here; for, though all the remainder of it was marked by talent and sagacity, not inferior to what he had already displayed, it was all tainted with deceit, trickery, and baseness, and closed, I fear, in treason. His first course, was under the pretext of punishing the islanders who had Medized to, and of levying a fund for the maintenance of future wars against the Persians, to enrich himself by pillage and extortion, the most barefaced and atrocious; and he did this to such an extent, that, after his exile and the transference of the greater part of his property to Asia, there were still found and confiscated above eighty talents, equal to about eighty-five thousand dollars, when before the war he had possessed barely three thousand. It is true, he prevented the iniquitous attempt of the Lakedaimonians, to keep Athens in a subordinate, if not subject state, by opposing the rebuilding the fortifications demolished by Xerxes; but this was effected by a degree of chicanery and falsehood, which, though it may in some sort be palliated by the necessity of the case, and the ill-faith of Lacedæmon, in no light redounds to the credit of the tricky diplomatist who planned it.

Shortly thereafter, his open corruption and overbearing arrogance of demeanor, as if assuming the whole merit of Xerxes' defeat, together with the growth of the opposite faction in the state, led to his ostracism, or temporary banishment; during which he remained at Argos; until the manifest treason of Pausanias being discovered at Sparta, and himself implicated in it, as appeared from the private papers of the Spartan leader, he was pursued both by the Lakedaimonians and Athenians with such rancor, that he escaped, not without difficulty, to the Asiatic continent; where he was received with the warmest and most honorable welcome by the king, who indeed used him as a private and familiar friend and associate, and allotted to him the revenues of three royal cities for his maintenance. Here he resided several years in luxury and ease, till Artaxerxes planning a new expedition for the conquest of Greece, and summoning Themistokles to advise with him, and aid him in his enterprise, the wise and wily Greek died, just in time to spare his memory the charge of overt and armed treason; as Herodotus writes, by poison, self-administered; but as Thucydides believes, to whom I attach more faith—not as more honest, but as less credulous—of disease engendered by the disappointment of his vanity, the frustration of his ambition, and the shame he must needs have felt at the thought of having once been the best citizen and savior, and being now the worst enemy of Athens.

In regard to his character as a statesman and strategist, there can be but one opinion—in both departments he was unsurpassed, if not unsurpassable. To him alone may be ascribed the preservation of the liberties of Greece, and the continued Europeanism of Europe. His strategy was of that class which relates rather to the management and manœuvring of forces out of the enemy's sight, than to their disposition or conduct in action. But his foresight of events, his selection of times and places, his calculation of results, seem to have been almost infallible, while his coup d'œil was certain, and his resources inexhaustible.

For his individual and moral character no one can have the slightest respect, or hold with him the slightest sympathy. To enemies and friends, whether it was actually traitorous or not, his course was invariably indirect and tortuous. And, even if it be granted, that, in view of the benefits conferred on his country, his ostracism was unjust and harsh; that his complicity in the manifest treason of Pausanias was unproved; that in the then state of the Hellenic mind he could have had no fair trial; and, that he had no other recourse for safety than flight to the Asiatic —still, when we look to his continual tampering with the kings of Persia, to his transference of his ill-gotten gains to Asia, previous to his own flight, and to the open manifestations of gratitude due to him from Artaxerxes, and paid even to excess of interest, I fear we must, impartially judging from the evidence, pronounce him a traitor, even as we have pronounced Miltiades an enemy, to freedom; even though it were the lot of both to save their country, and to win, perhaps, the two greatest victories on record in behalf of liberty.

At all events, a career so bright and glorious in its commencement, should never have been so dark, so doubtful, and so desperate, in its close; and if one were innocent, he would do better far to die nobly like Sokrates and Phokion, victims to calumny and ingratitude, than to live basely, a self-constituted object of suspicion, an exile in a hostile land, and the creature of a foreign tyrant, like Themistokles, the great, but alas! not good, Athenian.

IV.

PAUSANIAS,

THE SPARTAN.

HIS BATTLE OF PLATAIA; HIS CAMPAIGNS, CHARACTER, AND CONDUCT.

It is not a little remarkable, that of the greatest Hellenic captains, several, and those not the least distinguished of the early times, were what the Greeks termed *μονόμαχοι*, or single fighters, not in the usual sense of single combatants or gladiators, but men distinguished for their conduct in a single battle. Of this class were Miltiades, Themistokles, Pausanias, the subject of the present notice, Kimon, and others scarcely inferior to these in celebrity. This great and fortunate leader was of the royal blood of Sparta, though not himself a king, being the son of Kleombrotos, and so descended directly from Hyllos, son of Herakles; but, as cousin german and next of kin to Pleistarchos, son of Leonides, who had succeeded to his father's dignity although a minor, he was appointed to be his guardian, and to command the confederate land forces, after the battle of Salamis and the flight of Xerxes. His colleague Leotychides, the other king of Lakedaimon, was absent with the fleet which he commanded, and

7

which was now employed in liberating the Ionians of the islands, and observing the Persian squadrons in the Hellespont and on the coasts of Asia Minor.

We have seen above* that the battle of Thermopylai occurred during the celebration of the Karnean festival at Sparta, and the Olympic games at Elis—the coincidence of which shows that it took place in the beginning of the Athenian month Metageitnion, corresponding to the end of our August and the beginning of our September. The sea-fight of Salamis ensued in the October of the same year, and the flight of Xerxes with the main body of his host followed without an interval. Mardonios, however, was left behind with three hundred thousand picked troops, independent of camp-followers, composed of the Persian Immortals and horse-cuirassiers, all the Medes, Sakians, Bactrians, and Indians, both horse and foot, together with the best men of the other national contingents. These troops had all wintered in Makedonia and Thessaly, where all the Greeks had Medized, and where the fertile and extensive plains afforded grain for his men and forage for his numerous cavalry, which he could not have procured in the barren and limited territory of Attika, already devastated by the circumstances of the last campaign. Sixty thousand men, however, under Artabazos, having been detached as an escort to the king, had been employed during three months of the winter in the reduction of Potidaia and Pallene, which had revolted, had lost great numbers of their force by a violent and unexampled irruption of the sea, and had now rejoined Mardonios, greatly diminished in strength; though this loss was more than compensated by the alliance of the Medizing Greeks Thessalians, Boiotians, and Phokians, the latter of whom fought reluctantly and on compulsion. These Hellenic allies are computed vaguely by Herodotus at fifty thousand, in round numbers, though he states that they were never enumerated; and he

* Miltiades.

farther estimates the Persians at full thirty myriads, which can, of course, be considered merely as an approximation, since that is the exact force said to have been originally left by Xerxes, without any allowance for the heavy losses of Artabazos, or the unavoidable casualties of so large a body of men encamped in a foreign country.

The following campaign appears to have opened early by a descent on Attika, in force, made contrary to the advice of the Medizing Greeks, who strongly urged it on Mardonios to remain in a state of "masterly inactivity," trusting to the international jealousies and selfishness of the confederated Greeks, and to the influence of his bribery, for which he had unbounded means, in plate, coin, bullion, rich raiment, and the like; by which he might disperse the allied forces gathering at the Isthmus, and so reduce the enemy in detail. And such, it can hardly be doubted, would have been the result, had that sound advice been followed; but Mardonios, influenced partly by a puerile vanity, and partly by the desire of conveying to his king tidings of the re-occupation of Athens, by fire-signals through the islands, insisted on active operations; and, re-taking Attika, proceeded to destroy and lay waste all that had escaped the ravages of the preceding year. It is stated, by that enlightened traveller, Colonel Leake, to whose topographical researches I am largely indebted, that for the transmission of such fire-signals the following stations would have sufficed: Mount Hymettos, the isles of Tia, Syra, Myconos, Nicaria, and Samos, across the Aigean, and mounts Gallesos and Tmolus, in Asia Minor. It is not a little curious to contrast with this route, drawn up from actual survey by an intelligent and experienced geographer, the long line of fire telegraphs, described by Aischylos, in his Agamemnon,* over the same country, with

* It need not be premised that in the poetic narrative of Aischylos, the line of route, instead of following down the shore of Asia Minor to the narrowest part of the Archipelago, where the islands lie the thickest,

this exception only, that the one line runs from Troy to Argos, the other from Athens to Sardis; the starting places and terminations being respectively within a hundred miles one of the other.

Previous, however, to entering Attika, Mardonios sent Alexander of Makedon to treat with the Athenians, in the hope of inducing them to Medize; and so greatly were the Peloponnesians, then engaged in fortifying the Isthmus, alarmed at the prospect of their defection, that they also sent ambassadors, to promise aid and confirm their resolution. But there was no occasion

crosses directly to the European side, and descends the long indented coast of Thessaly and Upper Greece, the stations being so far apart, above sixty miles on the average, as to render the transmission of news by any ordinary system of lights impossible. The lines are, however, so spirited, and it seems so probable that the idea was suggested to Aischylos by this device of Mardonios, that I have not scrupled to introduce them here, from my own version of the noble tragedy named above. The Choreutes asks Klytaimnestra, what messenger could have conveyed to her, so speedily, the tidings of the fall of Troy, and she makes answer—

Hephaistos, forth from Ida sending light.
Thence beacon thitherward did beacon speed
From that fire-signal. Ida to the steep
Of Hermes' hill in Lemnos; from the isle
Zeus' height of Athos did in turn receive
The third great ball of flame. The vigorous glare
Of the fast-journeying pine-torch flared aloft,
Joy's harbinger to skim the ridgy sea,
Sending its golden beams, even as the sun,
Up to Makistos' watch towers. Nothing loth
Did he, nor basely overcome by sleep,
Perform his herald part. Afar the ray
Burst on Euripos' stream, its beaconed news
Telling the watchers on Mesapion high.
They blazed in turn, and sent the tidings on,
Kindling with ruddy flame the heather gray.

why they should have doubted that generous and high-spirited people, who with their open villages in ruins, their capital yet smoking, their sacred Akropolis and the holiest temples of their gods in ashes, their women and children safe in the Peloponnesos, and their government beyond the reach of the enemy, in Salamis, were little likely now to yield to an enemy who had wreaked on them the extreme bitterness of his fury, and could injure them no farther. And if they did doubt, the noble answer of the Athenians to Alexander and to their own delegates must needs have reassured them. "Go tell Mardonios," they replied, "that the Athenians, 'so long as the sun travels the same path which he now follows, never will submit to Xerxes; but, trusting to the gods and heroes, our allies—whose temples and whose statues, respecting none of them, he burnt with fire—we will go out in arms, and fight him to extremity"—and to the Greeks—"There is not gold enough on the face of the whole earth, nor any region so excellent in virtue and beauty, that to receive it we would Medize, and be the means of enslaving Hellas." And

Thence, nought obscured, went up the mighty glow,
And, like the smiling moon, Asopos' plain
O'erleaped, and on Kithairon's head awoke
Another pile of telegraphic fire.
Nor did the watchmen there, with niggard hand,
Deny the torch that blazed most bright of all.
Athwart the lake Gorgopis shot the gleam,
Stirring the guards on Aigiplanctos hill,
Lest it should fail to shine the appointed blaze.
Kindled with generous zeal, they sent aloft
The mighty beard of flame that streamed so high,
To flash beyond the towering heights which guard
The gulf Saronic. Thence it shot—it reached
Arachnes' cliff, the station next our town,
Down-darting thence to the Atreides' roof—
Child of that fire which dawned on Ida's hill.

AGAMEMNON. 331.

again—"Know, therefore, this, if you knew it not before, that so long as one Athenian shall survive, we never will submit to Xerxes." Such is the way in which men should speak, and so spoke the Athenians—and as they spoke they acted. But to the shame of the Peloponnesians, it must be recorded, that their noble confidence in their own valor and the good faith of their allies, elicited no corresponding generosity from the cold Peloponnesians. They promised, indeed, to send their full force to the rescue, and in conjunction with the Athenians, to deliver battle in the Thriasian plain before Eleusis, on the frontiers of Attika; but when Mardonios poured down his hundreds of thousands, through the passes of Mount Kithairon, into Attika, and re-occupied the Akropolis, and swept all the Megaris with his superb cavalry, their hearts failed them, or their selfishness prevailed—for the Isthmus was now fortified from sea to sea, with a strong wall and a system of redoubts—and not a man issued from their lines to succor Athens, in this her second calamity. Nor was it until a deputation came from Salamis, reproaching them severely with their bad faith and cowardly tergiversation, and informing them that if unassisted they had no option left but to Medize, and so escape extermination as a state, that the Peloponnesians perceived how surely, in spite of all their walls and fortresses, they must fall, should Athens join with the invader to attack. Then at length, nor then until after fresh delays on the old plea of sacred festivals—for it was now the Hyacinthia—they did bestir themselves, and sent out from the Lakedaimon, five thousand Spartans, the very flower of their fighting men, accompanied each Spartan by seven light-armed Helots, in all forty thousand combatants, and these were speedily followed by five thousand Lakonians of the surrounding country, each with a single attendant, and in rapid succession by the contingents of the other confederated cities.

Intelligence of this movement was conveyed to Mardonios, by

the Argives, who from hatred of Sparta had Medized, though tney dared not openly join the enemy, and he began to fall back deliberately on the friendly territory of Boiotia. Suddenly learning, however, that an advanced-guard of one thousand Lakedaimonians were already in the Megaris, he wheeled upon them in the hope of cutting them off before the arrival of their supports, and launched his horse over the open country to intercept and isolate them. In these movements it is stated by Herodotus,* that the Persian army reached the farthest western point it ever attained in Hellas—an error well corrected by Col. Leake,† for they had attempted Delphi, the preceding year, which lies at least forty miles to the westward, though almost as many north, of the Megaris. Had he said southern instead of western point, he would have hit the mark, but even the most accurate of the ancient writers have little idea of the comparative bearings even of places well known to them; and little reliance can be placed on their geography.

It was not long before the Persian commander learned that the whole Peloponnesian force had arrived at the Isthmus, when he called off his cavalry and retreated upon Thebes, at about six miles in front of which, on the northern or right bank of the river Asopos, and on the edge of the plain of the Platais, he established himself in an entrenched camp, containing something above a square mile of ground, palisaded and fortified with lofty wooden towers.

Here he was joined for the first time by the Phokians, to the number of a thousand hoplitai, who had as yet made no active movement in his favor; and so little was he satisfied with their tardy aid that he made a formidable demonstration of attacking them with his cavalry, which seems indeed to have been prevented from becoming something more serious than a demonstra-

* Herod. IX. 14.

† Travels in Northern Greece, Vol. II. 339. Chap. XVI.

tion only by the bold front maintained by the Phokian foot, who formed, what is termed the *synaspismos*, an order of battle in which only a foot and a half each way was occupied by every soldier, so that their large shields were in close contact, and their bristling spears were as close as quills upon the fretful porcupine. After this trial, however, they were amicably treated, and admitted to form a portion of the army.

The plain of the Platais, so named from the city of Plataia, situated on a lofty spur of Mount Kithairon, now Elatia, on its south-eastern verge, lies to the north of the main ridge of that mountain, which is four thousand three hundred feet in height, descending very steeply to the walls of the town, and an inferior branch of the same mountain, extending eastward to Mount Parnes, parted from it by a gorge called Dryoskephalai, the oak-heads, in which are some of the sources both of the Asopus and the Oërope, and through which wind two different roads from Megara, and the Isthmus northward.

In front of Plataia are a number of low spurs and ridges, the principal of which, at about a mile and a half eastward of the city, is the water shed between the straits of Euripos and the Korinthian gulfs, sending off the head waters of the Asopos, eastward to the former, and those of the Oërope, south-westward to the latter, their fountains which are large and numerous being nearly intermingled.

At about two miles distant, north-eastward of the city, lie the ruins Hysiai, and nearly at the same distance and on the same line, those of Erythrai, both on the Parnes ridge of Kithairon, eastward of the pass of Dryoskephalai, and the latter one mile due south of the main river Asopos, now the Vuriendi, which here runs nearly east and west, receiving the tributary from the oak-heads falling into it almost at right angles to the principal channel. To the west of this tributary, and directly in front of Plataia, with the temple of Here at the extreme northern point of the city overlooking it, lies what is termed in Herodotus, the Island; but it is no island, but a low flat meadow, intersected and luxuriantly watered by half a dozen rivulets, which form the river Oërope. Midway between Plataia and the oak-heads to the eastward, is the ridge Argiopios, of very inconsiderable elevation, with the shrine or Heroum of Androcrates, and the fountain of Vergutiani, supposed to be that in which Actaion saw Diana bathing, at its northern and southern extremities, and again nearly midway between the Argiopios and the tributary of the Asopos, alluded to above, is the fountain of Gargraphia, often alluded to in the account of the great action which ensued. Farther than this I have only to add that the plain of the Platais, measured to the northward from the pass of Dryoskephalai to the Asopos, is four miles in width, intersected by many rivulets and low hills, but every where suitable for cavalry operations. Beyond the Asopos, northward yet, the ground slopes upward very gradually in open downs, perfectly adapted to military manœuvres to the walls of Thebes, six miles distant. In length, from the ruins of Erythrai, to the western extremity of the island, the measure does not fall short of six miles. It must be observed, that all the positions and all the fighting in Pausanias' great battle was to the southward of the Asopos, although the Persian camp lay to the northward of it opposite Erythrai, and extending westward until nearly over against Hysiai. A careful reading and correct understanding of this geographical account is almost indispensable to a clear comprehension of what follows, as the manœuvres are as complicated as those of any ancient battle. I shall merely add, previous to entering on the details of the battle, that it is the opinion of Colonel Leake, which is of the greatest military authority as a distinguished officer of rank, that there is no reason, as has been repeatedly asserted there is, for disputing the number of the troops, as given by Herodotus, who were engaged on that day on the score of the incapacity of the Platais to contain them. Assuming the number of the Greek force at ninety thousand men at the very smallest, he says " for such an army the space was amply sufficient in each of the three positions which they occupied. In the first and second, the front was about three miles in length, with an indefinite space in the rear. On the day of battle the hoplitai formed three separate bodies, two of these had each a mile for their front, and there was nearly a square league of ground to contain all the light troops, together with those hoplitai, who had formed the centre of the Greek line in their second position, and who in the third were in the rear near the Heræum." Again speaking of the Persian host, he observes, " even on the supposition that they were three to one, there was sufficient space for them in the Platais, as none but the choicest infantry were immediately opposed to the Greeks, and the cavalry, as well as the light-armed, on both sides may have been spread over a space of twelve or fourteen square miles. Even in modern warfare, in which the range of missiles has created an order of battle much less deep than that of the Ancients, examples might be found of fields of battle as small in proportion to the numbers as that of Platæa," and in a note he adds—" at Borodino, two hundred and fifteen thousand men fought for fifteen hours, within the space of little more than a square league."*

This may be received in my opinion as perfectly conclusive whether we regard it as that of a clear sighted and intelligent eye-witness, or as that of a distinguished artillery officer whose judgment on matters of military science, range and distance, must be superior to that of the ablest civilian. And now, without farther preamble I shall proceed at once to the details and incidents of this most important and decisive action.

Mardonios then was encamped in his entrenched position,

* Travels in Northern Greece, Vol. II. 355.

north of the main Asopos, at the eastern extremity of the Platais opposite to the small town of Erythrai, on the spurs of the Parnes ridge of Kithairon, and his force, only approximated by Herodotus in his rating it at three hundred and fifty thousand, cannot reasonably be computed at less than three hundred thousand, account being taken both of Artabazos' losses, and of the accession of Greek auxiliaries.

To meet these the Peloponnesians marched out under Pausanias, the son of Kleombrotos, from the Isthmus, and were joined at Eleusis by the Athenians, who had crossed over from Salamis, led by Aristidles, when being well informed of the enemy's position on the Asopos, they advanced by the pass of the Oak-heads, and bearing to the north eastward of the large southern tributary of the river, formed line of battle on the left bank, opposite to the Persian camp, from which their centre was about fifteen hundred yards distant, their right somewhat advanced in front of Erythrai, and their left in about the same degree retired before Hysiai, and a large walled fount still extant. The whole of this position is on the lower spur of the Parnes branch of Kithairon, so often mentioned, and was in general nearly inaccessible to cavalry, of which they were themselves entirely destitute, not having even wherewithal to protect their convoys coming up from the Isthmus, or to cover the approach of reinforcements which were continually pouring in from the rear.

Seeing that the Greeks were resolved by no means to descend into the plain, Mardonios at once determined to launch his cavalry against them, which he did under the leading of Masistios, who was esteemed the second best man in the army. This splendid arm of the Persian service, which cannot, according to the usual proportion of horse and foot in Oriental armies, be computed at less than sixty or eighty thousand, came dashing up the steep and rugged banks, in all the pride and pomp of Eastern war, with barbaric music sounding—cymbals, and gongs, and kettle-drums—and hundreds of bright banners waving, and their full-blooded barbs literally shaking the earth beneath the thick-redoubled clatter of their furious gallop, and the clash and clang of the mail-coats of their riders, and kindling the very air with their furious neighings. On front and flank, at once, they charged almost upon the serried spears of the solid phalanxes, which met them everywhere, unmoved, on the brink of the stony heights, and hurled their sharp-barbed javelins, and shot their hail of arrows into the solid ranks; and wheeled, as if to fly, but in flying still shot and darted their clouds of missiles, and again charged home, and wheeled again, flitting and circling to and fro like clouds of sea-fowls; making no impression, it is true, on the firm array, but wholly unmolested by them; for the light infantry of the Greeks—never, until after the creation of targeteers by Iphicrates, a favored arm of the Hellenic service—was at this time especially deficient, for they had scarcely any archery, and it seems that aim was uncertain with the javelin, and the range short and ineffective. At length the Megarensians, to the number of three thousand, who were posted in a situation far more accessible to cavalry, and nearly on level ground, were so hard pressed by the horse, who rode in resolutely to their very spear points, threatening literally to tramplet hem under foot by their desperate and incessant charges, and so severely galled by the clouds of projectiles which fell on them in all directions, that they sent, still preserving their order and sustaining the attack with stubborn resolution, to the general for reinforcement. It is not stated by any of the historians in what part of the line the Megarensians were stationed, nor is it easy to discover this, as the lower spurs of the hill on which the Greek was posted, in a very obtuse angle, with the apex toward the enemy, are, apparently, nearly continuous and equally abrupt at all points; but on a close examination of the map, I am inclined

* Herod. IX., 21. Plutarch, Aristides, XIV.

to believe that they must have stood exactly in the centre, where the valley of a rivulet flowing northward to the Asopos, nearly bisects the position, and probably has some level ground on its banks, which would favor a charge of horse. If it be so, the attack was doubly formidable, and the danger imminent; for it would appear, that if the Megarensians should give way, the army would be cut in two, and the enemy's horse might have passed up the ravine, and so gained the rear of the whole army, which would then have been, of course, assailed in front by the infantry of the Immortals, and other picked troops of the enemy. At all events, the hazard seemed so great that volunteers were called for, and three hundred of the Athenian hoplitai, under Olympiodoros, the most active and eager of the captains, were detached, having bowmen mingled with their files, to their succor; and these, who had been on the advanced guard before Erythrai, rushed forward, cheering loudly, with so much impetuosity, and with so well sustained a flight of arrows, that the battle was restored. Still, however, the Persian horse fought undauntedly, and made charge after charge, as if resolute to break in upon the pikes of the phalanx; but, at length, the Greek archers shooting singly, and with deliberate aim, as the cavalry dashed in upon them rank after rank, the charger on which Masistios rode was pierced through the flank by an arrow, and, on the anguish of the wound, reared bolt upright, and unseated his gallant master. Then before he could recover his feet, being overloaded by the weight of his panoply—for he was armed not only on the head and breast but on all his limbs,* with gold, and brass, and steel—the Athenians rushed upon him, and captured his charger, which was bedecked with bits and necklaces of gold, and in the end slew him, resisting desperately, and well defended by a corselet† of gold scale armor, above which he wore a crimson tunic. For so well tempered was the armor that it turned

* Plut. Aristides, XIV. † Herod. IX. 22.

all their blows and thrusts, and he remained unwounded, until he was stabbed at length with the reverse point of a javelin, through an opening of his helmet and his eye, into the brain. He was the tallest man, it is said, and the handsomest, in the Persian army; and was held both by the Persians and the king as their most considerable personage after Mardonios. At first the Barbarians, who had not seen what had befallen him in the tumult, wheeled off and began to retire; but when they learned that Masistios had fallen, they brought all their horses round unanimously and charged, no longer in successive squadrons, but all abreast, in one great solid mass. Then the three hundred Athenians, seeing themselves completely overwhelmed by numbers, and finding themselves borne back, in spite of all their resistance, and compelled to abandon the body, shouted aloud for reinforcement to the army; and, the heavy hoplitai rushing in from all quarters to the rescue, the horse were no longer able to endure their onset with the pike, or to carry off the dead, but wheeling off on all sides, and rallying at about two stadia* distance, held council, what they were to do in this emergency. Then, after a while, they fell off, and retreated to Mardonios, as being now without a leader—leaving the honors of the day and the body of their commander as a trophy to the Greeks.

And the lamentation and mourning for Masistios was great in the Persian camp; for they not only wailed and howled for the slain, till all Boiotia was filled with the echo of their lamentations, but the men shaved off their beards and eyebrows, and cut off the manes and tails of their mules and horses, such was the mode and measure of their sorrow for Masistios.

And the Greeks only became acquainted with the greatness of the exploit by the emphatic grief of the enemy, for beside the leader they had slain but a few of the horse. Yet they exulted

* A quarter of a mile English measure.

greatly and prided themselves on their success in beating off such a cavalry. Nor did they so without good cause—for no horse on earth—not the Mamelukes against Napoleon's fire-breathing infantry at the Pyramids—not Milhaud's cuirassiers against the immovable British squares at Waterloo, could have behaved better than did the Persian cavalry, on the first day of Plataia. They charged home, not once, but repeatedly, on the pike-points of the phalanx, and no men can do more; for if the triple lines of a modern square, armed only with the short musket and bayonet, can fearlessly defy the onset of horse so long as they preserve their equal order, what must have been the effect of files eight deep, and sarissæ twenty-four feet in length, in resisting a similar attack. At the same time, we must remember that the Greeks had every reason to be proud of their steadiness on this memorable occasion; for if it is to this day held the most trying duty of infantry, and the highest proof of their soldierly qualities, to resist charging horse, even while the musketry of their rear rank is decimating their assailants with an incessant roll of fire; much more difficult and trying must it have been to troops, who, themselves harassed and cut up by the missiles of the cavalry, had no projectiles, and could offer only a passive resistance to an enemy, thus to them invulnerable. This action is further memorable, as one of the very few occasions in the ages of classic warfare, on which horses attempted to charge unbroken infantry front to front; and as the first instance on record of infantry charging cavalry in line, with the pike, and that too successfully; for such was the movement by which, after a repulse, they recovered the body of Masistios from his countrymen.

The consequences were important, though the loss on either side was inconsiderable, so far as numbers were concerned; for the Greeks were so greatly encouraged by their success in beating off the formidable horse of the Persians, that they now ventured to change their position, which was disadvantageous owing to the scarcity of water; there being but one small fountain, to the north east of Hysiai, in the rear of their extreme left, wherefrom to water the whole army, the right of which was at least two and a half miles distant. On the very afternoon of this sharp affair, therefore, after parading the armed body of Masistios in a chariot through their ranks, they countermarched, by the road from Athens through Phyle to Plataia, passing through Hysiai, and by several springs, where the modern village of Kriakuki now stands, at the opening of the Gorge of Dryoskephalai into the plain.

This circuitous route, in taking which they must have appeared to be in full retreat, they chose, because it lay along the steeper spurs of Mount Kithairon, and when it descended into the low ground, left both the river Asopos and its largest tributary between them and the enemy. On reaching the springs, they turned northward by the road to Thebes, and took up a new position, partly in the plain, partly on a series of low ridges divided by many rivulets falling into the Asopos.

It was at this stage of the proceedings, probably, that a dispute arose between the men of Attika and the Tegeatans for the post of honor on the left wing, which the Spartans at once decided in favor of the Athenians, as the conquerors of Marathon; for immediately afterward they formed line of battle by nations, in the following order.

The Lakedaimonians, holding the right wing, advanced from the Theban road, and formed line, in an obtuse angle, its apex pointing due east, and its upper limb facing the south-western corner of the fortified camp of the Persians. Its lower limb occupied a line of heights forming the west bank of the large tributary stream so often mentioned, having the fountain Gargaphia in the rear of its right, while the left rested on a strong stream running due north, close, and nearly parallel, to the Theban road.

The Spartans, Laconians, and Tegeatans, who composed this division, were eleven thousand five hundred strong of hoplitai, ten thousand of whom were from Lakedaimon; with them fought forty-one thousand five hundred light troops—seven helots to each of the five thousand Spartans, and one to every other shield —raising the full force of the division to fifty thousand soldiers. The centre, which lay on a line nearly at right angles to the general direction of the right, facing the Asopus and the north, was composed of five thousand Korinthians, three hundred Potidaians, and six hundred Arkadians of Orchomenos; Sikyonians, three thousand; Troizenians, one thousand; Epidaurians, eight hundred; and Lepreans, two hundred. From Mykenai and Tiryns came four hundred; Philius sent a thousand; Eretria, Styris, and Chalkis of Euboia, a thousand more; Ambroia, Anactorium, and Leukas thirteen hundred; Kephallenia contributed two hundred; Aigina, five hundred; Megara, three thousand; and, to conclude, Plataia gave six hundred. The centre was composed, therefore, of nineteen thousand two hundred hoplitai, with an equal number of light armed soldiers; or in all, of thirty-eight thousand four hundred fighting men. The left wing, consisting of the Athenians, eight thousand strong in shields, with as many more light-armed, were formed again in another obtuse angle, a little in advance of the left of the centre, with their own left resting on the north-westerly road to Thebes, and pushed forward to within a hundred paces of the Asopos. This division, therefore, contained sixteen thousand men of all arms; but to these must be added, I presume, eighteen hundred Thespians, who, according to Herodotus, were in the camp as supernumeraries, and these not hoplitai. The addition of these Thespians would raise the force of the left wing to seventeen thousand eight hundred men, and that of the whole army to one hundred and nine thousand two hundred soldiers, of whom thirty-eight thousand were completely armed hoplitai, and seventy thousand five hundred light armed skirmishers.*

The whole position which they now occupied, the two wings forming obtuse angles in different directions, like bastions, with a horizontal centre, like a flat curtain, between them included a semicircular space of ground surrounded on three sides, as by a wet ditch, by the Asopos and its tributaries. It was well supplied with water, by the fountain Gargaphia in the right rear of the right wing, by four large rivulets passing through the posi-

* Herod. IX., 28, 29, 30. The above enumeration is made up from Herodotus, who singularly enough has made an error in his summing up, which all his successors, even Colonel Leake, have followed, not having troubled themselves to verify his numeration. The following are his facts—10,000 Lakedaimonians, half Spartans, and 1,500 Tegeatans=11,500. Allied Greeks of the centre, 19,200. Athenians, 8000.—That is—11,500+19,200+8,000=38,700. And so he correctly states it. Then add for the 5,000 Spartans—seven Helots to each=35,000; add for every other Hoplites—for this 38,700 Hoplitai—5000 Spartans=33,700, one man each—33,700. Again, 38,700×35,000×33,700=107,400. Then add 1800 light-armed Thespians, whom he mentions subsequently, and we have 107,400+1800=109,200 men. This is precisely as he states it; for after enumerating the hoplitai at 38,700 shields, 5000 of whom were Spartans, he adds the following words: "But the force of the light-armed was as follows; to the Spartan band, 35,000 men, as being seven to each man, and of these every one was equipped for war; but to the Lakonians and the other Greeks, thirty-four thousand five hundred being one to every man." The error, it is true, amounts only to 800 men, and is scarcely worth altering, as it would be quite fair to reckon a force of 109,200 men, in round terms, at 110,000, particularly where the numeration, as in Greek, is made by so many ten-thousands μυριάδες; but when the particulars are so closely laid down, and the error lies merely in a miscalculation by the original writer; it is curious to observe how that error is perpetuated, and it proves how necessary it is to verify every quotation by actual examination, instead of taking it on the faith of any modern historian, how accurate soever he may be.

tion, two through the right, the others through the centre, besides the Asopus itself in the front and a considerable brook on the left of the Athenians.

The Lakedaimonians, who with their light auxiliaries formed nearly half the army, were the most securely posted on a series of moderate heights; the combined Greeks of the centre, and the Athenians on the left were in the open plain. On the whole it was a good one and well chosen, covering the pass of the Oak-heads by which their reinforcements and supplies would come up, covering the two principal roads through that pass to Athens, and having a retreat first on what was called the island among the rivulets and sources of the Oëroe, and thence to the strong heights around the walls of Plataia and the abrupt spurs of the true Kithairon.

In this second position the Greeks remained eight days inactive, their soothsayers promising them victory in case they should act purely on the defensive, besides which their leader must have been aware that without horse to cover his flanks, he could not advantageously advance the phalanx to attack across an open plain. Why Mardonios made no movement of any kind for so long a time is less evident, though it is stated that he also was advised by the Greek prophets in his army to remain on the defensive; but it is probable that the severity with which his cavalry had been handled and repulsed in the first affair, led him to adopt their counsels. On the eighth day, however, at the instance of Timegenides, a Theban, he sent off his horse across the Asopos, and probably along the same road by which the Greeks had countermarched to take their new position, turning their right flank, with orders to take post in the pass of the Oakheads, and to cut off the supplies and reinforcements which were continually coming up from Attika and the Peloponnessos. This movement, which he ought evidently to have made much earlier, was very successful, as the horse immediately intercepted a train of five hundred head of cattle, bringing up grain for the army from the isthmus, with all their drivers and followers. All these fell into their hands; and, till they were wearied out with slaughtering, they spared neither men nor animals. The result of this was soon visible in the straitening the Greeks of their provisions; yet their numbers still increased, and they remained so firm in their position, that Mardonios still felt unwilling to assail them in it; though he had already a powerful detachment of cavalry in their rear with which he might have created a most effective diversion in that quarter, by charging them from the higher ground while he himself attacked in front with his main force. It is remarkable, that neither does Mardonios appear to have been at all aware of the advantage he had obtained in thus turning their whole position with his formidable horse—the best arm in his service—nor did Pausanias at first discover the peril to which he was exposed by the establishment of such a power in his rear; at least he made no more attempts to dislodge it, though he might have been conscious of inability to do so, than did his antagonist to avail himself of it. The Persians never indeed appear to have profited at all by the superiority of their numbers or of their cavalry; as, had they possessed any strategetical ability, they might in almost every instance have made demonstrations at once, on every part of the enemies' lines, any or all of which might have been converted into true attacks, simultaneous on front, flanks, and rear. Yet they always appear to have trusted to direct attacks on the front; and what is more remarkable rarely with more than one arm at once, either attacking with their foot and holding their cavalry in reserve, or *vice versa*. The Greeks had, it would seem, no option, since they were at this time entirely destitute of cavalry, not having even a squadron to protect their convoys; and their light troops being singularly ineffective as compared with the admirable quality of their heavy foot. At this crisis of the manœuvres it is evident to me that the Greeks had the worst of it; as is shown by the great difficulty they had in maintaining a strong position on the first day when Masistios was slain, and by the fact that that accident terminated that affair; and I am inclined to believe that, if on that occasion, when the Megarensians wavered before the horse alone, Mardonios had ordered an immediate advance and attacked with all his forces along the whole line, he might well have been victorious; since the Athenians could in that case have sent no reinforcement to the weak point of their centre; and, had that once given way, the cavalry would have at once cut their position in two, and could scarcely have failed to destroy them. At this juncture, Artabazos and the Thebans also, since they too were falling short of supplies, pressed Mardonios to fall back on the fortified position of Thebes; and there lie at ease, feeding his host from the rich plains of Thessaly and Macedonia, contenting himself with straitening the Greeks in their position, whence they could scarce retreat with his troopers in their rear, and trying the effects of bribery, added to their natural jealousies and to their weariness of protracted and ineffective warfare, to bring about the dissolution of the confederacy. This was sound counsel, founded on sure and soldierly principles; for so long as his great force occupied the heart of Greece, unbroken, there was nothing to be gained by fighting, and the scheme of Artabazos was certain of ultimate success. But Mardonios was too arrogant and too confident of his numbers to brook the idea of retreat, and being aware that want of supplies must compel a movement of some kind, he determined to neglect the omens of the Greek soothsayers, and, abiding by the Persian customs, to cross the Asopos, and delivei battle on the plain. It was on the tenth day from the death of Masistios, that Mardonios took this determination, and on that same night Alexander I., of Macedon —who must not be confounded with Alexander the Great—

came alone on horseback to the outposts of the Athenians, on the extreme left, and informed them of the design of the Persians. These at once communicated the intelligence to the Spartans, when it was resolved to fight; but Pausanias requested the Athenians, on the passing of the watchword at daybreak, to countermarch from the left to the right wing, thus changing places with the Spartans; in order that, being accustomed since Marathon to the Oriental mode of fighting, they might be opposed to the Persian Immortals, the Medes and Sakians, while the Lakedaimonians should meet the Greeks in the tug of war. It is stated* that, at this juncture, the other Attic generals objected to being ordered hither and thither by the Spartans, as though they were Helots; but that they were reconciled to it by Aristides, who showed them that when contending for the post of honor they had been contented with the left wing; and, that it was now scarcely consistent to refuse the right, when offered to them voluntarily.

As soon as the day broke, this manœuvre was executed, by the rear of the centre, and was first discovered by the Medizing Boiotians, who were posted opposite to the Athenians, as these were advanced more closely on the Asopos, than the centre and right; for, when the Greeks broke up from their position at Erythrai, the Persians had quitted their entrenched camp, and followed along the right bank of the river, which divided the outposts of the two armies. They at once communicated the fact to Mardonios, who forthwith executed a similar movement, bringing his Orientals again to face the Lakedaimonians; and, thereupon, Pausanias again countermarched, returning to his old post on the right. Mardonios again followed him; and, as they once more stood as in the first instance, sent a Herald to the Spartans with an insulting message, challenging them to do battle with the Persians, in equal numbers man to man, and so

* Herod. XI., 46. Plutarch, Aristides, XVI.

to decide the quarrel in behalf of all Hellas. No reply was made to this defiance, and Mardonios was greatly elated, as if he had gained a bloodless victory. This narrative is remarkable, as it distinctly proves that the terror of the Medes and Persians, which Herodotus describes as universal before the battle of Marathon, had not yet subsided, in spite of their several defeats; and that they were still regarded as more dangerous antagonists than their Greek allies, both by those allies and by their enemies.

What is more singular, is this, that the Athenians were evidently held in greater awe, not only by the Orientals—as would be natural, since they had repeatedly beaten them—but by the Hellenic auxiliaries also, although the right wing in battle and the commandership of the fleet was given to the Spartans without dispute on the part of Attica, as if in acknowledgment of their superiority. Yet there is no other way of explaining the reluctance of both nations to sustain the attack of the Athenians, especially after the Spartans had shown their unwillingness to engage the Persians.

But now Mardonios delayed no longer, but launched all his cavalry against them, still without any infantry supports, and harassed them dreadfully, for many of his cavalry were horse-archers, Persians, Sakians, and Parthians; all of them, but the latter especially, the best bowmen in the world, and the rest strong and skilful javelineers, to whom the Greeks had no arm which to oppose, nor any means of repaying them the injuries which they inflicted. They kept their ranks indeed, unbroken, and lost no ground, though they were ravaged by the fierce hail of missiles, which wounded many and killed not a few; but all the left and centre of the army was deprived of the means of watering, for they were cut off from the Asopus by the intervening cavalry; and, to make affairs darker and more hopeless, the horse had taken possession of and blocked up the fountain of Gargaphia in the rear of the extreme Lakedaimonian right. By what forces this was accomplished, it is not stated; nor is it easy to discover how or by whom it was effected, unless it were by the horse detached for the blockade of the Dryoscephalai, which pass lay little more than a mile to the south of the fountain, with no covering force between. It is clear, on the other hand, by all the accounts, that the Oriental cavalry did not penetrate and break through the Greek position; nor can it be easily believed that they turned both flanks, or either of them; since to do so a detour of five or six miles would be necessary; and, if such a manœuvre had been effected, as it must probably have been by the Athenian left,* the Greeks would have been so completely surrounded, that the dullest enemy must have perceived the certain success of a simultaneous attack; nor even, if that were not attempted, could the manœuvres which ensued have been possible to the Greeks. In any event, whether we believe that the troops blockading the Oak-heads came down direct on the Spartan rear, and took possession in undeniable force of the spring, within half a mile of their right and directly behind it, or that the Persian right turned the Athenian left, and traversed the whole length of their position to the extreme right, with the same result, the fatuity is inconceivable, which could have induced them there to remain idle and inactive when a few vigorous charges must have obliged the Greeks to form a fresh front to the rear in order to oppose them, and must, if seconded by their infantry from the Asopos, have taken them between two fires, and could have hardly failed to annihilate them.

It is remarkable that Diodorus Siculus makes no mention of this second equestrian action, nor of the subsequent retreat of the

* According to Col. Leake's plan of the Plataiis, horse could scarcely have forced their way between the Spartan right, drawn up on steep hillocks, and the large tributary of the Asopos, as they must have done to turn the Greek right.

Greeks, but represents the latter as attacking, and on ground which compelled the Persians to fight in serried order, thus depriving them of the advantage of their superior numbers.* No authority of this writer can however invalidate that of Herodotus, who wrote within twenty years of the event; besides which, examination of the ground and other circumstances confirm his description of the affair.

It is evident, therefore, that the attack not only occurred, but that the Greeks were very severely pressed, and looked forward with dismal forebodings to the giving of the signal for general action, at this moment, by Mardonios. Why he did not give it, can never now be known; but that he should have done so, according to every principle of military science, is undoubted; nor can I imagine, even with all allowance for the superiority of the Hellenes in discipline and armature, how in that case he could have failed of victory. It was at this juncture, while the skirmish was still raging all along their front and in the rear of their right, that a council of war was held in the quarters of Pausanias; when it was determined, that should the Persians defer the attack to the next day, they would retreat to the island, as it is called, immediately below the steep slope from the walls of Plataia, where they could neither be cut off from the water, nor be taken in flank, from the nature of the ground; while they would present a much smaller front to the enemy. This new, or third position,† lay ten stadia‡ to the west of the Lakedaimonian position and the fountain of Gargaphia, and about twice as far from the Athenians on the left; and, in order to reach it, the Greeks should have marched by converging lines, the Athenians almost due south by the westernmost road from Thebes, the confederates of the centre south-westward, and the Spartans almost due west; since their second position occupied ground, though its faces were

* Diod. Sic. XI. 30. 31.

† Herod. IX., 51.

‡ Ten stadia, an English mile and a quarter.

angular, in the form of an irregular arc, the centre of which lay in the island.*

During that whole day, the Greeks had unabating toil and distress, the attacks of the horse never being for a moment intermitted; and with such eyes of eagerness, as the Duke of Wellington is reported to have watched for night or the Prussians, rejoicing, as hour after hour lagged away, and still his weary squares held out impregnable against the thundering charges of Milhaud's iron cuirassiers, at Waterloo, must the outnumbered Greeks have watched for night, and exulted, as hour after hour passed away, and signal was not given for a general assault. In several respects, indeed, this battle of Plataia was not dissimilar to that of Waterloo; for in like manner as the Anglo allies, so did the Greeks hold a semi-circular position, with its front to the enemy; in like manner, as Napoleon sacrificed and wore out his inimitable cavalry, against infantry on which he never made the least impression, so did Mardonios launch his unsupported horsemen against the Hellenic pikes; and, in like manner, were both battles won by a general charge of foot, and converted into unexampled routs by the want of cavalry to cover the retreat of the broken armies. Pausanias and Wellington both fought the waiting fight, and when the time at length arrived struck the decisive blow, which there was nothing left to parry. At nightfall, when it came, and when darkness set in thick and moonless, the confederates of the centre broke up, instantly, glad to get out of reach of the terrible horse—who, by the way, must have again fallen back, either to the Oak-heads or to the camp beyond the Asopos; since, had they still held Gargaphia, they must have perceived and prevented any movement—and marched, at their best speed, across the island, not halting according to order, but ascending the heights to the Heraion or temple of Here,

* Leake's Plan of the Plataiis; Travels in N. W. Greece, vol. ii. Herod. IX., 51.

beyond Plataia, and to the eastward of it, where they piled their arms, weary and hungry—for their supplies by the Dryoscephalai had been cut off—and had no share in the business of the morrow. Pausanias, seeing that the centre had marched, ordered his own troops to take up their arms and follow; but Amompharetos, the leader of the Pitanatean lochos, resolutely refused to move, insisting that it was disgraceful and infamous in Spartans to retreat before an enemy, and declaring that he and his lochos would stand their ground and die, although all the rest should desert them. Meantime, a messenger came over from the Athenians, who had not yet moved until they should know what the Lakedaimonians were about; for they had no great confidence in their adhering to their word,* and found them halted, in some confusion, their leaders wrangling one with another; when Pausanias bade the herald to go tell the Athenians what was passing, and request them to join him there, and co-operate with him in the retreat. But while they were debating day broke; and then Pausanias concluding that, when it came to the crisis, Amompharetos would follow the rest of the army, led the remainder, with the Tegeatans, by his own right, among the hillocks and on the lower spurs of the Kithairon, toward the position he had chosen, occupied a line of heights on a plateau called the Argiopion, having a temple of the Eleusinian Demeter in his front, and the fountain of Artemis, at the modern village of Vergutiam, the scene of Actaion's misadventure with the goddess, at his extreme right; and here Amompharetos soon rejoined him, but not until he was closely pressed by the Persian horse, who seeing the retreat, rode hard upon his traces. In the meanwhile the Athenians, who had nearly twice as far to march as the Lakedaimonians, in order to gain their post, fell back across the open plain, there being no elevations in that quarter of the field, except a high, solitary mound, on which stands the modern

* Herod. IX., 55. Plut. Arist. 17.

village of Platani, concealing them both from the Persians beyond the Asopos, and from their own allies on the Argiopion; but before reaching their proper station, they were overtaken and obliged to form in the low grounds, and prepare to resist the Medizing Greeks, who were marching upon them, near fifty thousand strong.

Mardonios, seeing the position of the Greeks vacant when the day broke, and supposing that all the Hellenes had lost heart and were in full flight, immediately crossed the Asopos at all points, and pursued with all his host, shouting as if already victorious, in loose and disorderly array; leading the chase himself on his conspicuous white horse of the Nisaian breed, at the head of the thousand chosen Persian cuirassiers of the Immortals, who bore gold balls on the reverse of their lances—whence their name of apple-bearers, μηλόφοροι,—and who were the best and most perfectly armed of all the Oriental troops. With these he made so terrible an onslaught on the Lakedaimonians and Tegeatans, who fought with them, numbering eleven thousand five hundred shields of heavy foot, with forty-one thousand five hundred light armed troops, that Pausanias sent a mounted officer to gallop for life to the Athenians, and entreat them to reinforce him with their Archery. This shows that little or no service was to be expected in action from the Helots, whom the Spartans were in ordinary times afraid to trust with arms, and who had neither discipline nor skill in the use of weapons. The Athenian light troops, on the contrary, were citizens of the poorer classes; but it is, I imagine, the Thespian skirmishers, who composed the whole contingent of that city, and were, therefore, probably of a very superior character to the ordinary light armed men, that did such good service on the first day against Masistios, and were now looked for by Pausanias, to repeat the duty of repulsing that terrible horse.

Aristides at once gave orders to his whole force, consisting of about seventeen thousand men—for the Plataians had joined them from the left centre, too brave to fly with the confederates—to march at once at double quick time to the relief of the Spartans. The Medizing Greeks, on seeing this, advanced on them, in a force traditionally stated, for they were never numbered, at fifty thousand, including a considerable body of Theban cavalry. Aristides thereupon,* stood forth beyond the lines, shouting to them vehemently, and calling all the Hellenic gods to witness, that they should give way, nor hinder those who would peril their lives for Hellas.

But when this availed nothing, but they still came on in array of battle, he lowered his pikes and charged in close column, compelled to give up his design of relieving the right wing. As he charged, the Lokrian, Phokian, and other Medizing Greeks gave way, as unwilling to encounter their countrymen in behalf of the barbarian; but the Boiotians, and Thebans more especially, volunteer traitors, instigated by hatred of Athens, shouted and charged home, shield to shield; and the tug of war was for a time difficult and desperate between them.

At this time the Lakedaimonians, on whom the brunt of this bloody battle fell, were suffering severely—for their sacrifices were ominous of ill, and forbade their fighting on pain of total defeat. They stood, therefore, immovable, covering themselves as best they might, kneeling under shelter of their great shields, while the Persian cavalry wheeled round and round them, pouring in their deadly hail of missiles, till many fell dead in their lines, and few but were wounded. Encouraged, too, by the inactivity of the Greeks, which they could not comprehend, the Persian infantry came up to within half bow-shot, and, piling their square wicker bucklers in an extemporaneous breastwork, shot from behind it their volleyed arrows with terrible precision and fatal execution. Again victims were slain, and again the signs

* Plut. Aristid., 18.

were unfavorable; until Pausanias, turning his head to the temple of Here, on the heights above his left, which he could see over the ruined ramparts of Plataia, burned the preceding year by Xerxes, implored the aid of the goddess with outstretched arms and flowing tears. Then, it is said, the sacrifices at once became propitious; and then, with the deep and solemn conclamation of their pæans, at length released from their unwilling inactivity, down from the upper ground, down, came the Spartans with their stout allies, in serried phalanx, eight shields deep; and forth to meet them, casting aside their bows, rushed manfully the Persians; and about the rampart of bucklers, and on the consecrated ground of Ceres, the conflict was severe and stubborn; nor were the Orientals inferior to the Greeks in spirit or in strength, but in their light harness, and short weapons, they were as naked* men against men clad in proof. But the Greeks keeping their order of linked shields, *synaspismos*, beat down the wall of bucklers, and thrusting their long pikes into the faces and chests of the Persians, bore them down by sheer force, but not without spirited resistance; for they strove hard to break the pikes with their bare hands, and did break many; and came in, hand to hand, with scymetar and dagger, and tearing away the shields of the Hoplitai, held the fight dubious for a long time and the victory in suspense. Then, as they began to give way and scatter before the irresistible pikes, Mardonios with the horse of the Immortals once again charged home, and was already making some impression, as he had done all day, wherever he charged in person, and the infantry rallied fast, favored by his diversion, when the Spartan Acimnestos, like Aias and Aineias, and other heroes of the epic ages, seized a huge stone, and hurled it with such violence and precision, that striking him in his face, it slew that gallant chief outright; and as all beheld him fall in the first ranks, disorderly flight and a

* Herod. IX., 67. † Plut. Aristides 18.

total rout ensued. For Artabazos, who had fought reluctantly from the first, and with disaffection to Mardonios, being now chief in command, made no effort to rally the men or retrieve the day; made no effort to defend the fortified camp, or even the Theban wall, but gallopped off the field with forty thousand fresh horse—all that were left of the gigantic cavalry, which had commenced the action with such a clang and clatter, and were still sufficient, if well led, to have trampled the Greek army into dust, and taking the road west of Platai, by Leuctra, Thespiai, and the edge of lake Kėphisis, over the plain of Chaironeia, made good his escape into Phokis, and thence by Thessaly and Thrace to the Hellespont.

In the meantime, the Athenians, in spite of the superior numbers and hard-fighting of the Thebans, had broken them, with considerable loss, killing three hundred of their best men, and were driving them off the field by the direct road to Thebes though held somewhat in check by their horse, when a messenger came up from Pausanias, informing them of the decisive victory he had gained on his wing, and requiring their aid, if they could give it, in storming the entrenched camp; for the Athenians were the most skilful of all the Hellenes at wall-fighting, and the storming of fortified places.

The Boiotians had by this time been beaten to their hearts' content, and as they showed no signs of rallying, as the Athenians relaxed their pursuit, but were already over the Asopos in full flight, Aristides led his forces over the site of the last night's position of Mardonios, down the right bank of the Asopos, and reached the encampment, just as the Lakedaimonians and Tegeatans were in check and wavering, so strenuous was the defence of the walls and the towers.

And now the Boiotian cavalry was retreating across the field whereon the Athenians had repulsed their countrymen, in order to rejoin them; when, having already done good service, in protecting the routed Persians, they fell in with the Megarensians and Phliasians in the plain—who, not having struck a blow in the action, now seeing the victory won, were rushing down disorderly to share the spoil—and charging them pell-mell, cut them to pieces, killing above six hundred; and, after chasing the rest to Kithairon, made good their own retreat to Thebes. Then, by the fierceness and alacrity of the Athenians the walls were forced and a great breach made, by which the whole Greek force burst in, and such a slaughter followed, as history nowhere else records; for, their walls once forced, the miserable Persians thought no more of resistance; and the Greeks, if they felt compassion, dared not display it, so much did the vanquished enemy still outnumber their whole army. So they butchered them, literally, like sheep; and it is confidently asserted that, of three hundred thousand Orientals, to speak in round numbers, only the forty thousand who fled early in the day with Artabazos, and three thousand who escaped from the camp, and were subsequently slain by Perdikkas in Makedonia, got off with their lives from that truly disastrous day.

Of the Lakedaimonians, who confessedly did the best that day, although the Athenians and Tegeatans fought undeniably, ninety-one fell; of the Tegeatans sixteen; of the Athenians fifty-two—so small was their loss, owing to their unbroken ranks and perfect panoply.* Plutarch complains of the silence of Herodotus† as to the other Greeks, and charges him with unfairness; as he alleges that of the Greeks, in all, there fell one thousand and thirty-six. But it must be remembered that Plutarch was a Boiotian, hostile both to Sparta and Athens; that he did not write until the fourth century after the battle, and that he states the dead of the Lakedaimonians, Tegeatans and Athenians, at the same number with his predecessor. The frankness, moreover, with which Herodotos, who was an Ionian, and no

* Herod. IX. 70. † Plut. Aristides, 19.

admirer in general of the Lakedaimonians, ascribes the glory of the day to them and to Pausanias, amply confirms his veracity, if confirmation were required. But the charge is false; for he does mention the fall of six hundred Megarensians and Phthiasians, though not in the battle; and it is notorious that the ancients never were wont to enumerate the loss of any, except hoplitai; wherefore, if it be a fact that a thousand and thirty-six Greeks fell, the number either includes all who fell in all the three days' fighting, or the light armed and Helots of the last day.

Thus terminated this most memorable and most important day.* Most memorable, because no equally well authenticated battle even approximates it in carnage, and because on it the Persian fleet and army at Mykale was utterly destroyed almost at the same hour. Most important, for it turned the whole tide of battle, and changed the scene of the Persian wars from European to Asiatic soil, so that when we again find Hellenes and Orientals in action, we shall see the former as invaders, and the latter struggling in vain to defend their soil against the western spear.

The conduct of Pausanias was, indeed, admirable throughout those three most trying and most desperate days; his resources are shown to have been extraordinary; his *coup d'œil* prodigious; and the manner in which he manœuvred infantry over open country, in the teeth of a vast and admirable cavalry, without losing a man, or having a rank broken; and kept them together under circumstances almost hopeless; and steady, under harassing attacks to which they could make no reply, reflect the highest lustre on his generalship, and on the immovable steadiness of the men he commanded. On two occasions—when the Per-

* According to Plutarch, it was the 16th of the Attic month Maimacterion, corresponding to the end of November and beginning of December, 2d year, of 75th Olym., 479 B. C.

sian horse were established in his rear on the second day, and when the cowardly withdrawal of his centre, in the last and decisive action, left his two wings separated by a gap of nearly a mile, by pouring their whole army into which, and so cutting his position in two, the Persians might have attacked him in detail—he ought to have been beaten, and that by no possible fault of his own; while it was by his own constancy and conduct, only, that he turned even disasters to his own advantage, and won a battle unequalled perhaps in any age of recorded history.

The spoil taken was enormous; the brazen manger of Mardonios was seized by the Tegeatans; his dagger, or acinaces,* and silver-footed throne, by the Athenians; the whole army was enriched with booty, and for years afterwards Persian Darics of gold became the ordinary currency of Greece. Of all the spoil, women, horses, coined and uncoined gold, furniture, dress, camels, all, one-tenth was given to Pausanias—and, alas! proved his ruin.

For, like Miltiades, like Themistokles, like so many other great and gallant Greeks, the luxury and wealth, added to his unbounded vanity and ambition, corrupted him, even to the degree of assuming the manners and dress of the Persians, and of traitorously corresponding with the king. At length, this splendid soldier, this superb commander, the greatest benefactor of his countrymen, who might have reigned immortal in the hearts of his fellow citizens, could he but have limited his overweening pride and vaulting ambition to the first magistracy of a frugal and poor republic—convicted of manifest treason—died miserably, a dishonest, and deplorable, if undeplored, death. Taking sanctuary in the temple of Athene, "of the brazen house," from which the awful religion of the spot prevented his removal, the door was walled up—his own mother laying the first stone—the roof torn off, and guards stationed around; till

* Pausanias, Attica, 27.

the most famous soldier and wealthiest man of all Hellas, died wretchedly, on the bare earth, of cold and famine.

It is not a picture to be dwelt upon; for, though it has a sad moral of the inconstancy of human things, even of human virtue, it is one of so constant occurrence in the early republics of Hellas, that we are half induced to suspect some natural ill inherent to their constitutions, which rendered inevitable, if it might not palliate, these constantly recurring instances of the noblest patriotism, polluted by the basest treason, in the person of a single individual. Heaven be praised, if such acts of devotion are rare of occurrence in these latter days—such treasons are impossible

V.

XENOPHON,

THE ATHENIAN;

HIS RETREAT OF THE TEN THOUSAND; HIS CAMPAIGNS, CHARACTER, AND CONDUCT.

Born an Athenian, in the borough of Ercheia, of the tribe Aigeis, this distinguished man came upon the stage of life at a busy and eventful period, both for his native city, and for the world at large—for it was in the second year of the eighty-third Olympiad, corresponding to four hundred and forty-five B.C., in the Archonship of Timarchides—the same year in which, after all the district of Attika had been devastated by the Lakedaimonians, and the city of Chaironeia fruitlessly captured by their own general Tolmides, who was afterwards defeated with the loss of his whole army, and himself slain at Koroneia, the Athenians were compelled to liberate all the cities they had gained in Boiotia, in order to procure the release of their own prisoners from the hands of the Thebans—that he first saw the light. His father's name was Gryllos; but little is known either of his family, or of his early years; beyond this, that while a very young man his personal beauty recommended him to Socrates, of whom he became perhaps the most favorite and distinguished pupil, certainly one of the very few, who neither

MARCH OF A GREEK ARMY.

p. 172.

disgraced the name and tenets of their preceptor by the grossness and immorality of their private lives, nor turned the profession of philosophy into sordid money-making charlatanry; for he, at least, used it rather as the daily guide and measure of an honorable, upright, and useful life, than as the means of dishonest profit, or the badge of vanity and arrogance.

A truce of thirty years was signed, on the year of Xenophon's birth, between the Athenians and Lakedaimonians; and so much were the former depressed by the results of the battle of Koroneia, that they moved but little in the public affairs of Greece for a considerable space of time; until, in the first year of the eighty-seventh Olympiad,* they became involved in a quarrel between the Korinthians and Kerkuraians, in the course of which they soon came to actual hostilities with the former people, at the siege of Potidaia, an Attik dependency which had been seduced from its allegiance by the joint influence of Korinth and Perdikkas of Makedonia, who was at this period actively revolutionizing all the Athenian colonies and conquests in Chalkidike.

Their blockade of Potidaia, by that able leader Phormion, was instantly seized as a pretext against Athens, by the Spartans and other Peloponnesians, who were anxiously seeking cause of war; and, after a mock examination at the isthmus, and the farce of sending evidently untenable demands and inadmissible propositions, they declared the truce to be broken by the Athenians, and so declared war upon them. In the following year, the Thebans commenced hostilities by the seizure of Plataia, the devastation of its territories, and the wholesale carnage of its rural population. This led to retaliation, and thence to the Peloponnesian war, which raged for twenty-seven years through every part of Greece, and at its close left Athens stripped of

* Diod. Sic. XII. 37. In the Archonship of Pythodoros, and the administration of Perikles.

power and almost of independence; and all the other states of southern Hellas, so thoroughly divided and exhausted, that they fell at once under the control of the absolute tyrannies of Epiros, Makedonia, and Thessaly; and ultimately sunk an easy prey to Rome, the very calmness of whose equable but iron despotism was received as a boon, and regarded almost as liberty and peace, by states worn out with the excitement of incessant warfare, wearied by the continuous succession of victory and defeat alike unavailing, and wishing above all things for repose, even if it were the repose of national and political annihilation. At this period Xenophon was in his fifteenth year, and from the early age at which the Greeks were wont to enter upon political life, as also from the energy and activity of his subsequent career, we should expect soon after this to hear of him in public; but it is not till eight years later, at the defeat of the Athenians by the Boiotians, under Pagondas, before the walls of Delion, that we find any mention of him, and that only in the shape of a vague and unauthenticated rumor, that fighting desperately he was struck down and would have been slain, but for the prompt rescue of his preceptor Sokrates. The same story is also told, however, with the name of Alkibiades introduced for that of Xenophon, in relation to the same battle, so that little reliance can be placed upon it; though there is something more of probability in another tradition of his being captured not long afterward in another battle, the name of which has not, nor indeed any other traces of it, been preserved in history; and of his being long detained a captive in Thebes, where he is said, by Philostratos, in his life of Sokrates,* to have studied philosophy with Prodikos of Kos, and where he perhaps formed that intimacy with Proxenos the Boiotian, which induced him to join in the expedition of Kyros against Artoxerxes. It is, indeed, not a little remarkable that, with the exception of these two uncer-

* Anthon's Bibliotheca Classica; art., Xenophon.

tain notices, both of which in some degree lack confirmation, nothing definite or certain should be known of the way in which the youth and early manhood were spent of one, who was destined afterward, when his maturity had somewhat passed its prime, to come forth as it were self-made, and blaze up at once, without visible experience, a thorough and consummate general. For seven and twenty years, as I have already stated, beginning when he had already completed his fifteenth year, war, continuous and unmitigated, raged through the Peloponnesos, through Attika, Boiotia, through all the seas circumadjacent, through many of the neighboring isles of Greece, Sicily, the richest and the most remote, not excluded; his native country was devastated five times, far and near, by Peloponnesian armies, the flames kindled by whom could be seen from the very walls of Athens; was decimated by the most fearful pestilence recorded, unless it be perhaps the great plague of London; underwent all vicissitudes from the most splendid glory, to the most abject gloom; and was, in the first year of the ninety-fourth Olympiad,* compelled to surrender to the Spartans, under Lysander, who razed her long walls to the earth and put an end to her supremacy for ever. Of the first twenty years of this war, we have, complete to this day, the finest specimen of contemporaneous history that ever flowed from a vigorous, eloquent, and impartial pen; I mean of course that of Thukydides—of the remainder, Xenophon himself has left us the narrative; but in neither of these works, nor in that of Diodoros, is there the slightest allusion to any military services, or any exploit of Xenophon himself. That a man of his parts, energy, intellect and courage could possibly have been engaged in warlike duties for twenty years, without attaining any command, or performing anything worthy even of a passing notice, would indeed seem impossible; and it is not to be imagined that he would have

* 404 B.C.

remained, even had he been permitted to do so, quiet and inactive, while it was debated in the most desperate strife whether his own country was "to be or not to be," and almost decided in the negative. Nor does he again appear in history, until he joined the expedition against Persia, in the year after his return, commanded with so much ability by his friend Agesilaos. Even in this, we know not what part he played or what rank he bore; and in the like obscurity rests his conduct at Coroneia, although the fact that he served there, and by that service lost the favor of his countrymen, is patent.

It avails nothing, however, to inquire or examine, where and how Xenophon acquired that military skill, which he afterward displayed in so eminent a degree. How he became so much attached to the polity, and such an admirer of the character of the Spartans—how such an intimate with Agesilaos, an active enemy of Athens, must ever remain an insoluble mystery: and we can only marvel where the military wisdom had its school, which conducted the most remarkable retreat, and in its line the greatest military achievement, recorded on any page of any history.

To return, however, a little, in order to throw some light on the state of affairs in Persia, which led to the expedition of Kyros, in the last year of the eighty-eighth Olympiad, corresponding to four hundred and twenty-five, B. C., died Artoxerxes, surnamed Longimanus, the son of Xerxes, and to him succeeded Xerxes II.; who was murdered within a few months by his own natural brother, Sogdianos. He in his turn was again deposed and put to death by a third illegitimate brother, Darios II., who had previously been known as Ochos, the two reigns falling within the space of a little over a single year. Darios II. reigned nineteen years, during which there was but little stir in the affairs of Asia, with the exception of some unimportant victories gained by Kyros, his younger son. He dying in the year four hundred and four, the same which saw the termination of the Peloponnesian war, was succeeded by his eldest son Artoxerxes II., who had previously been named Arsakes, being born before his father's accession to the throne, and at a time when that event seemed wholly improbable; but Darios left a younger son also, Kyros, who had already obtained not a little military distinction, and who was full of ambitious aspirations himself to assume the imperial tiara, Nor was he entirely without some sort of pretext for aspiring to it; since, although the usages of Persia favored primogeniture, it was well known that Xerxes I., son of Darios Hystaspes, had been preferred to his elder brother Artabanos, partly through the influence of his mother Atossa, partly on the same plea that Artabanos, born while his father was a private individual, was not the son of a king, nor heir to the kingly title. Such a quibble would really appear almost too transparent; but conscious that he had his mother Parysatis, whose favorite he was, on his side, Kyros, even before his father's death, had entertained hopes of obtaining the succession by his father's bequest. Nor is it altogether improbable that he would have obtained it, had he been on the spot in time. For, when he felt himself to be on his death-bed, Darios summoned Kyros, Artoxerxes the elder being present, to come up from his satrapy of Asia Minor, which he had bestowed on him with the command of all the Greek and other forces assembled in the plain of Kastolos; and though he came up with all speed, carrying with him as his near friend, Tissaphernes, and escorted by three hundred Greek hoplitai, commanded by Xenias the Parrhasian, he arrived only to find his father in the death agony, and to be a witness of his brother's inauguration. At this juncture, Tissaphernes, who, whenever he appears on the page of Xenophon's most interesting narrative, is marked with some peculiar brand of falsehood, treachery and cowardice, accused Kyros to his brother of compassing his death; on which the prince was arrested, condemned to death, and only not executed, owing to his mother's tears and obsecrations, which prevailed not only to obtain his pardon, but to preserve to him his satrapy,* whither he was commanded forthwith to retire.

The fuller particulars state that it was the usage for Persian monarchs, at their investiture, to visit the temple of the goddess of war, corresponding to the Greek Athene, and having there partaken of a solemn repast, consisting of a kind of marmalade of figs, preserved nuts of the terebinth, and sour milk, to assume the royal garb, and with it the authority of king. While Artoxerxes was making ready, with his brother, for this ceremonial, Tissaphernes introduced one of the inferior priests of the temple who had given information of an ambush, which Kyros, he said, had prepared for the king, in order to slay him so soon as he should put on the robe of state.† Some insinuation has been made to the effect that the priest was suborned; but the probability is the other way. The affections among relatives, born in the precincts of the harem, are to a proverb as frail and transitory, as their jealousies and animosities are vindictive and enduring; nor are brothers, in oriental dynasties, even to this day, particularly scrupulous in the use of the drugged bowl or the assassin's knife, for the removal of a tenant of the throne.

The subsequent conduct of Kyros, especially in the battle of Kynaxa, shows something more than the unscrupulous intent to wade even through fratricide to empire, for it was marked by a savage animosity, and a sanguinary determination to slay with his own hand. The shrewdness and sagacity, moreover, with which he had long courted the Spartans in preference to the Athenians, as always the more ready to traffic with the barbarian; and the secresy with which he had been collecting and maintaining small bodies of Peloponnesian mercenaries at various points under the pretext of an intended expedition against the barbarians of Pisidia, so that when he required it he was at the head of a Hellenic power at a moment's notice, all go to prove

* Xen. Anab. 1. † Plut. Vit. Artox. 4.

that he was resolved, long before these events, to throw for empire at the risk of life. There is little reason, therefore, to doubt the willingness of Kyros to have recourse to stratagem and a single dagger's stroke, instead of trying the chances of war, and affronting the proverbial fickleness of military fortune. And this the rather that, in Asia, there was no such sanctity in the bond of brotherhood, as to render the crime of fratricide the most appalling of atrocities, or the intermarriage with a sister the most shocking of incests ; both being matters of every day occurrence, and the former—the latter being the rule, rather than the exception—being regarded pretty much as the taking off any other dangerous, political antagonist, or formidable rival.

Both these young princes appear to have been naturally amiable, rather than the reverse; and the younger unquestionably possessed in a very high degree that most princely power of conciliating all affections, and of fascinating all who came within his sphere.

He had by far the greater talents also, for he was not only generally accomplished and a rare proficient in the use of arms, but was a general, not unjustly, of considerable pretensions.

Artoxerxes, on the contrary, was weak, wavering and undecided, in his character, though not deficient in personal courage; and lacked the practical commonplace wisdom, which should have induced him either to conciliate his brother by a total avoidance of all show of suspicion, and a complete and generous confidence founded on oblivion of the past; or by strong measures and deprivation of all power political, and military authority, to have rendered him for the future incapable of open rebellion, if not of secret sedition. Instead of doing this, while he so far pardoned him as to dismiss him unhurt and with an almost independent command, to his own satrapy, he yet treated him with such coolness, and with marks of displeasure and suspicion so strong, that it was natural enough for Kyros to deem himself one marked out for future jealousies, perhaps destined for present destruction—since then as now, in the East, it was an usual method when kings apprehended the disloyalty, or dreaded the exuberant power, of their most puissant satellites, rather to let them be taken off while on the route to their distant provinces—a casualty which might well be ascribed to chance indisposition—than to summon them to open trial; and so give them an opportunity of resorting to open resistance.

Whether Artoxerxes entertained such designs or no, cannot now be discovered, but that Kyros was filled with doubt, dismay and animosity combined, was stung almost to madness by the sense of merited or unmerited disgrace, and was now if not earlier, resolved on striking for empire, is evident from the preparations which he began at once to make with equal energy of purpose, and shrewdness in avoiding suspicion.

We find, for instance, that, in order doubtless to lull his brother's suspicions to sleep, he condescended to solicit favors at his hands through the intercession of his mother Parysatis, and succeeded in obtaining the government of several wealthy cities in Asia Minor, for which his old enemy Tissaphernes was a rival applicant; while at the same time, he was diligently collecting the materials for an auxiliary force of Hellenic mercenaries, whom he levied, maintained, and employed in various places and under various leaders, apparently unconnected with himself and with each other—until the time should arise for exhibiting himself in his true colors, and taking the initiative in offensive operations.

He was moreover in secret treaty with the Lakedaimonians, whose ephori had promised him active aid, so soon as he should be ready to strike, a promise which they failed not to keep; since it was their constant and true policy to hold the hands of the Persian monarchs full at home, whereby to deprive them of leisure for intermeddling in the affairs of Greece; nor were they at all so scrupulous as to be troubled about the morality or justice of any expedition which should subdivide the power of the king, and disturb the integrity of his dominion.

The first pretext of Kyros was the *quasi* war with Tissaphernes, which ensued on the king making over to his brother the Ionian cities of the coast, which had formerly belonged to that satrap, and in which he had been for some time exciting revolutionary movements to the detriment of the prince's authority. As if to counteract these movements, he now collected a force of Hellenic mercenaries, and at once laid siege to Miletos, being careful to pay over regularly to the king the tributes of all those disputed cities; so that, until his plans were entirely matured, no suspicions of his motive seem to have arisen.

Besides this force he had already a considerable power of Peloponnesian mercenaries on foot, under the command of Klearchos, a political exile from Sparta, and Aristippos of Thessalia, to whom he had advanced payment for the levy and maintenance of four thousand men for six months, who were under arms across the straits in the Thrakian Chersonesos, as if warring on their own account, there and in Thessaly. Now, moreover, he summoned Proxenos of Boiotia, to levy Greeks, as if for the subjugation of the Pisidians, a semi-barbarous tribe in the mountains toward Upper Asia, while he employed Sophainetos the Stymphalian, and Sokrates the Achaian, in besieging Miletos, which was occupied by the allies of Tissaphernes.

It would appear that some three years were consumed in the preparation of these forces, and in other preliminary arrangements; for it was not until the 4th year of the 94th Olympiad, in the archonship of Exainetos, and the military tribuneship of Publius Cornelius, Caius Fabius, Spurius Nautius, Caius Valerius, Manlius Sergius, and Junius Lycurgus, corresponding to B. C. 401,* that the expedition actually commenced.

For this end, in the spring of that year, Kyros marched from

* Diod. Sic. XIV., 19. Arnold's Rome, vol. I., 346.

Sardis, the capital of his Satrapy, with Xenias the Arkadian, commanding four thousand shields of heavy foot, the garrisons of the maritime cities; Proxenos the Boiotian, with whom came Xenophon—not as a general, nor captain of a band, nor private*—at the head of fifteen hundred shields and five hundred light infantry; Sophainetos of Stymphalos,† at the head of a thousand shields; Sokrates the Achaian, having five hundred shields; and Pasion of Megara, leading three hundred hoplitai and five hundred targeteers, a new arm of the service, intermediate between the heavy infantry and the *gymnetai*, recently introduced by Iphikrates of Athens, and used by him with effect and execution.

At the end of four days' march he arrived at Kolossoi, a large city of Lydia, where he halted seven days, and was joined there by Menon the Thessalian, leading a thousand shields of heavy foot and five hundred Ainianian, Dolopian, and Olynthian targeteers. Thence he marched three days' journey further to Kelainai, a city on the junction of the Maiander and Marsyas rivers, where he abode thirty days, awaiting Klearchos, who came up here, together with Sosis the Achaian, and Sophainetos the Arkadian, leading in all two thousand three hundred heavy infantry, eight hundred Thrakian targeteers, and two hundred Kretan bowmen. And this completed the whole of his Greek contingents which he reviewed here, and found them to amount in all to eleven thousand shields of heavy foot, and about two thousand targeteers and archers.‡ The actual forces, as enumerated above, amount to ten thousand six hundred shields, and two thousand three hundred light troops, part of whom were

* Xen. Anab. III., 1, 4.

† This chief must not be confounded with Sophainetos the Arkadian, mentioned hereafter; for Stymphalos, though an Arcadian city, seems at this time to have belonged to Argolis.

‡ Xen. Anab. I. 11, 9.

probably equipped as hoplitai during the march, in order to equalize the numbers of the phalanx. There is, however, some discrepancy in the numbers, throughout; for although Kyros was farther strengthened by the junction of Cheirisophos the Lakedaimonian, at Issos, within the Kilikian gates, bringing up seven hundred* Spartan infantry sent by the Ephori, we find that in the battle of Kynaxa, the shields were but ten thousand† four hundred, while the targeteers amounted to twenty-five hundred —the only loss recorded being that of two lochi of Menon's men‡, who were either cut to pieces while plundering, or deserted, to the number of a hundred shields. The march into Upper Asia occupied, it seems, above six months; and it is not improbable that over and above the ordinary casualties of so long an expedition, many of the Greeks were corrupted by the luxuries of the Oriental cities in which they halted, and so became lost to the army. Even for ordinary losses, however, the difference is not excessive, amounting only to six hundred deaths, or desertions, over and above the recorded loss of Menon's men, in a march of ninety-three days, halts not included, and of two thousand‡ miles.

When they reached Tarsos, at the pass between the mountains and the sea into Upper Asia, Kyros was again compelled to halt for twenty days, since the Hellenic bands began to be refractory, and showed much disinclination to proceed farther into the country, suspecting that they were to be employed against the king. At the end of these days, however, they were brought over by Klearchos, who was the only leader fully in the confidence of Kyros, and by the representations of the prince himself, that he was only about to march against Abrokomas, a personal enemy of his own, who lay on the Euphrates, some twelve marches distant. Persuaded by these considerations, and by an

* Xen. Anab. I., iv. 3. † Anab. I., vii. 10. ‡ Anab. I., ii. 25.
‡ Anab. II., ii. 6.

increase of pay, they marched onward five days farther to Issos, where, as above stated, the army was joined by Cheirisophos, sent thither with the Spartan fleet. And here Xenias the Arkadian, and Pasion of Megara, took ship and deserted, through resentment at the defection of many of their men to Klearchos, during the last halt; but it does not appear that any, beyond their personal attendants, if even these, joined them in their disaffection. From this point they marched quietly to the rich city of Thapsakos, twelve days farther—no one positively aware, even yet, what was the object of the expedition, says Xenophon;* yet it is scarcely possible to doubt, especially when we perceive how immediately all their scruples vanished before the exhibition of increased pay, that not only the generals, but the soldiers of all ranks, must have been absolutely certain, if only from the secresy with which it was conducted, what was the real object of their march. At Thapsakos, however, all their doubts, if they entertained any, must have terminated; for here Kyros himself explained all his purpose to the leaders, and they, calling an assembly of the army, to the soldiers. But these affected great indignation at their own officers, as if they had been deceived by them; but on receiving the promise of a bonus of five silver minæ—equal to about twenty pounds sterling, or a hundred dollars, to speak in round numbers—to every man, in addition to his full pay, from their departure until their return into Ionia, so soon as they should arrive at Babylon, they relented as usual, and proceeded without further hesitation, across the Euphrates, and along its eastern bank, to the city of Karmanda. There they fell in with the first signs of the enemy, in the trail of about two thousand horse, preceding them and devastating the country; there, too, Orontes, one of Kyros's most trusty chiefs, was convicted of manifest treason, in endeavoring to carry the cavalry over to the king, and was led away as if to execution; from

* Xen. Anab. I. iii. 16.

which time, alive or dead, he was never seen of men, nor the place of his sepulture. Thence entering Babylonia, they marched yet three days, when at midnight Kyros reviewed his whole force on the plain, and arranged his order of battle; for he expected his brother to deliver battle on the morrow; and to Klearchos he gave the leading of the right wing; to Menon that of the Greek left, and to himself he reserved the command of his Orientals, one hundred thousand strong, with all his cavalry, which appears to have been unusually feeble, and twenty scythed chariots. But while the review was yet in process, deserters from the king arrived, announcing the approach of the royal army, rated at one million and two hundred thousand combatants, besides six thousand cuirassiers of the Immortals, led by Artagerses, and two hundred scythe-armed chariots. Of these, however, but nine hundred thousand were present under arms, being three out of the four equal divisions, each three hundred thousand strong, commanded by Tissaphernes, Gobryas, Arbakes, and Abrokomas—the last of whom did not come up until the fifth day after the decision of the campaign by the battle of Kynaka.* All that day the army marched in battle order, until they arrived at a vast recent trench, five fathoms wide and three deep, running twelve parasangs, or nearly fifty English miles up the country, till it reached the Median wall, where it met all the canals, four in number, about four miles apart, and a hundred feet in width, well bridged, which were constructed for the passage of the corn-ships from the Tigris into the Euphrates. The trench could be passed at one point only, on a causeway, twenty feet wide, along the bank of the Euphrates; and it was so evident that the king had originally intended to fight here, but that his heart had failed him, that, having thus far advanced in array of battle, no sooner had they entered this formidable line of defences, than the army relaxed its discipline; Kyros himself riding in his

* Xen. Anab. 1., vii. 11, 12.

chariot, and the Greek hoplitai advancing in loose order, with their shields borne for the most part in the baggage wagons, or on the backs of the beasts of burthen.

Thus they continued all the next day; but on the third, Pateguas, a Persian, confidant of Kyros, came panting in from the van, announcing the royal army close at hand. This was about the hour of full market, or from nine to eleven o'clock, A.M.; and then all was bustle. Kyros leaped from his car, and armed himself, with his javelins in his hand, and mounting his charger ordered his people hastily. To the Greeks he gave the right wing of the whole army; to Ariaios, with the Lydians and Phrygians, and a thousand horse, the left; and to himself, as before, he reserved the centre with ten thousand Persian infantry, and six hundred chosen horsemen, armed cap-a-piè with corslets, casques and thigh-pieces and Grecian sabres, and riding horses accoutred with chafrons on their heads and poitrels on their chests, whom he led in person, armed like the rest, but wearing on his head a tiara only, as seems to have been the usage with the Persian kings.

Of the Greek right wing, which he rightly esteemed the flower of his whole force, and to which he looked for the best service, Klearchos had the extreme right, along the river bank, which he occupied with all the targeteers, and a thousand Paphlagonian cavalry attached to his command by Kyros. Next to Klearchos, fought Proxenos the Boiotian, with whom served Xenophon as a volunteer; then the rest of the Hellenic infantry, and on the left, next to the barbaric centre, Menon the Thessalian, with his men.* And it was now mid-day, but no enemy were yet in sight.

It is remarkable that, up to this time, Xenophon, the able narrator of this expedition, and afterward its main stay, has not

* Xen. Anab. I. viii. 1–6. Diod. Sic. XIX. 21–22. Plut. Vit. Artox. IX.

made his appearance on the scene; and it is only by one casual expression of his own that we learn whether he bore any part at all in the action, in which he seems to have acted as a sort of aid-de-camp to his friend Proxenos, serving on horseback.

It was already afternoon, when "there appeared dust like a white cloud, and not long afterward black shadowy masses covering the whole plain. But when they were come nigher the flashes of the polished bronze were visible; and then the lines of spears and the ranks came into sight. And there were, on the enemy's left horse, with white corslets, said to be Tissaphernes' men; and next to these Persians with wicker targets; and next to these, again, heavy foot with wooden shields covering them to the feet—and it was said that these were Ægyptians; and beyond these other horse again, and again other archers, and in front of all a continuous line of war-chariots with scythes projecting from the naves and underneath the axles. Kyros, indeed, when he had previously harangued the Greeks, told them that they must endure the shouts and wild war cries of the barbarians, but he erred in this, for they came not on with a shout, but as silently and quietly as possible, at a slow pace, and with an even front. But now Kyros gallopped along the front with Pigres the interpreter, and three or four others, and shouted to Klearchos that he should oblique to the left, and charge, with his whole force of Greeks, full on the enemy's centre, for that the king fought there; 'and if,' he cried, 'we may conquer there, we shall have conquered everywhere.'" But when Klearchos observed the density of the Persian centre, and learned that the left wing of the royal army overflanked the whole Greek power, while the extreme left of Kyros' entire army was still to the right of the king's centre, he did not deem it advisable to leave a gap between his own right and the river, through which the masses of the enemy's left could have broken in force and gained his rear. Wherefore he contented himself by replying that he would arrange all for the best. And, at this time, the army was advancing orderly and evenly, when, Kyros careering along the front surveyed both hosts, of his friends and enemies, whereupon, Xenophon, the Athenian, gallopped out and inquired if he had any orders; and he reining up desired him to inform all men that the sacrifices were favorable and the omens propitious. While he was yet speaking, a great clamor ran along the Hellenic ranks, that he inquired what meant the clamor, when Klearchos replied that the watchword was passing now the second time; and he, surprised at this, asked again what was the watchword, and Klearchos answered, "Zeus the Savior and Victory." Thereupon, Kyros replied, 'I accept the omen and so may it be,' and gallopped away to his own station. At this time the armies were about three stadia apart, when the Greeks raised the Pæon, and levelling their pikes to the charge, rushed forward. Then, as part of the Phalanx hurried its step with overboiling ardor, so that the front was a little shaken, those who were left behind charged on at double quick time to equalize their advance, and catching ardor each from other, and influenced by their own rapid motion, all shouted at once the battle cry of Enyalios, and bore down with a fiery rush, clashing their spears against their brazen shields to terrify the cavalry. And, long before they were within bowshot, the Persians broke and fled in confusion, the Greeks pursuing them as rapidly as they could, without breaking their own ranks, and in fact chasing them too far off the field before wheeling on the rear of the royal centre. The charge of the scythed chariots, as usual, proved fruitless, for many were driven back on their own masses, many rushed through the Greek ranks, which opened to give them passage, empty and overset, without harming any one; and in fact thus far the victory was bloodless, for of all the Greeks, one man fell only, shot with an arrow in the left wing. Of the Persians, Tissaphernes alone did not fly, but charged through the targeteers and

Paphlagonian horse, along the river bank on the extreme right of the Greek lines, and gained the rear where he united with the royal right which had wheeled round the left of Kyros' whole array, and broke into the camp which they sacked mercilessly, regardless of the fortunes of the main battle. None of the targeteers had fallen in the headlong charge of Tissaphernes, for they had opened their lines and suffered the cavalry to pass through, galling them so terribly with their long weapons that they had no inclination to renew the conflict, but swept away uselessly to the rear, while the Greek light troops hurried on and overtook their victorious comrades. At this moment the field was in utter confusion. Each army had outflanked and turned one wing of the other, and gained its rear, while their two centres were still reeling in desperate and balanced fight. For Kyros, when he saw the Greeks victorious and in full pursuit on his right, and Ariaios gradually winning his way with the left, esteemed himself victorious, and being already hailed as king, charged headlong on the Immortals of the king's centre, with his own picked horse, killed Artagerses with his own hand, and by that single onslaught must have decided the whole battle had he kept his own men together, or had the victorious Greeks wheeled to their own left in due season. But neither of these things fell out*—the Hellenic allies were in full chase; the prince's body-guard got scattered in the melée, and fought in little knots of ten or twelve wherever they could overtake a flying foe or find one resisting; while Kyros himself, riding a fiery and hard-mouthed horse, drove pell-mell through the broken enemy, till he recognized his brother, and was recognized by him simultaneously. Then they both charged, spear to spear, and Kyros wounded Artoxerxes sorely in the breast, and unhorsed him, so that his followers believed him dead, and, taking him up

* Xenoph. Anab. I. viii. 24–29. Plut. Vit. Artox. XII. Diod. Sic. XIV. 23.

severely hurt, bore him away to a neighboring hillock where he slowly recovered his senses, all his men flying hither and thither in confusion. Still separated from his own people, Kyros rode up and down exulting in his victory and saluted king by many of the enemy, even by some of the king's eunuchs, till at last, his tiara falling off, he was wounded near the eye with a javelin by one Mithradates, a Persian youth, ignorant of his person; and a stone soon afterward striking him down, he was killed by a spearthrust at the hands of some ignorant camp followers. His body was at last casually recognized by Artasuras, called the king's eye, and carried to the presence; whereon, his head and right hand being cut off, and the news proclaimed, the royal horse began to rally, and seventy thousand men were soon collected about the person of Artoxerxes, who had of late so nearly lost both life and kingdom.

By this time Ariaios, who until now had been fighting well, learned the death of the prince, and drawing off his own troops by a route far to the left of the camp which the enemy were plundering, made his way back unpursued to the post which he had occupied on that very morning, a day's march in the rear. And now Klearchos and his phalanx returned from their pursuit, expecting that all was over; and as they traversed the ground on which the centre and left of the king had stood, until routed by their own charge and that of Kyros, they discovered that their camp was in the hands of the enemy, and advanced to recover it. But Tissaphernes, and they who had taken it, avoided an engagement, and passing to the Greek left along the river, over the ground held by Klearchos in the morning, hurried to the hillock occupied by the king; where they again showed front as if to receive battle. But when the Greeks once more cheered and charged, both armies being now in the same relative positions as in the morning, though nearer to Babylon than in the first action, the Barbarians again fled, and the hillock, on which were the Greeks and the king's banner, with a golden eagle flying, was deserted by the enemy, and the whole plain abandoned to the Greeks, who weary, hungry and supperless, for their encampment had been thoroughly sacked, remained masters of the bloody field, wondering whither the prince could have gone, and anxiously looking for his return.

The battle itself was ill-fought on both sides, and displays nothing but the indisputable valor of the Greeks, and their great superiority to the Orientals, both in armature and discipline. Plutarch insists that it was lost by the disobedience of Klearchos to the prince's orders, to oblique upon the enemy's centre; not by the rashness of Kyros; and on that text bitterly censures the Lakedaimonian leader. Possibly, had Klearchos so charged, he might have won the battle; for the fall of the king and the breaking the centre often, with Oriental armies, decides everything. Still to have made an oblique movement to such a length, exposing his own column to a flank attack, and leaving the whole right wing of the army open and unguarded, in the teeth of an admirable cavalry, would have been to the last degree an unsoldierly and unscientific movement; for executing which, even if successfully, he would have deserved not praise but censure. His determination to cling to the river with his right was just and sound, and his charge in itself masterly. His error, and it was a gross one, lay in chasing to the rear, instead of wheeling leftward on the centre; which could have decided the battle in season and placed the crown on the head of Kyros. In like manner, had that prince, on the fall of Artagerses, and the dispersal of the immortals, rallied his body-guard and held them in hand; or had he even fallen back alone on Ariaios, after unhorsing the king, and as he probably believed killing him, he would have been found master of the field by Klearchos, on his return, and his entire success would have been the consequence.

The loss of the battle—for by the death of Kyros it was

virtually lost—ought then to be ascribed rather to the want of concert, which naturally occurs in combined armies, acting without unity of command, than to any lack of individual judgment, courage, or conduct.

On the following morning the Greek leaders received intelligence of what had occurred, and of his own whereabouts, from Ariaios, with an invitation to join him, and retreat together by a different route into Ionia. This plan at first displeased the Hellenic troops, who regarding themselves as victors offered the crown to Ariaios, and halted where they were, breakfasting, as best they might, on the beasts of burthen which they slew, cooked on the wooden shields and missiles of the enemy, which they used as fuel. While thus engaged, they received a summons from the king commanding them to lay down their arms, when in the spirit of Leonidas they bade him "come and take them." And shortly after the dismissal of the heralds, the reply of Ariaios reached them, declining the crown and urging them strenuously to join him and commence their retreat forthwith. This they did, entering his camp on that same night, when they piled their arms, and, the generals and captains of bands entering in to Ariaios, a treaty was sworn between the Greeks and the Barbaric followers of Kyros, that they should be true friends and allies, neither betraying the other, and the Persians promising farther, that they would guide them truly home into Ionia. And this oath they ratified, slaying an ox, a wolf, a boar, and a ram, upon a shield, and dipping into the blood, the Greeks, their sword blades, and the Persians, their spear heads; a ceremony so solemn, so ancient, and supposed of such awful and appalling sanctity, that Aischylos* in his fine tragedy of the "Seven against Thebes" has ascribed it to the Argive leaders, in verse so striking, and terms so similar to the above, that it may be agreeable to

* Aischylos. Ἑπτὰ ἐπι Θηβαῖς.

my readers to compare it with this passage of history, even through the imperfect medium of an English version.

For heroes seven, impetuous champions strong,
Bull-slaughtering on a black-bound brazen shield,
And dipping in that carnage-cup their hands,
By Mars, Enyo, and blood-loving Dread,
Have sworn, these ramparts violently ta'en,
Either to sack the Kadmian town to earth,
Or dying here to glut this soil with gore.
Then for their parents on Adrastos' car,
With those same hands memorial gifts they crowned,
Weeping, but in their faces ruth was not.
For like to lions who spy the front of Mars,
Their souls were iron, hot with manly rage.

Such was the nature, and such the fearful obligation, of the oath to which both the Greeks and the Asiatics swore, whom community of friendship for the dead Kyros, and community of past toils, and present perils, should have linked together, without oaths, in permanent and true alliance. With the Barbarians however, the oaths were a mere pretext; and, as has been invariably the case in all compacts between men of European and Oriental origin, wherever it was for the interest of the latter to break them, the Greeks were sacrificed, blind victims to their own good faith, and the inveterate treachery of the Asiatics. This treaty concluded, they marched together, on the following morning, having the sun on their right hand, in the hope of reaching the Babylonian villages at nightfall. But as twilight was closing in, they saw what at first they took to be cavalry, which turned out, however, to be herds of horses grazing; and, so soon as darkness fell, the whole was explained, for the villages all around were full of watch-fires, and it was evident that they were close to the encampment of the royal army. On that night there was a panic in the Greek camp, which was appeased by the presence of mind of Klearchos; and on the following day messengers came from the king with proposals for a treaty. After this, the Greeks and their Persian allies awaited Tissaphernes, about three-and-twenty days, while nominally he was consulting the king as to terms and conditions; and at the end of this period Tissaphernes returned, with Orontes—both at the head of their contingents, as if bound homewards—when a treaty was concluded, and regularly sworn to, with plighted hands and solemn sacrifices, that the Persians should guide and convoy the Greeks in safety through the country, furnishing them with an open market, where they might buy supplies; but that, the market failing, the Greeks should be free to forage for themselves; and this on the bare condition that the mercenaries should travel through the country peacefully, and do no evil to the inhabitants, or injury to the crops, or cattle of the several districts. The Persians of the king also, and the Persians who had fought with Kyros were reconciled, and thenceforth they encamped with Tissaphernes and Orontes, by themselves, and the Hellenes by themselves also, at about a parasang or something less apart; both mounting guards, each against the other, and both apparently suspecting the good faith of the other.

From this simple narrative, as well as from what follows—for Xenophon states distinctly, that from this day forth the friendship of Ariaios declined visibly—it can hardly be doubted that the Persians, who had fought side by side with them, were false to their late allies from the beginning; and that the very first march, leading them into the very camp of the king instead of away from it, was the first step of a treason, which was intended to involve the massacre of the whole force.

Notwithstanding these suspicions, however, the Greeks marched nineteen days' journey—ninety-six parasangs, or about three hundred and sixty miles—in company with the Persians of Tissaphernes and Orontes, until they reached the river Zapatas, where they halted three days. And at this place the mutual distrust and dissensions became so alarming, that Klearchos apprehended an open rupture; whereupon he went manfully, and in good faith, to Tissaphernes, hoping to obtain an explanation, and bring about a perfect understanding. Availing himself of this, the wily Barbarian induced the honest Spartan to bring the leaders of the expedition, and the captains of the lochi, to his tent in the morning, promising to inform them who it was that had belied the Greeks to him, and to surrender the person to their vengeance.

Klearchos doubting nothing, and violently suspecting Menon the Thessalian of ill-faith, would have taken all the generals and captains of bands with him; but some of the private soldiers interposed, and insisted that *all* their officers should not go, as they had no faith in the barbarians.

And here it is worthy of notice, that in all cases where European officers have been induced to capitulate, trusting in the honor of Orientals, the privates have clearly discerned the treason which escaped the more acuminated vision of their superiors, and have always implored them to put trust in their arms only. Such was the case when a British regiment in Ceylon laid down their arms to the Kandyan savages, and were massacred to a man. Such, when in the fatal campaign of Ghizni, the English officers were induced to confer with the Affghan leaders in their tent, and were incontinently murdered by the hands of their hosts—and such, in the instance now before me, was the result.

In the end, Klearchos prevailed with four of the generals, and twenty of the captains of bands, to accompany him; the former being, in addition to himself, Proxenos the Boiotian, Menon the Thessalian, Agias the Arkadian, and Sokrates the Achaian; and in addition to these about two hundred of the soldiers escorted them to the Persian camp, unarmed, with a view of attending the market. The generals were at once admitted to the tent of

Tissaphernes, while the captains were detained without; until, on a given signal, those within were arrested, and those at the doors cut to pieces; while the cavalry made a wide sweep over the plain, after killing all who had entered the camp, and cut down every one whom they encountered, whether slave or freeman. The Greeks looked on, at first, in amazement, not imagining what this display of careering cavalry should mean; till one Nikarchos, an Arkadian, came in grievously wounded in the abdomen, and carrying his bowels in his hands. Then they all ran tumultuously to arms, expecting to be attacked immediately; but in a little while Mithradates, Artaozos, and Ariaios, all late friends of Kyros, rode up, and once more endeavored to persuade the Greeks to lay down their arms; telling them that Klearchos had been convicted of perjury and intent to break the treaties, wherefore he had been slain; but that Proxenos, Menon, and the rest, were in high favor with the king. This device was, however, too transparent to deceive, and was answered by Xenophon—who received the delegates, in the absence of Cheirisophos, he being out with a foraging party, together with Kleanor the Orchomenian, and Sophainetos the Stymphalian—by a demand for the instant release of Proxenos and Menon—"to which," said he, "there can be no objection; since, as you aver, they are in favor with the king."

To this, there was no reply; and after debating long among themselves, the treacherous barbarians rode away, frustrate of their end, and disappointed. The generals had, of course, all perished—Klearchos, Proxenos, Agias, and Sokrates—beheaded as overt enemies to the king; of whom Xenophon has left elaborate characters, and many interesting anecdotes, which I regret that my limits will not permit me to extract. They were all good and practised soldiers and strategists, "whose valor and conduct no enemy ever laughed at in battle, no friend ever found insufficient;"* but Klearchos, especially was a soldier, by habit, by choice, and by profession; seeking out every opportunity of active service, at home and abroad; a strict disciplinarian, an enthusiastic lover of arms, and in all respects a great captain and an honest, though stern and hard-visaged, man. Menon, on the contrary, was not allowed the luxury of a speedy or honorable death, but was consumed by slow tortures, which were protracted through the space of a whole year; though on what account he was punished by Artoxerxes, it is somewhat difficult to understand; since Xenophon more than hints that he was false to the Greeks; and if false to them, he must, at least, have endeavored to serve the king.

That night, when they knew that their leaders were taken off, the Greeks were in the greatest consternation and despair, nor that without good cause; "considering that they were almost at the palace doors of the great king, with numerous nations and cities surrounding them on every side, all hostile, with no one who should guide them on their way, no one who should furnish them with a market of supplies; and they above ten thousand stadia distant from Greece, with many vast and formidable rivers between, alone, betrayed by the barbarians who had marched up with them under Kyros, and unprovided with cavalry, so that if victorious in any action, they would be unable to follow up the success, if beaten they must needs be annihilated. When they thought over these things within themselves, they were utterly disheartened, and few of them tasted food that evening; and few kindled any fires, and there were many who did not muster at the shields that night, but laid them down, each where he chanced to be, unable to sleep from grief of spirit, and desire of their countries, their parents, their wives, their children, whom they never thought to look upon again.

So great indeed was the confusion and so complete the dis-

* Xen. Anab. II., vi. 30. Diodorus denies his death, xiv. 21.

organization of the whole Greek army, that if the Persian cavalry had fallen in upon them there and then, they would have encountered little if any resistance, and must have cut the Greeks to pieces. Even on the morrow, they would have gained an easy victory, but for the ready wit, stirring eloquence, and exuberant resource of one man, who from that day was the soul of the army, and who approved himself, wherever or however he learned the rudiments, a thorough master of the art of war in its most difficult details. For to him alone, and his over-boiling bravery, undaunted decision, and never flagging spirit, is it due that the bones of the ten thousand did not whiten the deserts of central Asia. That man was Xenophon—having fallen at length, like his comrades, into a slumber which yet was not sleep, so great was the perturbation of his spirit, he was startled by a strange, and as he imagined supernatural dream; and so soon as he was awake, musing deeply on their affairs, he saw that their only hope lay in energy, promptitude, and bold reliance on their own arms and valor; and forthwith rising from his bed, he called up the captains of Proxenos' division, to all of whom he was personally known, and addressed them with such convincing power of truth and common sense, and with such passionate soldierly heat, as is best suited to persuade soldiers. And when they had heard him out, they all clamored to be led forward, except one Apollonides, who spoke the broad Boiotian dialect, and who had voted at the first to give up their arms to Artoxerxes. Him they degraded speedily, from the captain of a band to be a baggage-bearer, for while Xenophon was displaying some choice powers of invective at his expense, the soldiers observed that his ears were bored as if for ear rings, and hooted him from the ranks as a Medized Greek. And this little incident, which otherwise I should scarce have recounted, proves what a change his words had produced, and how new and keen a spirit they

* Xen. Anab. III. I. 1.

must have diffused into those hearts late so dejected, that they could already descend to notice individual eccentricities, and jest with hearty soldiers' glee at such a moment.

And now these men—it was by this time about the middle of the night—went through the ranks, and called up every general, and when the generals were slain, then every second in command, and all the captains of the bands, to council—and all the generals came, and captains about a hundred. And Hieronymos of Elis, the eldest of Proxenos' lochagoi, addressed them, and told them wherefore they had thus assembled, and called them to co-operation, and then bade Xenophon, "Speak thou to these, as thou hast spoken unto us." And he spoke to them even so; and so convinced them, that Cheirisophos the Lakedaimonian—and Lakedaimonians were not over wont to give even due credit to Athenians—cried out, "Hitherto, O, Xenophon, I have known this much of thee only, that I heard thou wert an Athenian;* but now I praise thee much for what thou hast said, and done, and I would that there were more like to thee; for it would be for the common good." And he proceeded at once to collect all the soldiers, that they might elect leaders in place of those who were slain, and stand at once to their arms. Then were chosen in the place of Klearchos, Timasion the Dardanian; and of Sokrates, Xanthikles the Achaian; and of Agias, Kleanor the Arkadian; and of Menon, Philesios the Achaian; and of Proxenos, Xenophon the Athenian—and this latter election is remarkable for this, that in almost all the other instances a chief was chosen of the same nation with him who had fallen, or with the majority of the troops he commanded. But Xenophon was an Athenian, chosen by Boiotians, who of all men were most inveterately hostile to Attika. To his merits only, was his election to be attributed; and, whether there was need of action or of counsel, he still proved the choice to be wise and just,

* I am by no means certain that this was not intended as a half sneer.

which had fallen on him; for, in truth, he was thenceforth the head and front of the whole campaign, whether strategetics or tactics were the question, and whether the vanguard or the rear guard was assailed, there shall we find Xenophon, ever detached to meet the enemy.

Then Cheirisophos first addressed the soldiers, and as he concluded, Xenophon arose, full-armed for battle and decorated in all martial bravery, and spoke to them words of fire, lending them cheer and courage; so that when Cheirisophos put it to the vote, all shouted unanimously "let us march—let us march without delay." On Xenophon's proposal, therefore, it was resolved to proceed in an oblong hollow square, with the camp followers and baggage in the centre; and to Cheirisophos, as being a Lakedaimonian, he attributed the leading of the van, two of the eldest generals commanding the flank battalions of the square, while, with Timasion, he took to himself, as they the youngest, the rear guard, which in retreat is the post of danger as it is of honor. This all determined, the soldiers burned their tents and wagons, and all the superfluous baggage which they could not conveniently carry, and then cooked and piled their arms for breakfast. While they were thus engaged Mithridates came up with about thirty horse, pretending good will, but evidently sent to reconnoitre and gain information. To him Cheirisophos replied once for all, that if permitted to do so, it was their intent to march quietly through the country, doing no wrong to any; but that, if hindered on the way, they would fight to the uttermost." As soon as they had breakfasted, they stood to their arms, and, fording the Zapatas,* marched in order, with their baggage and beasts of burthen in the centre; not far had they gone, however,

* The great Zab, a large river of Kardouchia, now Kurdistan, flowing in a great semicircle northerly, westerly and then almost southerly, from the mountains below lake Urmia, now Oroumi, into the Tigris, about forty miles below Mosul.

before Mithridates again made his appearance with about two hundred horse, and four hundred bowmen and slingers, lightly equipped, active and fleet runners. At first they approached as friends, but, so soon as they got near enough, both horse and foot deployed on a sudden, and began to shoot and sling, into the closely ordered ranks of the Hellenes, with terrible execution. And the rear guard were cruelly cut up and harassed, and very many wounded, for the Kretans could not shoot half so far as the Persians; and were moreover so slightly armed that they were obliged to keep within the ranks of the hoplitai; nor could the javelineers hurl a spear so far as to hit the slingers, who whirled their missiles into them as fast and furious as a hail storm, though with far more fatal execution. Then perceiving how much confidence the enemy gained, and how severely his own people were suffering, Xenophon charged with a portion of the rear guard, both hoplitai and targeteers, and endeavored to pursue the enemy, who did not attempt to resist his onset, but fled, still shooting and slinging as they retreated. So that, after a time, having slain or captured no one, the Greeks were compelled to fall back in turn, and fight their way, not without loss of brave men, and much difficulty, to the main body which they would hardly have accomplished, had it not halted until they regained their station. That day they scarcely made three miles on their way, since there was a perpetual skirmish from dawn till it was dark; and at first Cheirisophos and his colleagues were inclined to blame Xenophon for his charge, as if he had rashly risked himself and his command without injuring the enemy or bettering the condition of the army. But he admitting the rashness of his zeal, showed them clearly that, circumstanced as they were, the army must be lost, since they could not disperse an enemy superior in light-armed troops, nor forage, nor even cover their own retreat if broken; and then, with sound and clear capacity, indicated a remedy in the creation of cavalry, and a more efficient army for skirmishing, all which he accomplished satisfactorily from so small means, as at once showed the quickness of his resource—one of the greatest qualities of a leader. His suggestions of that night were carried out on the next day, during which they halted, by drafting all the Rhodians who chanced to be in the army, to the number of two hundred, to form a band of slingers—for the Rhodians at this time were what the Balearic islanders were in the latter days, all slingers from their childhood using leaden bullets instead of ragged and clumsy pebbles—and by mounting on the spare chargers of the officers, on some horses left by Klearchos at his death, and some, his own private property, and yet others which had been taken in action and were now used as beasts of burthen, fifty picked men, who were equipped with breastplates, buff-coats, and all the other harness of well-appointed troopers, and to whom Lykios, the son of Polystratos, was named commander. On the next day, they again marched early, having a deep and difficult ravine to pass, at which they anticipated an attack from the bowmen and cavalry of the Persians, but they had crossed the gorge, and were about a mile distant on the plain, when Mithridates again made his appearance with a thousand horse and four thousand slingers—and it is said, that he had promised Tissaphernes with that power to compel the Greeks to surrender on that very day. But he found the Greeks now well ordered to receive him, for a certain force of targeteers had been ordered to follow up the slingers, and of hoplitai again to support the targeteers. And, so soon as Mithridates deployed in their rear and about their flanks, and sling-shot and arrows began to fall in the ranks, the Hellenic trumpets sounded, the Rhodians wheeled into line and dispersed the archery in an instant with their deadly missiles, the cavalry charged home, the Persian horse scattering before their unexpected onset and flying headlong to the broken banks of the ravine for safety; but fast and fierce the targeteers fell on, and the great shields of the heavy infantry came on like a wall in support; and, confident in their near aid, the Rhodian slingers ran at their utmost speed and slung into the mass of fugitives, and the troopers spurred hard upon their horse; and very many of the barbarian foot fell unavenged that day, and in the gulley of the torrent eighteen of their cavalry were taken alive by the Greek troopers.

That was a memorable skirmish, though the gain and the loss were actually but small. It gave the prestige of a first success to their newly levied troops, converted in one night from heavy foot into cavalry and slingers, which they never lost during the retreat. It established the superiority of the Hellenes in these, as in the more solid arms, of the service. It taught a lesson to the enemy, who had before considered their light troops, and above all their splendid horse almost invincible, from which they never entirely recovered; and it was, so far as we know from history, the first display of Xenophon's various and almost unrivalled resources and capacities as a great and genuine soldier. During the whole of that day, they met no farther annoyance from the enemy; but as they marched onward they found that their order of march in a hollow oblong column was inconvenient, in as much as at times in passing bridges or defiles, the hoplitai were so closely pressed together as to be useless, and again at times when the wings extended the centre was unduly weakened. This again was remedied by the appointment of six bands, or lochi, of a hundred each, with the proper officers, who, when the column was pressed together on the march fell into the rear, and again marched up on the outside the wings; and on the other hand, when the wings were extended, and the centre opened, filled up the spaces, forming a front of single, double or quadruple files as the nature of the case determined. After marching nearly all day thus, they entered some broken and hilly ground, when the enemy again showed himself in force in the rear, and as the Greeks descended from the summit of one knoll into the hollow, before mounting another, the light troops crowned that which they had just quitted, and galled them so severely that the Peltasts were again rendered useless and shut up within the heavy columns. These knolls were, it seems, the spurs of a lofty ridge on their right hand, as they marched northerly, with the Tigris on their left, running down to that river; and the difficulty was soon overcome by detaching all the peltasts from the right flank of the column to the heights above, by which means the enemy, fearing to be cut off, kept at a prudent distance, and during the rest of that day the column marching over the hillocks, and the light troops moving along the mountain side on their right and a little in their rear, they arrived unmolested at certain villages, where they halted several days to care for their wounded, of whom there were very many, and to recruit their men and horses with the food and fodder prepared for the royal army. From this time, moreover, they adopted a new plan; for so soon as the enemy appeared in pursuit, they halted at the first convenient village, and did not attempt to fight him on the march; but keeping a sufficient force under arms to repulse and pursue him, should he attempt to skirmish, passed the day at their ease with refreshment; and then, when the shades of night began to fall, while the enemy were yet hovering about them, sounded "boot and saddle." For experience had taught them that the enemy dared not encamp nearer to them than six or seven miles, for fear of a night attack; since, as Xenophon observes, an Oriental army is of all others the most liable to a panic, and to what is worse, that peculiar sort of panic, known on our prairies as a *stampede*, affecting hobbled or tethered horses; so that to them a night-surprise is almost a sure defeat. Then, when they were assured that they were once fairly off, they yoked their baggage-cattle and marched so far forward as the enemy had fallen back; so that it was not until the third day that they were again molested by them, and then but slightly. On that night, however, a party of the barbarians slipped past them in the dark, and occupied a very strong rocky hold on the summit of a mountain, below which their road lay. But in the morning, when Cheirisophos in full march discovered them, he halted the heads of the column, and ordered up Xenophon with his targeteers from the rear. Xenophon rode up at once, but did not bring up the troops, since the rear was also threatened by all the horse and archery of Tissaphernes, who led them in person; and no sooner had he arrived than he perceived not only the evil but its cure; for there was yet another and loftier height above that occupied by the enemy, which taken, they would be forced to retire. Hereupon, Cheirisophos giving him his choice, whether to lead the van to the assault, or to remain with the main body, he at once chose the former, and was supplied with a thousand targeteers from the van and centre, since his own men could not be spared from the rear-guard, and with three hundred more, picked soldiers of Cheirisophos' own body guard.

Then, at once, he set off at such speed as he was assured he could maintain; and the barbarians on the hills, seeing his object, set off likewise for the upper summit, hoping to anticipate him; and there was a wild and panting race, up those dizzy heights, between them, for the mastery—each army cheering its own detachment, till all the crags re-echoed with the stirring clamor. And Xenophon, gallopping beside his men, cheered them to breast the hill, as it needs a soldier to cheer soldiers. "Men," he cried, "Men, remember that the race is now for Hellas, now for your wives and children!—that striving now for a short space stoutly, we shall march henceforth at our ease!" Then one Soterides of Sikyon, made answer, "We are not on one footing, you and I, O Xenophon; for you are carried easily on your charger, I toil wearily with my heavy shield." Then

Xenophon sprang from his horse, and pushed him from the ranks, snatching his shield from him, and led faster than before, though he was armed in heavy horseman's panoply, so that he was overburthened by the shield—cheering the foremost to press on, and the rear to close up; so that it was hard for them to follow. Then the soldiers abused Soterides, and struck and pelted him, till they forced him to resume his shield and his place in the ranks; and Xenophon, mounting again, rode so far as the ground would admit of riding, and then led on foot, and of course, won the heights; for what soldier would not follow so game and soldierly a leader. The winning of the pass, of need won the passage bloodlessly; for the barbarians leaped down the rocks, save themselves who could! and Tissaphernes drew off his men in the rear, and the Greeks descended into the plain near the Tigris, which was full of rich villages. In the evening, the horse again made their appearance in the low grounds, and cutting off a few foragers, began to fire the villages; but the Greeks, seeing that the villages were the king's, not their own, began to fire them likewise; so that the Persians, seeing themselves the losers at that game, desisted, and withdrew for the night.

On the following day there was much doubt and dismay in the host; for in front their way was barred by precipices which they could not scale, and on their right was the Tigris—in the hope to turn which they had journeyed hither—unfordable, nor to be sounded by their longest spears. In this predicament, they turned back toward Babylonia, ravaging and burning the country far and near, while the enemy looked on in amazement, without daring to attack them. Then, after questioning their captives concerning the nature and inhabitants of the districts around them, they learned that the mountains directly to their north were inhabited by various Kardouchian tribes, savage, independent, and, though often assailed, never conquered by the king, who had often invaded them to no purpose, a hundred and twenty thousand strong. Beyond these again, they were informed, lay the rich and fertile plains of Armenia, where they might either turn or ford the sources of the Tigris; and yet a little farther off were the head-waters of the Euphrates, in like manner passable by the army.

Now it must be remembered, that on their way up from Sardis, they had crossed the Euphrates by a deep ford at Thapsakos, said, and probably with justice, to be the only place where it was fordable, about midway between their point of departure and the termination of their expedition on the field of Kynaxa—that, after the battle, while yet friendly to Ariaios, they had been informed—and it is not to be doubted, again, justly—that the country wasted by their up-march could, by no possibility, support them on their return; and that, while under safe-conduct from Tissaphernes, they had crossed the Tigris at Sittake, on a bridge of thirty-six boats, to the right or eastern bank, by which, they had been led to believe, lay their best homeward route. This, doubtless, was a piece of Persian treachery, followed up by the murder of the Greek generals on the banks of the great Zab. After this event it was that the Greeks resolved to persevere in their northern route, principally induced by the consideration that they had no means of crossing those two great rivers in the face of the enemy; the rather that the country afforded no timber for bridge or boat building, even had other means been abundant. Under these circumstances, the generals had no choice but to persevere, since the Tigris to the left or westward was impassable, while to return southward was to rush back into the lion's mouth, at Babylon; and, to march eastward, to turn their backs absolutely on their own country. The road northward led to the sources of the rivers, which they must head, since they could not cross them, and thence with victory and safety home.

I have thought it well to point out these facts here, since I have recently met with a critique on this retreat, attributing it as a fault to the leaders, that they held their course too directly northward, and attributed to the Pontos Euxeinos, or Black Sea, a situation too far to the eastward. Now it is clear, first, that they could not march further west of the north than they did at this point; and secondly, that they did not miscalculate the bearings of the Black Sea, since they struck it without material deviation from their line, at Trebizonde, above a hundred miles westward of its eastern extremity. It should be remembered also, that instruments, maps, compasses, were not in those days; that the Greeks were in a hostile land, where no European foot had ever trod; had no guides but captive enemies, no pilots but the eternal signs of heaven, and the wonder is that they accomplished at all a retreat, which has nothing comparable to it in the military history of all ages, and which is a prouder trophy of true generalship, than the most brilliant campaign ever won by mortal genius. They plunged at once into the rugged wilderness of craggy rocks, pathless ravines, and torrent-beds, unknown even to this hour, which forms the modern district of Kurdistan, and the Turkish Pachalic of Van, to the south of the great lake of the same name, and forced their way through it—having destroyed all their superfluous baggage and released all their captives, with the exception of the female hetairai, who followed them in great numbers—by desperate and incessant fighting, in the space of seven days. At first they suffered terribly, for the weather was dreadful, and the inhabitants had all fled to the hill-tops, and thence galled the rear-guard with the most fearful archery they had yet encountered; for they fought with six-foot bows and cloth-yard arrows, which no casque or corslet could withstand; so that Xenophon lost two of his best hoplitai—Kleonymus, a Lakedaimonian, shot clear through shield, buff-coat, corslet and body; and Basias, an Arkadian, through the head.

This was in some sort the fault of Cheirisophos, who, deceived by the guide into the belief that there was no other pass, attempted to make his way forward by dint of sheer fighting, and left his rear-guard to shift for itself; so that the march of Xenophon was, in his own words, all but a flight. At the council which followed, the latter chief, who well knew the greatest secret of mountain warfare, that there is no position which may not be turned somewhere—and whose constant motto, through this fearful time of trial, was, that the greatest object here is not to win with the greatest glory, but to come off with the least loss—insisted on this plan for the future campaign. Then he extorted from one of two captive guides, though not till the other was slain before his face, the admission that he knew a higher defile, as is ever the case in hill-fighting, by the occupation of which the position of the defenders would be rendered at once untenable, and the passage of the army easy.

Volunteers were detached that very night to occupy the topmost hill of all, taking with them the guide in chains, with orders to blow their trumpets at dawn, should they succeed in their mission; while Xenophon, to distract the attention of the enemy, advanced as if to enter the usual passes, but they were impregnable, the enemy rolling down rocks upon them as large in diameter as wagon wheels; and when it became quite dark he drew off the rear guard to supper, for they had tasted no food that day. But in the mean time the volunteers, favored by the darkness and a timely fog, carried the height unseen, owing to the night, and at daybreak sounding their trumpets, charged and cleared the way. Then Cheirisophos with the main-guard forced the regular passes without difficulty, and Xenophon with the rear, followed the new path, domineered by the hill which the volunteers had taken. He soon, however, reached another peak, which he was compelled to storm in deep narrow fronted columns, sometimes, I believe, in Indian file; having carried this, and seeing another yet in front, he left a guard on it, lest it should be retaken, carried the second, and discovered yet beyond, a third peak, loftier than that forced by the volunteers, occupied by the enemy, who fled, however, on the instant, leaving it to be taken by Xenophon in person, with a few of the younger men only. For he had ordered the rest to halt, until the rear should rejoin them, and then proceeding down the slope, to pile arms in the plain at the bottom. Before this could be done, however, the savages had overpowered the post left on the first hill, so that but few escaped leaping headlong down the rocks, and then encouraged by this success, followed up so closely, that, as the rest descended the last hillock into the level land, they rolled down rocks upon them, and did some damage. In the plain, at the foot, they found villages with comfortable dwellings, and good provision, and much wine; but in order to recover their dead, which was a point of the most awful religion with the Greeks, they were compelled to treat with the Barbarians and to release their guide. The next day they marched again, with no one to direct them, but by adopting Xenophon's plan, they gained more ground and with less loss either of time or life. For when the way of Cheirisophos with the van was obstructed in any defile, Xenophon turned it by the mountains, and so cleared the route; and when Xenophon's men thus converted into the van, were brought to a stand, Cheirisophos in the like manner manœuvred by the upper ground to open the road in his turn. Still there was hard-fighting, for the same terrible archers met them, who drew their bowstrings not to their breasts as the Greeks, but bearing their weight on the left foot pulled the cords downward to the left ear, exactly as the English archery, so formidable in the middle ages, and like them pierced the strongest shields and breastplates out of ordinary bow-shot. The whole of this great passage was conducted on true military principles, every successive post of the enemy being carried by the main body without loss, after being turned on the right, where the ground was higher, by the rear guard. Whether the whole movement might have been performed more easily and with less loss, by a constant advance with the right wing thrust very far ahead, so as to turn all the positions in succession, is doubtful; but probably, considering the very limited range of ancient missiles, and the corresponding diminution in value of dominant heights, which could command only within the range of arrow-shot, and taking into account the nature of the enemy who, turned or not, would have fought till the missiles fell among them, Xenophon's passage of the mountains of Kurdistan, could be little improved upon, even at the present day; and, as in the late desperate battles in Affghanistan, not very far removed from the same scene of action, every defile must have been forced, or turned in succession.

At length they descended into the open plains on the bank of the Kentrites, now the Khabour, which was at that time the boundary between Armenia, the king's province, and the independent tribes of Kardouchia. It would appear that the point at which they left the Tigris and entered the hill country could not have been far from the modern city of Mosul; as ruins, supposed to be those of Mespila, described in the Anabasis,* exist there still; that they passed near the site of the present Amadieh, and came down on the upper waters of the Khabour, to the eastward of the site of Tigranocerta, now Sered, at about fifty miles distance west of the southern end of lake Van; for it is quite clear that they were never in sight of that great sheet of water which Xenophon, so singularly exact and minute in his details, could not have failed to mention, had he seen or even heard of it; while it is even more certain that they could not have gone east of it, since in that case they would have crossed neither the Kentrites, nor the Tigris, if they did cross the latter at all, which I hold doubtful. The never mentioning of this Palus Arsissa, or

* Anab. iii. iv. 9.

Lake Van, is in fact one of the most remarkable things connected with the expedition, as it is probably the largest lake he or any other Greek had ever seen, being about sixty miles in length by half the breadth, and as their route must have lain for several days across a level country, within a few miles of its southern and western shores. Here, once more, they beheld their old enemy in the shape of the showy and well-accoutred cavalry of the Persians; being Armenian, Chaldaian, and Mardonian mercenaries, with the Satraps, Orontes and Artouchos, arrayed in all the pomp and pride of oriental war, and ready to prevent their passage of the river; while in their rear, covering the slopes and sides of the craggy hills they had passed so laboriously, swarmed the fierce hordes of the Kardouchian archers. Never were the Greeks in a worse predicament, as it appeared, than now; for the only ford they had discovered was more than breast high, and the stream ran like a torrent over large slippery stones, utterly impassable to men carrying arms, especially when opposed to an active enemy. A second ford was, however, accidentally discovered above, and by some very skilful manœuvering, Xenophon kept the Persians on the farther shore, in doubt as to which ford they intended to use, until Cheirisophos was well over it; and then, distracting them by a feint of crossing below and surrounding them, put them to flight without striking a blow. Then rapidly moving up to the practicable ford, he formed front to the Kardouchians, who had come down into the plain, and covered the passage of the baggage and camp followers, until these were well over also. That accomplished by a feigned charge with pœans and clash of spear and shield, he drove the Barbarians back to their hills, and wheeling at a preconcerted signal of trumpets, which lent wings to the terror of the savages, carried all his rear guard safely over without the loss of a man, a few only who had pursued too hastily coming in wounded.

There is no finer record of a river passed by a *coup de main*—

and all through excellent manœuvering, with a superior force of cavalry in front defending the fords, and an inveterate pursuer, imminent, and intent on destroying the rear—than this of the Kentrites; and it is clear that, from the discovery of the ford by his foragers, to his own passage, almost the last man, the merit is all Xenophon's own. To increase their pleasure Lykios, with his handful of cavalry, had overtaken the Persian baggage-guard, and gained rich booty of garments and gold and silver plate. Thence they marched twenty miles over a fair and level plain—for there were no hamlets nearer the river through dread of the Kardouchians—and passed the night at their ease, billeted in convenient dwellings, at a large village near the Satrap's palace, where they had all necessaries in abundance. Some sixty miles thence they thought they crossed the sources of the Tigris, but the true sources lie considerably to the west of their route, although two or three considerable tributaries of that river do in fact arise in the plains to the west of Lake Van, which the Greeks were probably led to believe the true head-waters of that river. This was in the district of western Armenia,* and in the Satrapy of Tiribazos—now the southern verge of the Pachalic of Erzeroum—who now approached them with a splendid array of horse, and sent interpreters, offering them a safe passage, and liberty to forage, so they would abstain from plundering. And the generals agreed, and a truce was concluded and ratified by libations. As seems to be the fate, however, of all such truces, this also was immediately broken by the Barbarians; for on the third or fourth night thereafter, during a fearful snow storm which drove the men to cover in some hamlets near their bivouac, an alarm arose that fires were seen burning on the hills as of a great army; so that the leaders withdrew the soldiers from their comfortable quarters into the open air again. The snow, however, fell to such a depth, and the cold became so

*Xen. Anab. IV. 4. 4.

terrible that they were forced to seek shelter a second time, when they sent out Democrates of Temenis, who had at various times before approved himself an active and trustworthy scout, with men under his orders, to examine the hills where the fires were reported to be seen; and, on his return, he stated that he found no fires; but he brought in a prisoner, armed with a Persian bow and arrows, and an Amazonian battle-axe, who admitted himself to be one of Tiribazos' army, which he said lay in the mountains, at the only defiles by which the Greeks could pass, and consisted of the Satrap's regular power, besides Chalybian and Taochian mercenaries, levied of very purpose to set on them in the gorges. As soon as it was light, therefore, the generals marched with their best troops, intending to anticipate the Persians, and occupy the pass, leaving Sophainetos the Stymphalian in command at the camp, and taking their prisoner with them as a guide. Then, when the targeteers had crossed the mountains, they perceived the barbarian camp below them on the other side, and without awaiting the arrival of the hoplitai charged down at once with their battle-cry, the enemy flying on all sides without a blow, though some of their men were slain, and twenty horses taken in the pursuit. The camp afforded rich booty, and Tiribazos' own tent was captured, with his silver footed couches and golden goblets, and his cup bearers and carvers, proving the truth of their captive's narrative. Notwithstanding this brilliant success, however, they tarried not to enjoy their spoils, but marched back that same day, to their own people, determined to break up at once, and pass the defiles without giving the enemy time to collect his forces. And on the next day they did so with success, halted for the night in the deserted camp of Tiribazos, and after marching three days' journey over a desert country, forded the Euphrates, waist-deep, its sources being reported to them as not far distant.. The mountains here spoken of are evidently those running due west from the north-western extremity of Lake Van, which divide the head waters of the Tigris from those of the Euphrates; the former rising in their own western slope, the latter from the southern spurs of Mount Ararat, two hundred miles to the north-eastward. The river, which the Greeks here forded, as the Euphrates, is the Arsanias, now called the Morad, its greatest southern branch, and as I should judge the true river, though the sources of that noble stream are usually ascribed to the northern branch rising near Arze, the modern Erzeroum in the Pachalic of that name. It is remarkable that both of this and its sister river the Tigris, Xenophon names the south-eastern branches as the true streams; and, to judge from the comparative size on the maps, his nomenclature, at least in the former case, appears to be more correct.

Up to this moment, the general direction of the retreat is as true as if it had been made by compass for Trebizonde, then Trapezos, a Greek colony on the Black Sea; and had that direction been produced it would have passed through Arze, even then a considerable town, on the true Tigris, and would have struck the Euxine within a few miles of their mark. From this point, however, for some reason which we cannot decide, they bore away to the north-eastward, and—having suffered dreadful extremities from cold, losing more men in those vast marshy plains, now covered five feet deep with snow, than in all their previous skirmishes and marches, and being saved from total destruction only by the energy of Xenophon, who stayed by the sufferers, protected them, and brought them safely in, when Cheirisophos, with the van, had hurried forward recklessly, leaving the men to fall asleep and die where they fell, as in the disastrous retreat of Moscow—at length struck a stream, which Xenophon calls the Phasis, as he does the tribes dwelling on it, the Phasians; but which is in fact the ancient Araxes, or modern Aras, a principal tributary of the great river Kur, which falls into the Caspian Sea, south of the Volga. It would be agreeable here to pause and consider the details of their long and hospitable entertainment by the Armenians, who, alone of the nations and tribes, through whom they marched, entreated them with kindness; but neither these nor any of the truly interesting accounts of the countries through which the ten thousand passed, their natural products, curiosities or inhabitants, will the design or limits of this little work admit; and for all such I must refer my reader to the admirable work of Xenophon, a work abounding with all the interest of the wildest romance, the fascination of the most graphic travels, and the truth of the gravest contemporary history, the whole clothed in a style never surpassed for ease, elegance, simplicity or grace.

Soon after crossing the Aras, on coming to the ascent of the mountains from the plain—here they must have discovered the error of their course in having too much northing, and turned short westward, for no where else do the hills approach so nearly to the course of the Araxes—they found the slopes occupied by a hostile array of Chalybes, Taochoi, and Phasianoi, who offered a desperate resistance. Here again the passage was forced by the same manœuvre as before, turning the enemy's position by night, and gaining the upper ground; and by the same captains Aristonymos of Methydra and Agasias the Stymphalian; but in this case, there was some hard fighting on the upper hill, and it was necessary for the Targeteers to charge, supported by the heavy foot, before they could clear their way. Soon afterward they fell short of food, for the Taochoi retreated with their wives and children and all their supplies, to inaccessible hill fastnesses, a few of which were carried rather by desperate personal valor and emulation among the captains of Lochi, especially those named above, than by much skill or science. Still it appears that Xenophon again suggested the movement by which the most difficult was taken. The desperate character of

* Anab. IV. v 24–36.

these people was evinced by their casting down their wives and children, and leaping themselves headlong from the rocks when they saw their hill forts carried—as did the Chimariots when Suli was stormed by Ali Pacha—rather than submit to enemies, who, to their eternal honor be it spoken, never had recourse to a single act of cruelty or wanton devastation during this long and desperate retreat, when provoked to the utmost by the treachery of the unrelenting foe, who appeared set on hunting them to destruction. Thence, they entered the Chalybian country, the men being very bold and hardy, fighting with the Greeks hand to hand, armed with pikes twenty feet in length, and cutlasses like the Lakonian swords, and wearing linen corslets, with head pieces and greaves. From these people they could win no food or forage, but were supported by what they had taken from the Taochoi, until, reaching the Skythinian district, they halted for three days and foraged unmolested. The next tribe, occupying a large, populous and wealthy city, sent a guide who promised to bring them within five days, through an enemy's country which he begged them to burn and devastate, to a mountain from which they should perceive the sea, and that he was willing to die in case of failure. And on the fifth day, he brought them to the hill, which is called Theke,* according to Xenophon, while Diodorus makes it Chenion.†

I am not aware that this hill has ever been identified by personal observation, but it is clearly one of the northern spurs of the ridge of mountains in which the Euphrates rises, and which Strabo‡ designates as the northern branch of the Taurus; and it is not a little remarkable that at the foot of such a spur, immediately above Trebizonde, and on the stream which forms the harbor of that once famous city, there is to this day a village of

* Anab. IV. vii 21. † Diod. Sic. XIV. 29.

‡ Anthon's Class Dict. Art. Euphrates.

Tekeh which may well retain a vestige of Xenophon's appellation Theke.

On reaching this point, the rapture of these men, home-sick, travel-worn, and heart-weary, can be imagined better than described, but of all descriptions, his must needs be the best, who saw the welcome sight, and shared the rapture which he witnessed. "When the first men," he says, "reached the summit and beheld the sea, a great shout arose; and when Xenophon and the rear-guard heard it, they supposed that a fresh enemy had attacked the head of the column; for at this time they were pursued hotly by men from the country they had wasted; and the rear-guard had killed some and taken others alive, of the enemy, in an ambush, besides capturing about twenty shaggy bucklers of raw bull-hide. But when the clamor constantly increased and became nigher, and when all who approached rushed up the hill at full speed, and joined those who were still shouting, and swelled the shout themselves, till it waxed very mighty, Xenophon conceived that it was something of greater import; and mounting his charger he galloped up, leading Lykios and the cavalry, as if to the rescue; and soon they heard the soldiers shouting "The sea! The sea!" and plighting their vows to heaven. Then all the rear-guard rushed up the hill, and the cavalry in full career, and even the beasts of burthen. And when all were at the summit, they embraced one another, and their generals, and the captains of their bands, weeping and speechless; and suddenly, as if to perform the vow of some one, the soldiers brought together stones and built a vast column, and hung upon it bull-hides, and their staves, and the shields of the enemy, which they had taken."*

How could any scene have been more striking or at the same time more affecting; indeed, so enthusiastic and contagious were their transports, that the barbarian guide, whom they afterward

* Anab. IV. vii. 21. and 26.

dismissed splendidly rewarded, partook their joy, and himself helped to erect the trophy, and cut the shields, and called upon the others to do likewise.

Never, I think, to borrow the noble words of Aiskylos,* was—

> "The land seen of men
> Shipwrecked and hopeless on the deep, the morn
> Breaking resplendent from a night of storms,
> The crystal fountain in a burning waste
> To the lone wayfarer,"

a spectacle so blessed and joyous as that far glimpse of those wild and inhospitable waters, heaving to the blasts of the fierce north wind which had dealt with them heretofore so roughly, but which they were now ready to adore, since every sweeping gust should bear them back to happiness, to home, to Hellas.

To me that simple and brief narrative of Xenophon, with that electric and electrifying shout "the sea! the sea!" has been, as Chevy Chase was to Sir Philip Sydney, such, that I might say with him, "I never heard it, that I found not my heart moved more than with a trumpet;" and at this day a picture of the scene, which I saw years ago, when I was a mere boy—I think, by Etty—is distinct before my eyes, with every detail, as when I saw it. The artist had chosen the moment when Xenophon reaches the summit, on his panting horse, and the whole scene is before him, the whole tale told at a glance. Some shouting, weeping, clasping hands, embracing, vowing—but all straining their eyes, all pointing their arms to that far blue misty line, which instinct rather than eyesight told them was the sea! The painter, too, had caught one incident, which the great penman has forgotten to insert—for it must have happened, since there were many hetairai in camp; some who had followed, doubtless, from unforgotten Greece; some captives only, but all now loved by

* Agamemnon, 983; Herbert's Translation.

their lords, if only from community of hopes and fears, and pains and perils—a soldier, the most prominent figure in the piece, lifting his mistress high in the air, that she too might behold the Sea! the Sea! and catch from it one inspiration from loved and lovely Hellas. To each one of them all, that sea was*

> "As a friendly hand
> Stretched out from his native land,
> Filling his heart with memories sweet and endless."

To each one of them all it seemed, doubtless, that all his toils were ended, all his perils over, the port already gained, the home of his youth before him—for Xenophon tells us elsewhere that these men were not mere hireling soldiers, but men of character, with property, homes, children, parents, wives; men who had followed Kyros partly from admiration of his great renown, partly from love of glory, partly from love of adventure, least of all from love of lucre; and the truth of what he tells is evident by the fury with which they turned on their leaders, whenever they suspected them of an intent to detain them in Asia—and yet how few of them ever saw home or country—how few ever filled a Grecian grave, which perhaps above all things all desired.

But not to anticipate—although their way was now not long to Trapezos, there were still difficulties to be surmounted; for after the Makrones had given them a free passage—owing to the curious fact that one of Xenophon's targeteers, who had been a slave at Athens, was originally a captive from that tribe, and still spoke their language—the Kolchians defended their hills with desperation, and were only conquered, after some sharp fighting, by Xenophon's favorite movement, of dividing the phalanx into columns of the several lochi, each a hundred strong,

* Longfellow—Building of the Ship.

with a front probably of four shields, and a depth of twenty-four, as more flexible and less liable to be broken and clubbed by difficulties of broken ground. In eight days they reached the sea near Trapezos, now Trebizonde, a Greek city, the easternmost on the Black Sea, and a colony of Sinope, the most powerful place and indeed the metropolis of all the Hellenic colonies on the Euxine. Here they were hospitably received, and rested awhile from their toils, and celebrated their return in safety, to what doubtless appeared to them Greece, by sacred games and festivals.

Thence Cheirisophos took ship for Herakleia, where he hoped to find vessels whereby to transport all the men home together; and the rest, meanwhile, were compelled by necessity to sell their swords to the colonists against their barbarous enemies, on whom they foraged, having neither markets sufficient to supply food for so many, nor means to purchase, had there been markets. And here they had some desperate fighting with the Kolchian enemies of the Trapezuntians, and lost many good men, but won much booty, which they sold to their entertainers, and from the profits furnished themselves with supplies, and with shipping for the sick and the soldiers, above forty years, the women, the children, and the baggage, whom they sent by sea, under the command of Sophainetos and Philesios, the oldest of the generals, to Kerasous, now Kerezoun, a sister colony from Sinope—whither the remainder of the army marched by land. Here they halted three days, and numbered the troops at a review under arms, when they were found to be eight thousand six hundred men—survivors, as Xenophon states, from about ten thousand—the rest having perished by the hands of the enemy, and in the snow, and some few by disease. In this enumeration there is clearly some confusion, since at the midnight review before Kynaxa, in which battle only one man fell, the number of hoplitai alone amounted to ten thousand four hundred shields of heavy foot, and twenty-five hundred light troops in addition; and again, at a much later period of the retreat, after heavy fighting with the Mosynoikians, when the army broke into three divisions, it is stated to have consisted of eight thousand six hundred and forty men. It is possible that in this place hoplitai alone are intended; but I consider it more probable that Xenophon has anticipated, and stated here the full force which passed over the Bosphorus, all losses included. Another difficulty is in this, that on the heavy infantry—better defended and less exposed, in hill-fighting, than the targeteers—the heaviest actual loss fell; they having lost three thousand men, for fifteen hundred of the others; but this may probably be explained by their greater sufferings in the snow. These discrepancies cannot, however, be explained—many, perhaps, are owing to errors in transcription of the manuscripts; and in no point of these do more mistakes occur, even in this age of printing, than in the articles; nor in any other are authors, especially the ancients, more careless; sometimes stating round numbers generally, as if they were intended to be accurate, and again exact numbers so loosely that they are taken to mean round ones.

The whole distance of their march from Babylonia and the battle-ground to Kotyora, their next halting place after Kerasous, he states at one hundred and twenty-two posts, or days' march—six hundred and twenty parasangs—eighteen thousand six hundred stadia; these distances by various measures agreeing nearly enough to prove their correctness, since eight stadia are a little more than one mile English, and one parasang a little less than four. The time consumed was eight months.

And here practically, and in a military point of view, this grand retreat may be said to have terminated—and that in safety and success.

With the miserable dissensions which followed, the ambition and treachery of the leaders, the base tergiversation of the Lakedaimonian admiral, the jealousies of the Greek colonies of the Black Sea, Xenophon had nothing to do, save that he nearly fell a victim to them; nor do they properly belong to the history of the retreat, which was in truth ended, so soon as the ten thousand had fought their way through all their barbarous enemies, had reached their countrymen of the Greek colonies, and the sea by which they might have obtained transportation to their native shores.

Still it may be well to trace his connection with the ten thousand to its close, for we find him in many and strange vicissitudes, owing to that connection. We find him arraigned before his own soldiers and acquitted honorably and by acclamation; we find him implored to accept the sole command, and resolutely declining it; we find him deposed from the station he had held since the death of Proxenos; reduced to his own small separate command; rescuing the very men who had deposed him; raised to the sole command involuntarily; carrying the army over the Bosphoros in safety, quitting them when all seemed well with them, returning to them when in distress; at one time well nigh stoned to death, because he desired to found a colony at Kalpe in Bithynia; at another offered the supreme government of Byzantium and declining it; but always playing the part of a good soldier, a good general, a good man, and what is more an honest, religious, conscientious, and consistent man, if ever there lived one in ancient or modern history.

In the end, he delivered over his men to Thibron, the Spartan General in Asia Minor; and they were amalgamated with the Greek force fighting against Tissaphernes and Pharnabazos, under his orders, from which time forth they had no separate existence, as an army.

Xenophon himself returned in the following year to Asia with his friend Agesilaos, but of what he did or what station he held we know nothing. Subsequently he was engaged in Greece, under the same general, against the Boiotians at the battle of Coroneia ; and this so displeased his countrymen, the Athenians, that they banished him ; but to be banished was to any Athenian a matter of too common occurrence to be much dreaded or deplored ; and to one who had been so great a wanderer surely no extreme punishment. Still he appears ever to have felt kindly to to his country, and to have rejoiced and gloried in the name Athenian, though he was indebted to the Lakedaimonians for his beautiful home, and rich estates at Skilluns, in Elis, where he lived the remainder of his days, happy and peaceful, in the practice of philosophy and piety, in the possession of easy affluence and literary leisure, in the society of his sons and his wife Phitesia, up to the advanced age of ninety-three years ; when he died as calmly as though half his life had not been spent in the most tumultuous of tempests—that of human warfare. Were I asked to sum up his character in a few words, I should say that so far as we know or can learn of him, he lacked no quality which a soldier, general, or man should have, nor possessed any which they should not have. As a general I should rate him not lower than the third of all the old world ever saw ; Hannibal being first beyond compare, and perhaps Epaminondas second, though between Xenophon and him I doubt. If it be objected, that he did little by which to hold so high a place in arms, I would reply that there was much, if not all of strategy, in that little ; that it is qualities, not opportunities, which make the general ; and that, judging from all that he did, I can conceive nothing which he could not have done.

As a philosopher he is the only Greek, unless it be, perhaps, Plato, for whom I have any considerable degree of respect ; most of their private lives were filthy, infamous and odious ; most of their pretensions to philosophy were mere cant, mere dogmatism, and mere humbug—most of themselves—might I not say all ? so tainted, not excluding Socrates himself, with quackery, buffoonery, and charlatanry, that we scarce know whether to loathe them as Tartuffe, laugh at them as Grimaldi, or scorn them as any one of fifty humbugs of our own day.

In one word, and to conclude, I fear that as a man in moral duties, and—so far as light was vouchsafed to him—in pious faith and practice, also, many a professed Christian might look for an example in the heathen Xenophon.

VI.

EPAMINONDAS,

THE THEBAN.

HIS CAMPAIGNS, BATTLES OF LEUKTRA AND MANTINEIA, CHARACTER, AND CONDUCT.

WITH the life and career of no one man, in the ages of authentic history, were the prosperity and pre-eminence of his native city ever so exactly contemporary and co-existent, as those of Thebes with those of her best and greatest son, Epaminondas. For, previous to his coming upon the stage, and taking the lead in the administration of her affairs, she had never aspired to more than a secondary position among the independent states of Hellas, little indeed, if at all, superior to that of Korinth, Arkadia, and Argolis, nor dreamed of contesting the supremacy with Attika, or Lakedaimon. Yet, so soon as this great man rose to the head of her affairs, she sprang at once to the leading and mastery of the Greek states, which she wrested from the iron hands of Sparta, then at her loftiest pitch of power; and still maintained it, sometimes at the head of her allies, oftener single-handed, so long as his political wisdom and moderation ruled her councils; so long as his military science fought her battles.

In what year he was born does not appear distinctly, but we know that, with his friend and brother in arms, Pelopidas, he was of one among the noblest of the Boiotian families. It is to be regretted, that of this highly interesting period, and this its most interesting personage, we possess fewer and far less authentic documents than of the events and characters immediately preceding and succeeding it. Of Plutarch's lives, Epaminondas is one of the missing; and. as the biographer was a fellow countryman of the general, and himself by no means destitute of patriotic and party spirit, it is not to be doubted that he had laid himself out on the career and character of this, the greatest soldier and statesman of his nation. We may therefore esteem this a real loss; although, in general, Plutarch's lives are to be regarded rather as gossipping collections of stray anecdotes, and pleasant compilations, than as authentic histories. And it is to be regretted, the rather, because the magnificent and most veracious history of Thukydides closes before his career began, unless it was in the first fight at Mantineia that he drew his maiden sword; and because Xenophon, who continued that great work in his Hellenika, has, from partiality to his friend Agesilaos, described the campaigns and battles of his rival with a brevity and lack of appreciation so different from the minute and graphic details, the energy and life, which we meet in every page of the Anabasis, that we recognize neither the author, nor the glorious actor, whom he deals with, I regret to say, almost in a spirit of detraction.

It was in the second year of the ninetieth Olympiad, B. C. 419,* if we may believe Plutarch, that the Thebans, being then

* Plut. Pelopid. IV. Such is the narrative of Plutarch. I must, however, regard it as apocryphal; since this battle of Mantineia being fought B. C. 419, that of Leuctra in 371, and the second battle of Mantineia, when Epaminondas fell, in 363, allowing the friends to have been but fifteen, at this period, Epaminondas, at his death, must have been at least seventy-one years old; whereas there is no hint to be found in history that he was at all advanced in years; but, on the contrary, a general report, that he was young at Leuktra, and that he died, cut off in his mid career.

in close alliance with the Lakedaimonians, and sending an auxiliary force to serve with them, Epaminondas and Pelopidas fought side by side in that first fierce battle of Mantineia, in which Agesipolis defeated, with so terrible a slaughter, the combined forces of the Argives, Mantineians, Arkadians and Athenians. In the shock of that dreadful encounter, the chosen band of Argive youths a thousand strong, broke the left wing, in which the Thebans fought, and drove a large portion of it clear off the field; but the two friends, as he asserts, with some comrades, linking their shields, resisted desperately, when all around them were in full flight; and, when Pelopidas fell, with seven wounds all in front, Epaminondas stood over him, though he believed him to be dead, defending him and his armor, until he too had received a spear-thrust in the breast and a sword-cut in the arm, when they were rescued, timely, by the arrival of Agesipolis from the right, where he had carried all before him, who now came up, restored, and won the battle. From this time forth, we are told, the young men were inseparable friends; for they both recovered from their wounds, to do their country better service; although it was not until after the lapse of several years that we find them again acting together, as it were, with one hand and a single spirit.

This I have inserted as a pleasing story, illustrative both of the times and of the character of the men of whom it is narrated; as popular traditions, if they are apt to err, like this, in preserving exact synchronism, are wont to adhere very closely to the veri similitude of things and the individuality of characters; and this it is, which renders it at times difficult to discriminate between them and authentic history.

In the first year of the ninety-fourth Olympiad, B. C. 404, the Peloponnesian war, which for the space of twenty-seven years had raged incessant throughout Greece, was closed by the surrender of Athens at discretion, the demolition of her walls, and the subversion of her constitution by Lysander—thirty tyrants and an oligarchical form of government being imposed on her, in lieu of her fierce, untamed democracy. From that day her supremacy in politics was at an end—although she recovered her independence—and Sparta was, in her stead, the dominant power of Hellas.

From this time, for several years, the changes of polity and intermutations of alliances are intricate and incessant, so as almost to defy unravelling, among the Hellenic states; for, within a year or two, the Thebans assisted Thrasybulus and the Athenians in banishing the thirty, and re-establishing their ancient government; so that when the Boiotic war arose, between Thebes and Phokis—Sparta taking part with the former—Athens and the Argives espoused the cause of the Thebans, and the tide of war began again to turn; the walls of Athens having been rebuilt by Konon, then serving as Persian Admiral for Teribazos, with the aid of the Boiotians. Thus matters continued, with continuous versatility, continuous war and slaughter, for seven and twenty years, though with no decisive effect nor any unity of purpose, except on the part of Sparta; which persisted in winning her way steadfastly, and in spite of all opposition, to universal dominion—so far, at least, as Greece was concerned—the other states offering no concerted resistance to her ambitious plans, but fighting now for her, now against her, as the whim of the hour might dictate. But at the end of this period, in the third year of the ninety-eighth Olympiad, B. C. 386, Phoibidas the Lakedaimonian general, while marching through the Boiotian territory, then at peace with it, treacherously surprised the Kadmeia, or citadel of Thebes, which he occupied with an armed garrison, and banished about three hundred of the most eminent citizens of the democratic and patriotic party, who found hospitality and protection in Athens. So ill was this act of treacherous aggression taken by Greece at large, that Lakedaimon, not so completely absolute but that she had some fear of popular opinion, went through the farce of fining Phoibidas in a large sum of money, for his conduct; while they by no means forgot to retain the Kadmeia with a powerful Spartan detachment, and to enforce the edict of banishment against all the patriots.

Among these was Pelopidas, but Epaminondas was suffered to remain in the place—for in some sort they despised him, as a philosopher, and yet more, they regarded him as powerless, from his want of means. Plutarch records this capture of the Kadmeia, and banishment of Pelopidas, as immediately consecutive to the first battle of Mantineia; yet thirty-three years had intervened; so that had these men then distinguished themselves, as he relates, they must have now been between fifty and sixty years of age, when the whole context of the narrative points to them as young, active, and enthusiastic men; and when, to complete the absurdity, Plutarch names Epaminondas as among the youngest of the exiles. During this time, mindful of the countenance which the Boiotians had shown them during their own time of trouble with the thirty tyrants, Athens refused resolutely, in answer to all the expostulations of Sparta, either to expel or injure the exiles; and when, after awaiting their opportunity, they at length determined on striking a blow, they aided them with arms, and sent them forth with their good wishes, promising armed assistance, should their stratagem prove successful.

It was in the fourth year after the capture of the Kadmeia, that Pelopidas, with twelve confederates, entered the gates of Thebes by night with hounds, and hunting nets, and boar-spears; and, having contrived to remain in the city all the next day, undiscovered—partly by means of their disguises, and partly under favor of a wild gale and snow-storm—the next evening broke in upon the tyrants Archias, Leontidas, Hyphates, and Philippos, while they were feasting, with song and dance, clad in feminine attire, and slew them without mercy. As soon as the deed was done, Epaminondas and Gorgidas, who had been mustering the youth of Thebes, came to their support with a considerable power; and, as soon as the news of it could reach them, the main body of the confederates, who had awaited the result of the conspiracy in the Thriasian plain, on the confines of Attika and Boiotia, marched into the gates in full armor, and summoned the people to assemble, which they did, with shouts of joy and triumph; receiving the men as their benefactors and deliverers. Thereupon Pelopidas being elected one of the Boiotarchai,* with Mellon and Charon, proceeded at once to raise counterworks against the citadel, and to threaten it with assault; on seeing which the Lakedaimonian garrison, no less than fifteen hundred strong, surrendered, on condition of being allowed to march out with their arms and with military honors. This was a wise and well-judged act of moderation on the part of the confederates, on the principle of building a bridge of gold for a flying enemy; for, although they knew it not, there was already a great power afoot under the command of Kleombrotos, the Spartan king, marching upon Thebes, and so near as the frontiers of Attika and the Megaris. Had they refused terms to the garrison of the Kadmeia, it is probable, at least, that they would have stood a long siege, and supported themselves until the arrival of reinforcements; so at least argued the Lakedaimonians, for they put to death two out of the three harmostai, or colonial governors, who were in the citadel, Herippidas and Arkesos, and banished Lysanoridas, the third, from the Peloponnesus, after making him pay a heavy fine.

That was a bold and dashing exploit of Pelopidas and his friends; and, although it may be thought to verge too narrowly

* The military leaders of all the independent confederated states of Boiotia, one elected by each subordinate city, two or three by Thebes, were called *Boiotarchai*.

upon individual assassination, to meet the unqualified praise of this more enlightened age, yet the slaughter of the tyrants was so immediately connected with an armed military expedition, and that was again so enthusiastically hailed by a unanimous and universal popular rising against the foreign force which alone opposed it, that the irregularity of the proceedings may be overlooked in consideration of the obvious necessity of the case, and unequivocal absence of any private animosities against the persons sacrificed to the common weal. It is said, that Epaminondas, with a sense of delicacy and perception of true right and wrong almost too nice and too correct for that age, refused absolutely to be a participator in the bloodshedding of fellow citizens, however great their political error, however flagrant their criminality against the state; but that he willingly took up arms against the foreign oppressors, who held their power by no right, except that of might. But this I believe to be one of those rhetorical inventions with which such writers as Nepos and Plutarch abound, and to which less credit is due than even to those traditional anachronisms of which I have spoken above, since they, unlike the former, are inconsistent with the spirit of the times, and therefore, not with the veracity only, but with the verisimilitude of history. What is perfectly true, however, of this daring and successful enterprise, is the fact, that from that night forward Sparta began to decline; that the prestige of her moral superiority was counteracted; and that her ascendency was never again perfectly established as the ruler both by sea and land; but that she gradually sunk into a secondary state, while Thebes grew up in her stead to be the arbiter of Greece, until all the nations fell at once into the shadow of one vast and consolidated power, which could be resisted by no casual combination, but only by a unity of force equal to its own.

This truth was proved without delay, by the defection of many of the Spartan allies, as the Chians, Byzantines, and Rhodians, and their instituting a senate at Athens, to act in behalf of all the confederates;* nor was the matter allowed to rest long in words and councils only, for Sphodriades, the Spartan admiral, at the suggestion of Kleombrotos, making an attempt on the Peiraios, at the head of ten thousand men, which was repulsed, and being subsequently acquitted, the Athenians declared the truce with Sparta broken, and at once selected their three best men, Timotheos, Iphikrates, and Chabrias, generals, with a force of twenty thousand foot, five hundred horse and two hundred war-ships.

The Spartans, however, were determined not to yield without a blow, but sent Kleombrotos, with a considerable force, to support their interests in Boiotia, although it was in the depth of winter; intending to cross the ridge of Kithairon by the pass of Eleutherai, which was occupied strongly by Chabrias, with the Athenian targeteers. On perceiving this, Kleombrotos made his way by Aigosthena, between the sea and the western slope of Mount Elateia, across the river Oëroe, near Kreusis, and thence by Plataia to Thespiai, and thence to Kynoskephalai, where he encamped within a mile of Thebes, and remained there sixteen days, expecting, probably, that there would be some rising of the oligarchical party in Boiotia, of which he might take advantage. Nothing, however, of the kind occurring, he fell back again to Thespiai, where he left Sphodrias at the head of a third part of the allied forces—with instructions to raise mercenaries, and prosecute the war—and then retreated by the road he had come, by way of Kreusis and the western passes of the Kithairon, where he lost some of his men and many of his baggage-train, by a storm so terrible that it blew the shields† out of the soldiers' hands, and cast the loaded animals headlong from the precipices. But shortly afterward Agesilaos was sent from Sparta to replace Kleombrotos; and, entering by the same pass of Kithairon as his

* Diod. Sic. XV. 28. † Xenophon, Hellenika, V. iv. 18.

11

predecessor, advanced to Thespiai, where he found all the plain fortified with field works, mounds, palisades, and trenches, with narrow openings, from which the Theban light troops and cavalry sallied out and galled him not a little; on his attempting to bring on a general action, Chabrias thwarted him, it is said, by a new arrangement of his men, whom he caused to kneel with their shields grounded and pikes presented, much, it is to be presumed, as modern infantry receive cavalry in square; but, in spite of all this, Agesilaos forced them in the end to evacuate their positions and devastated the country up to the very walls of Thebes. Notwithstanding this success, however, the royal leader was able to produce no great or permanent result, but retired, loaded with booty, into the Megaris; where he dismissed his army to its respective countries.

The details of a warfare so petty and unprofitable as this are tedious and uninteresting alike to the writer and the reader; yet it is in such small fields that the first exercise is often passed, and the first experience gained, by which are made great generals. Such is not often the case in modern times, or as relates to modern armies; for at the present day the art of war is too perfectly and purely a science, that any man without patient study and stern discipline can become a great strategist—once a partizan always a partizan, would seem to be an inevitable law now-a-days, yet such was far from being the case in the times of which I write, and there is the strongest reason to believe that it was in this paltry skirmishing that the first ideas of generalship, the first rudiments of military science dawned upon the youthful genius* of Epaminondas. No sooner had Agesilaos and his great army—the second great army which had invaded the Thebais in the course of a single year—retired ineffectual, than the Theban leaders, choosing their time, fell upon Phoibidas' out-posts, and cut off two hundred of them, when that chief,

* Plut. Vit. Pelop.

rushing out of Thespiai, where he had a good garrison, attacked the enemy on his return, who, turning on him suddenly, destroyed no less than five hundred of his men, himself falling* gallantly as he fought hand to hand with the foe, perhaps unwilling to survive the defeat he had undergone; the rather that he had experienced already the justice of the Lakedaimonians, being condemned to pay a fine as the reward of his success in capturing the Kadmea. On the news of this disaster reaching Lakedaimon, Agesilaos was again put at the head of a sufficient force, and for the third time in that one year the Spartans invaded Boiotia, for though it was early in the following spring, twelve months had not fully elapsed since the first irruption of Kleombrotos. At first the Spartan king manœuvred as if he would have entered the Thebais from the Plataiis by way of Thespiai, as before, but so soon as he perceived that the enemy were concentrating their forces on the Southern passes of Kithairon, he countermarched suddenly in the opposite direction, by Erythrai, making two days' marches in one, passed the entrenchment which had been thrown up before Skolos, without giving the enemy time to occupy it, and devastated all the eastern part of the Thebais, so far as to the frontiers of Tanagra, which was at this time occupied by his friends. Thence he marched upon Thebes, which, however, he did not attempt, but passed it to the northward, having the walls on his left hand, and thence proceeded up the valley of the Schoinos, now the Kanavari, to a difficult position called the Graias-stethos, or the old woman's breast, which the Thebans had fortified with a trench and palisade as if against an enemy descending the same valley from Thespiai. In front of this position they were now so strongly posted that Agesilaos did not judge it wise to assail them, but alarmed them by a clever movement by his left flank towards the city, which, it seems, had been left defenceless, so

* Diod. Sic. xv. 34.

that they quitted their position, and hurried at their utmost speed along the road through Potniai to Thebes, closely pressed in the rear by the cavalry, and Skiritai, or royal body guard of the Spartans. There was some sharp but indecisive skirmishing along this line, in the course of which one of the Spartan Polemarchs was slain by the Theban javelineers, and afterward some few of the Theban rear were cut up by the enemy's horse. As the former, however, faced about and offered battle under their walls, while the Skiritai retreated at double-quick time, they claimed the victory and erected a trophy, though it should seem with but little reason; since, in fact, Agesilaos had succeeded in his object, having dislodged the enemy's force, in the presence of which he did not dare to scatter his troops on their work of devastation, and shut it up in the city. On the following night he occupied the camp at Graias-stethos, which they had evacuated, and thence retreating at his leisure, laying waste the country as he went, upon Thespiai, he returned through the passes of the Kithairon upon Megara, where he dismissed the allies, leading the native force back to Sparta. These three consecutive expeditions appear to have been singularly ineffective and unworthy of the reputation of Agesilaos as a great warrior; for it would certainly appear from the context that he had a fair opportunity of carrying Thebes itself by a *coup de main* in the absence of its defenders, and thus terminating the war at a blow. But it must be remembered that the Lakedaimonians were never either very skilful or very successful in the attack of walled places; and this is probably the true cause of their not attacking a town when unprovided with defenders and unprepared for defence, which had so little real strength of fortifications which to defend, that Alexander, a few years later, carried the walls by assault, and then stormed the citadel, within the space of a few hours only, although he was met by a stern and vigorous resistance. Agesilaos, however, though rash to a fault in the councils which preceded and often induced the hazards of a dangerous and destructive war, appears to me, on a careful review of his principal campaigns, to have been a cautious, wary, and perhaps slow general in the field, preferring long and certain operations with distant results, and a cold and dilatory policy, to sudden and decisive blows. Such was the whole line of his clever and successful campaigns in Asia, in the course of which, without delivering any general battle, or fighting any one remarkable action, he separated nearly the whole of Asia Minor from the Archipelago up to the Kilikian Gates from the empire of the king, and reduced it to the condition of a Hellenik province. In the present instance, though he missed the opportunity of planting a fatal and decisive blow, he reduced the Thebans to very serious straits from the scarcity of grain and provision, their whole district having been twice ravaged with fire and steel in the course of a single twelvemonth, and two seed-times and harvests thus rendered absolutely fruitless. This last time, indeed, the work of havoc had been most systematically and thoroughly performed throughout all her confines, from the borders of the Tanagrice on the north and east, to that of the Plataiis and Megaris to the westward and southward; so that, had the Spartans tarried in the Thebais, it appears to me that the Thebans must have come out and delivered battle in the open plain, which the Spartans at this time, confident in their as yet unconquered infantry, most desired.

So far as these campaigns are concerned, it is clear that the generalship of the Theban leaders was on the whole superior to that of the Spartan king, since by gaining time they were exercising and disciplining their raw levies into soldiers, and were preparing their state for the glorious career of victories which it was shortly destined to enter upon; while he by neglecting to strike when he might have crushed—as I hold it certain that he might—gave them the opportunity to prolong the war and retrieve its fortunes, as they did disastrously for Lakedaimon on the terrible fields of Leuktra and Mantinnia.

In the following spring a Peloponnesian army marched as before; but Agesilaos, who was lame of one leg from his birth, was suddenly afflicted with a severe aneurism in the other, while ascending from the temple of Aphrodite to the council chamber in Megara, whither he had advanced with the power under his command. The swelling became inordinately great, and the pain intolerable, whereupon a Syrakusan surgeon opened the artery near the ancle and he all but bled to death, after which he continued ill during all the summer, and far into the winter. In his lieu, therefore, Kleombrotos was again sent out, and attempting, as before, to cross the Kithairon, with his targeteers in the van, was repulsed, with the loss of about forty men, by the Thebans and Athenians, who had anticipated them, and occupied the summits in advance. Upon this he gave up the attempt in despair, and dismissed the allied contingents, retreating homeward, as if the passage of the Kithairon was impracticable against defenders. These clumsy and insufficient proceedings created considerable indignation among the allies, when it was determined to blockade the port of Athens, and having compelled her by famine to surrender, to transport their forces into the Thebais either through the Phokian country or by way of Kreusis, the harbor of Thespiai. This plan, however, though it was tried, proved abortive, since the Athenians under Chabrias defeated Pollis the Lakedaimonian, with his sixty blockading galleys, opened the port, and brought in their corn-ships safely; after which, when the enemy would have attempted the Theban coast, they sent so powerful a squadron around the coasts of the Peloponnesos, as succeeded in capturing the large island of Kerkyra, now Corfu, and effectually prevented the Spartans from attempting anything beyond the isthmus.

In the autumn of that year, which was the second after the

accident of Agesilaos, Timotheos again beat the Lakedaimonian fleet under Nikolochos, and set up a trophy for the victory; and in the meantime the Thebans,* having been free from internal troubles, had conquered and reduced all the neighboring cities of Boiotia, which had been held by Spartan garrisons, as Thespiai, Plataia, and the wealthy city of Orchomenos, and were now as strong in territorial power, and stronger in moral and physical military strength than at any previous period of the war. During this time, several efforts had been made by Artoxerxes, king of Persia, to bring about a reconciliation and general peace among the Greek states; for he was now busily occupied in making war on Egypt, which had revolted from his authority, and thought to prosecute it with greater effect, by employing Greek mercenaries, whom he hoped to attract to his standards in great force, should universal peace be proclaimed throughout Greece.

Many of the states were well enough disposed to this end, for, of the leading powers, Sparta was disgusted by her continued want of success, and her really serious losses; and Athens was discontented with the conduct of her Theban allies, between whom and herself no true cordiality ever existed, and who were now elated by their unwonted victories over the armies of Lakedaimon, hitherto deemed invincible. But for a time circumstances rendered such a reconciliation impossible; for in the first place the pride of Agesilaos and the Spartans induced them to insist on the restoration of independence to all the Boiotian cities by Thebes, as a condition of peace, while naturally the Thebans felt that being victorious it was for them to dictate conditions rather than submit to them; and in the second an accidental collision between the fleets caused the Spartans to suspect Athens of foul play, and in consequence, the war was further protracted.

Two years more of disasters and naval defeats on the part of

* Xen. Hellenika, V. 4. 66.

Lakedaimon, and of increasing disgusts on that of Athens, to whom her old and steady allies of Thespiai and Plataia had appealed for aid against the vengeance of Thebes, put an end to such difficulties, and peace was concluded, ambassadors from all the states being assembled at Sparta. Here, Epaminondas appeared on the behalf of Thebes—a man, says Plutarch,* of great philosophy and learning, but one who had as yet displayed no *military genius*—*for it appears that* hitherto the confederated forces had been commanded in chief by an Athenian, either Iphikrates or Chabrias, the Boiotian leaders holding subordinate rank only. Of him Agesilaos, it seems, inquired whether he esteemed it right and just that the cities of Boiotia should be free and independent—in reply to which he asked quickly and boldly, while all the other ambassadors cowed before the haughty Spartan, whether he esteemed it right that the Lakonian cities should be free and independent. Hereupon Agesilaos leaped up in a rage and demanded a categorical answer, would he declare Boiotia independent? and Epaminondas replied as curtly and as haughtily, "If you will declare Lakonia independent, aye!" This terminated the conferences, for a general peace was at once ratified, Thebes alone being excluded from its operation, and all her allies at once deserting her, either to join in open hostilities against her, or at best to maintain a doubtful and suspicious neutrality.

At this period there was a Peloponnesian army in Phokis on the borders of Boiotia under †Kleombrotos which had been sent thither, the preceding year, to check the invasion of that country by the Thebans, who had fallen back before it and contented themselves with guarding the avenues to their own country. To this army orders were now sent to invade Boiotia at once, and compel the Thebans to declare all the Boiotian cities independent and restore Thespiai and Plataia, which they had

* Plut. Vita Agesilai, xxvii. † Xen. Hellen. VI. iv. 2.

destroyed; and when the Thebans positively refused to listen to any such terms, it marched with ten* thousand shields of heavy infantry and a thousand horse† to Koroneia, a town of Boiotia situated between the streams of Phalaros and Kyralios to the southward of the lake Kephissis, just where the northernmost spurs of Mt. Helikon subside into the plain. Two gorges‡ open from the hills below the city sending down each a torrent to unite and form the the Kyralios, the one running southeasterly, and giving direct access to the plain of Thebes through Zagara, Askra, and Thespiai; the other trending due south, through the heart of the Helikonian ridge, to Thisbe, and thence to Kreusis the port of Thespiai on the Oëroe, from which there was a direct road by Plataia into the Thebais. This city was already famous to the Lakedaimonians and consequently infamous to the Boiotians, for the single victory which Agesilaos had there gained over the confederates, by which indeed the pride of Thebes had been for many years humbled and her power broken.

This fact, perhaps, tended to increase the dismay which seems at this time to have prevailed in that city, which was now entirely deserted by her allies, and pitted single-handed against the most puissant of all the Hellenik states. They did not quail, however, in the emergency, but electing Epaminondas as their Boiotarches, and giving him five others as councillors and subordinates, besides Pelopidas, the captain of the sacred band, sent him out with about six thousand heavy infantry, and a cavalry greatly superior in quality and composition, if not in numbers, to that of§ the allies. As they passed the gates of Thebes, the army encountered a herald bringing in a blind man, a ‖fugitive either from servitude or from justice, which for some reason or other

* Plut. Vit. Pelopid. xx. † Diod. Sic. xv. 52.
‡ Leake's Northern Greece, Maps, vol. I. & II.
§ Xen. Hellen. VI. vi. 10. ‖ Diod. Sic. XV. 53.

was esteemed as an omen of most evil import; so that the veterans all cried out that it portended ill to the expedition, while the younger men fearing that such words on their part would be construed into signs of cowardice, held their peace; and then it was that Epaminondas shewed himself nobly superior to the superstitions and prejudices of his day, for he cried out in a loud voice, borrowing the noble sentiment ascribed by Homer to the patriotic Hector—Εἶς οἰωνὸς ἄριστος ἀμύνεσθαι περὶ πάτρης—

The fairest omen is your country to defend.

He led on, undeterred by that, or the more calamitous auguries which succeeded to it, and took post in an exceeding strong position within the mouth of the gorge leading from Koroneia by way of Askra to the city, through which it was expected that Kleombrotos would advance into the Thebais.

Kleombrotos, it would seem, was at this juncture almost compelled to give battle, for he had been suspected—not of what might have been fitly laid to his charge, want of moral courage, energy, and that decision which strengthens men to meet the risk of responsibility—but of a treasonable inclination to favor the Boiotians,* because in the year of his first invasion he had not devastated the Thebais, when encamped at Kynoskephalai, and because subsequently he had retreated from the passes of the Kithairon after a very slight check of his vanguard by the targeteers of Chabrias.

On this account he felt, probably, that not to fight at all, and to fail in fighting, would be to him nearly equal—the preference, if any, pointing to the latter alternative. This consideration it must have been which caused him to hurry his movements, and to deliver battle, without awaiting the arrival of Archidamos, the son of Agesilaos, who was already on his way to join him.

* Xen. Hellen. VI. iv. 5.

with reinforcements so powerful as to have rendered victory almost certain.* It was necessarily the object of the Thebans to anticipate the coming of these succors, and as they had no allies whom to expect, a victory only could prevent an armed coalition against them. Both armies, therefore, desired battle, and yet, owing to the great natural strength of the Theban position, which they did not choose, and that very wisely, to quit, in order to attack or offer battle in the plain, the engagement was yet farther deferred. For Kleombrotos, not daring to engage himself in the passes so formidably defended, broke up from his post at Koroneia, and making a series of forced countermarches through the gorges of Mount Helikon, upon Thisbe, surprised the harbor of Kreusis, now Livadhostro, near the mouth of the Oëroe, on the gulf of Korinth, and took twelve Theban triremes, with their crews. Thence, wheeling short to his own left, he ascended the course of the Olmeios, and entering the plain of Thebes above the head waters of the Asopos, now the Vurienda, found the Boiotian force, which had made a corresponding movement to frustrate his manœuvre, encamped on the heights of Leuktra, still between himself and the city, where there was a monument to the daughters of Skedasos, who were known throughout this region as the Leuktridai. These it is said were certain damsels of the country, to whom violence had been offered by Spartan envoys,† very long ago, probably in the heroic ages, who had refused to survive their dishonor, and on whose tomb, in this place, their father failing to obtain justice at Sparta, had slain himself, with awful imprecations on the country of the violators. From this cause

*Xen. Hellen. VI. iv. 26. Diodorus Siculus states—xv. 54—that Archidamos had come up with succors previously to the action, and that his arrival caused Kleombrotos to break a treaty, made with the Thebans, at the suggestion of Jason of Thessaly. Xenophon, however, was a cotemporary, and I prefer his account.

† Plut. Pelop. XX. Diod. Sic. XV., 54.

there had been given forth to the Spartans an oracle, awful from remote antiquity, that they should beware the divine wrath at Leuktra; but the meaning of this oracle had escaped the Lakedaimonians, since there were two other places of the same name, one a Lakonian fortress on the sea-shore, and the other in Arkadia, near Megalopolis; the Boiotians, however, had kept the religion of the spot, and now crowned the monument with wreaths. A further tale concerning this tomb is recited by Plutarch, to which I give place, as singularly characteristic of the times, and as showing the alacrity with which the leaders caught at anything that might avert the evil omens which had accompanied their march from the city, and the pains they took to cheer the spirits of their soldiers, shaken by such disastrous auspices.

Pelopidas, thus runs the story, while sleeping in his tent, with the enemy before him, dreamed that he saw the girls, weeping and uttering imprecations on the Spartans, and Skedasos commanding him to sacrifice a yellow-haired virgin, upon the tomb of the damsels, if they would conquer the Spartans. And concerning this dream a great strife arose; for although the custom of human sacrifices had in a great degree fallen into disuse, yet instances were not wanting of such horrors, even in recent time; and the ill-success of Agesilaos was attributed by many to his disobedience in not sacrificing his daughter, as Agamemnon had done in the heroic ages, to the goddess Artemis. The priests, therefore, were urgent that the dream should be followed to the letter; and the chiefs were discussing the question eagerly, and Pelopidas was greatly troubled, when suddenly a beautiful bay filly foal came careering up from a herd of horses in the vicinity, and gallopping through the lines, halted as if she had reached her goal; and all were struck by the peculiar and brilliant glitter of her glossy yellow coat, and the pride of all her motions, and the bold tones of her voice; and on seeing her, Theokritos the seer cried out to Pelopidas, "Fortunate man, your victim has arrived, wherefore let us await no other virgin, but thankfully receive the omen and the offering which the gods have given you." Then they crowned the filly with sacrificial wreaths, and leading her to the tomb of the virgins, slew her, with votive prayers, rejoicingly. And the news of Pelopidas, his vision, and his offering, went abroad through the army; and in the breasts of all the men was enkindled a confidence that they should gain that day a mighty victory, by the giving of the gods. And what such confidence avails an army on the day of battle, when it is not blindly shared by the generals, to the neglect of discipline or strategetics, every soldier knows. It was this confidence which rendered the followers of Mahomet invincible, while the creed was yet young, and the only choice vouchsafed to their enemies that between the Koran and the sword. It was this, more than their coats of plate, that rendered Cromwell's ironsides impregnable to the charge of the high-couraged cavaliers. It was this that carried the veterans of Napoleon unscathed over half the world, earnest believers in the doctrine of the soldier's star, "the sun of Austerlitz." And this confidence it was, in no small degree, which conduced to this great victory, one of the most fatal that ever was won from the Lakedaimonians—one of the most bloody ever gained by Hellenes from Hellenes, in all the history of Greece.

The field of Leuktra is well marked to the present day, "by a tumulus and some artificial ground on the summit of the ridge which borders the southern side of the valley of Thespiai; this position being exactly in the line between Thespiai and Plataia, as Strabo intimates Leuktra to have been."* This isolated ridge was, beyond doubt, the position of Kleombrotos, and the barrow or tumulus on its brow is the Polyandrion, or general sepulchre of the Lakedaimonians who fell in the action. The height, on

* Strabo, p. 414, quoted by Leake, Northern Greece, XIX.

which the Thebans were encamped, was evidently a spur of the ridge of hills forming the southern wall of the valley of the Schoinos, or Kanavari river, which it separates from the plain of Leuktra, on which the battle was fought, and containing, some four miles to the northward, between itself and the river, the strong position of Graias-stethos, already mentioned. On the southern declivity of this slope, and to the eastward, probably, of Kleombrotos' camp, as so interposing between him and Thebes, lay Epaminondas, awaiting eagerly an opportunity to deliver battle. The plain between these ridges does not exceed a mile in width from north to south, except at the eastern end, where there occurs a gap between the ridge of Leuktra and the foot of the downs, on the summit of which stands the city of Thebes, by which it extends southerly nearly thrice that distance, to the upper waters of the Asopos, or Vurienda ; and by these alone it is divided from the Plataiis—the scene of that other yet more memorable battle, of Plataia, whereby Pausanias decided, for the last time on the soil of Greece, the question of Hellenik or Persian superiority in arms—from east to west it runs nearly five miles, and is an admirably chosen spot for a pitched battle, since the face of the country is perfectly open, without rock, wood, or water, to impede the shock of combatants, and the hills are wide sheep-walks to the top, of no very great altitude—that of Leuktra more especially—and perfectly adapted to military movements, though perhaps scarcely accessible to charging cavalry.

So soon, therefore, as Epaminondas saw Kleombrotos preparing to descend into the plain, as if to offer battle, he advanced with alacrity, and met him half way, confident in the spirit of his men, and relying much on the undeniable superiority of his Theban and Thessalian horse.

Epaminondas, however, was not the man to rest content with such advantage, or to neglect any precaution which might ensure the victory against an enemy so formidable as a Lakedaimonian army, numbering in their ranks no less than seven hundred Spartans; he therefore devised a new and excellent scheme of tactics,* says Diodoros, and won through his own peculiar strategy that very famous battle. This scheme of tactics, which is no other than the celebrated oblique formation, of which, before this day, no trace is to be discovered in history, was unquestionably the invention of Epaminondas; that unrivalled Greek commander, whom Plutarch from some favoritism, the cause of which has escaped us, describes as second in military genius to Pelopidas, at best but a brilliant and daring subaltern, and whose splendid achievements Xenophon in his affection for Agesilaos, and his admiration of the Spartans, has related with such brevity and lack of detail, that in his conqueror of Leuktra and Mantineia, we recognise anything rather than the originator of a new military system, which has endured to this day still unaltered and unimproved, to which one of the greatest judges of the art of modern warfare, Frederick the Great of Prussia, was so much attached that he considered it irresistible, being wont to say, after his splendid victories, that he had only been fighting over again Epaminondas' battle of Leuktra; a system which, if adhered to by the Duke of Brunswick, as he at first intended, would almost certainly have converted the doubtful cannonade of Valmy into a French disaster; which, if adopted on the heights of Landgraefenberg, might have given a different result, despite the colossal genius and wonderful resources of Napoleon, to the dreadful field of Jena.

On the fifth day of the month Hecatomboion, in the second year of the one hundred and second Olympiad, corresponding nearly to the twentieth of July, B. C. 371, Kleombrotos descended into the plain with his cavalry in front of his hoplitai, who were drawn up in line, each enomoty having three shields

* Diod. Sic. xv. 55.

in rank and twelve in file, the king himself having command with the Spartans about his person, on the right wing.

Perceiving this disposition, and knowing, from the immovable valor and perduracy of a Lakedaimonian army, that a general attack along the front would only lead to a measuring of personal strength between the files opposed to each other, and would probably result in the defeat of his own men as numerically much the inferior body, Epaminondas formed his men on an entirely new principle. Selecting all his best warriors, and especially his best file-leaders, he drew them to the extreme left, where he arranged them—considerably in advance of the centre and right, which he purposely withdrew—under his own command, no less than fifty shields in depth, intending by this extraordinary weight of his column, to bear down and cut in two the Lakedaimonian right, and to crush at a blow the king himself and his hitherto unconquerable body-guard of Spartans. His own right and centre were drawn up in much shallower order, probably not exceeding the usual depth of eight shields, for it was his object, if possible, to induce the enemy to extend their own left unduly, and being actually inferior in numbers, while he had reduced his general strength yet farther by the extraordinary concentration of his masses on the left, he was obliged to make his right shallow, even to feebleness, in order to keep up the semblance of an even front. The details which have come down to us of this action are, as I have observed, but brief and indistinct, yet it appears from Plutarch's statement, who gives the whole glory of this battle to Pelopidas, even while he ascribes the oblique formation, the value of which he did not comprehend, to Epaminondas, that the general had strengthened his centre, so as in some degree to compensate for its numerical weakness, by the three hundred known as the sacred band, who were never beaten until they fell to a man with all their wounds in front

* Plut. Vit. Pelop. 23.

"on that dishonest field of Chaironeia, fatal to liberty," and lay as they fell

> "With their backs to the field and their feet to the foe,
> And leaving in battle no blot on their name,
> Looked proudly to heaven from the death-bed of fame."

But that day of disaster had not yet arrived; and in this furious hand to hand encounter, they with their gallant leader did their duty well, and merited so much of the honors of the victory as belongs of right to those who are intrusted with an office of the highest faith and moment, and who do not disappoint the trust reposed in them—they were, in fact, as the strong hands which execute that which the wiser head has planned; and, although they have every right to share, have none to claim, much less to monopolize, the honors of a victory, which, but for the strange and new formation in which they fought, must almost to a certainty have been a terrible defeat. From that day forth, this oblique method was the constant, and almost constantly successful array and order of the Thebans, until at Chaironeia it was turned against themselves by Philip of Makedon to their total discomfiture, and thenceforward was one of the favorite manœuvres of his heroic son Alexander.

To return to the battle before us, however; no sooner were the two armies in the plain, the Thebans with their left advanced so as almost to feel the enemy's right, while their own right was so far retired as to be very distant from the Lakedaimonian left the cavalry trumpets sounded, and the horse on both sides encountered between the main bodies in full career.

At this period the Theban cavalry was in admirable condition, on account of the wars which they had been so long carrying on against Thespiai and Orchomenos, as well as the auxiliary Thessalian horse of Jason, which were the most celebrated of all the Greek cavaliers. The Lakedaimonians were at this time, and indeed generally, if not always, miserably deficient in this arm of the service; for none but the richest men of the state kept horses, and these did not serve on horseback, but when the troops were called out, a certain number were allotted to this service, and arms and horses were assigned to them; so that neither the riders were accustomed to their chargers, nor the chargers to their riders, which is of all things the *sine quâ non* to the efficiency of a cavalry force; while the possibility of drill or discipline was entirely out of the question, if indeed these were ever insisted upon, which appears to me very doubtful, by the Hellenic nations, among whom—previously, at least, to the age of Alexander and Philopoimen, both of whom made great use of their cavalry—this arm was exceedingly weak and inefficient. In addition to all these disadvantages, it may be added, that in the Lakedaimonian armies, the choicest of the levies being reserved for the ranks of the hoplitai, the weakest and least spirited of the soldiery were mounted on those chance-selected horses, and served as troopers.* The consequence of this difference in the nature of their cavalry services, was the almost instantaneous defeat and scattering of the Lakedaimonian horse before the Thebans, and their falling back into the lines of their own hoplitai, which they threw somewhat into disorder before the encounter of the main battles. This must have occurred, I imagine, toward the Theban right, where the interval was the widest between the opposing armies, and the space between the hills the narrowest. For since the signal for the onset of the infantry seems to have been given as soon as the cavalry were no longer interposed, if the Spartan right, which first came into contact with the Boiotians, had been much shaken—as they must have been, had their broken horse disordered them in that quarter—they could never have made such a resistance as they did to the terrible onset of Epaminondas,

* Xen. Hellen. VI., iv. 11.

with his column of fifty shields. The cavalry on both sides, therefore, of which we hear no more during the action—as is by no means unusual in narratives of ancient battles—must have swept away, I conjecture, the Lakedaimonians in full flight, and the Thebans in reckless and inconsiderate pursuit, down the plain toward Thespiai eastward, and no portion of either, it is probable, re-appeared on the field until the victory was decided.

In no respect, indeed, do the ancients appear to have been so far inferior to the moderns—nay, but even the Greeks to the Orientals—as in their ignorance of the true use of cavalry and of its proper tactics. In nine cases out of ten, there were in every general battle two several independent actions—one of the horse, which had for the most part no influence on the result of the whole, and one of the infantry, which was decisive. The battle of Delion was indeed won by Pagondas, who brought up reserves of cavalry which deterred the Athenians from prosecuting a half-won victory, and ultimately converted it into a defeat; but even this appears to have been the result of chance rather than of design, and it has scarcely a parallel in the annals of ancient warfare, until the days of Alexander in Greece and Hannibal in Italy, with both of whom horse was a favorite and effective arm.

The holding a reserve of horse in hand, whether to complete an impression made on an enemy's battle, to turn his undefended flank, to surround and charge his rear, or to cover the retreat of its own infantry, was a thing, it would seem, never thought of. Horse, indeed, rarely charged home at all, merely skirmishing as javelineers;* and it is very doubtful to me, whether they were ever trained to come in all abreast with an even front; whether they had any regular number of files or order of working; and whether they were aware of the most obvious rules of cavalry exercise, such as the leading of the charge at the pace of the

* Xen. de Re Equestri, passim.

slowest horse, the never suffering themselves to be charged except in the act of charging, and the like—now axioms understood by the dullest subaltern of the worst horse service in the world. At least it is certain that Xenophon in his elaborate treatises on horsemanship and cavalry service, hints at nothing of the kind, but directs all his precepts toward the making of individual or partizan troopers.

To compensate for this, their infantry tactics were almost perfect—perhaps, as regards troops fighting entirely with the standing pike and sword, and using no missiles except as a distinct arm of service never employed in the actual crisis—actually so. Nor was this ever more distinctly shown than in the present instance, for the Lakedaimonians exceeded the Thebans by nearly one half in numbers, and I presume nearly as much in individual strength and prowess; for their very best men fought here, and man to man, Spartans appear to the last to have been all but invincible.

So soon as the trumpets sounded, the Lakedaimonians led forth at charging pace along the whole front; their left hurrying their advance, in order to close with the Theban right, which rather fell back than advanced, though still preserving their connection with the left, which met the Spartan right with levelled pikes and their battle cry, at a full run. There the battle raged fiercely, hand to hand, and was for a long time stationary, since there Epaminondas met the chosen Spartans, with Deinon, Sphodrias, and Kleombrotos their king, who would not yield a step, nor turn, but sustained the shock of his deep column with their *synaspismos* of linked shields, until their spears were broken, and it came to the closest single combat, with their short stabbing swords. In the meantime their left, which had been disordered somewhat by its own flying horse, and shaken by the rapidity of its own advance, endeavored to extend still farther to the left, in order to outflank and surround the Theban right, with which it was not yet fairly engaged. All manœuvring with so heavy and unwieldy a body as the phalanx, in the face of an enemy, was difficult; and if attacked when in the act of deploying or changing its front, that array, at other times so formidable, was the most defenceless and helpless of masses; and at precisely such a moment, and in the middle of such a movement, Pelopidas rushed headlong with his three hundred of the sacred band, serried in the closest combination, upon their centre, giving them time neither to extend as they desired, nor to contract their files in order to meet his shock, so that they wavered visibly, and though they still fought stoutly, were momentarily falling into confusion.

By this time, however, the extraordinary depth, and consequent weight and impetus, of the terrible column of Epaminondas began to tell; the pressure of the rearmost files bearing the foremost bodily onward, and if the front men fell, others succeeding to their places, almost as it seemed ad infinitum. And now Sphodrias was down, and Deinon; and Kleombrotos had fallen, fighting worthily of his Herakleidan blood, and all the adjutants and four hundred of the seven hundred Spartans; and as the head of the assailing column met less resistance, it fell in with wilder shouts and a more fiery impetus, and broke the Spartan right into shattered and defenceless fragments, outflanking it, moreover, and thereby turning the right of the whole array. But no sooner did the Lakedaimonian centre, already shaken, and their left, which had scarcely felt the enemy, see the defeat of their right wing, than they turned also; and the forces opposed to them assuming the offensive, no time was given them to rally, and the confusion and route became general along the whole front; except where in a knot the surviving Spartans fought so desperately around the body of their king, that Epaminondas judged it wiser to suffer them to withdraw it, as their point of honor, than to risk a renewal of the action with an enemy ever formidable, now rendered desperate. The loss of the Lakedaimonians was prodigious, considering that there was no long flight, or fierce pursuit, with execution of the flying—no onslaught of horse, plying them with their bloody sabres, but only a short stern retreat, up the height on which they had encamped, until they had crossed the ditch which guarded their camp, when they faced about with presented arms and serried shields; and even held debate among themselves, whether they should not rather risk a second conflict than suffer the Thebans to erect a trophy, so high and valorous were their yet unbroken spirits.

Prudent councils, however, prevailed; for above a thousand Lakedaimonians, four hundred of whom were Spartans,* lay dead on the plain below them, without enumerating the slain of the light troops, who were not included in the order of battle, or those, I presume, of the allies, who are said to have been greatly dispirited by the action. Diodoros states the whole loss of the Lakedaimonians at four thousand, and that of the Boiotians at about three hundred; but these numbers cannot be exactly relied on, although if the light-armed Helots and the allies be included, the number cannot be regarded as excessive as compared to the loss of the native hoplitai. At all events, it was the severest defeat ever as yet inflicted by one Hellenic nation on another, and the most notable victory won by Greeks from Greeks. The Thebans restored the Lakedaimonian dead under treaty, who were buried in the polyandrion mentioned above, as still visible on the heights of Leuktra, and permitted them to retire peacefully homeward. But they, trusting to secrecy and promptitude, rather than to the faith of treaties, for their safety, marched that same night through the passes of the Kithairon to Kreusis, and thence to the fortress of Aigosthena, in the Megaris, along the

* I am clear that this is the meaning of the text—Xen. Hellen. VI., iv. 15—although Mitford understands it to mean a thousand *and* four hundred; Plutarch agrees with this view. Vit. Ages. XXVII.

same wild and perilous path over the southern cliffs of Mount Elateia, above the Korinthian Gulf, in which Kleombrotos had suffered so severely from a tempest seven years before the battle which put an end to his career. His death was that of a hero, and sufficiently disproved the charges which had been unjustly brought against him of personal cowardice, or of disaffection to his country. It was moral decision, not individual valor, that he lacked; and if he failed in generalship against Epaminondas, it were a reproach to few tacticians who have ever lived, to say of any one of them that, so matched, he was* *impar congressus Achilli.*

Immediately after the battle, a herald was sent crowned with bays to Athens, to demand the aid of the people and announce the result of the action, but he was very coldly received and dismissed without a reply, in regard to the assistance requested, so that it was evident that they had no friendship to expect in that quarter. The Lakedaimonians having escaped unmolested into the Megaris encountered there the powerful reinforcements sent from Sparta, under Archidamos the son of Agesilaos; but not feeling themselves equal to any farther operations, re-entered the isthmus, dismissed their allies, and returned to Sparta, never again to recover from the moral consequences of that overwhelming defeat, or to recover their station among the Hellenic nations, although they still made a stout struggle for pre-eminence, and long maintained their independence. Without losing a moment's time or suffering the prestige of victory to pass into oblivion, the Thebans took possession of Orchomenos, the inhabitants of which they were half disposed to sell as slaves until persuaded to milder counsels by Epaminondas, and made preparations to prosecute the war within the isthmus, having been joined by the Phokians, Aitolians and Arkadians, who had recently defeated the Spartans under the walls of the Mantineian Orchomenos. In the following

* A proverbial phrase of any one overmatched, taken from the com bat of Hector with Achilles, in the Iliad.

year, Epaminondas entered the isthmus with no less than fifty thousand men, and burst into the Peloponnesos in four several columns of attack, devastating the country of their enemies in all directions, having appointed a general rendezvous at Sellasia a city of Lakonia, northeast of Sparta,* situate in a valley between two hills, known as Euas and Olympos, commanding the road down the valley of the Oinous, running direct to Sparta. At this town they all arrived in due season, having met with little opposition except that offered to the division of Arkadians by Ischolas, who rather chose to die like a second Leonidas in defence of the post entrusted to him, than to return dishonored home. Thence they entered Lakonia, cutting down all the fruit trees, burning the country far and wide, driving the cattle and destroying the crops up to the very suburbs of Sparta, whose boast it had always been that her women had never seen the smoke of a hostile fire, and that no enemy had ever been beaten back from her unwalled and unfortified metropolis. Now, however, her boast stood as nought, for not only were the flames of conflagration seen reddening the horizon in every quarter, but the enemy with Epaminondas at their head were in full view endeavoring to ford the snow-swollen torrent of the Eurotas; and they came so near to taking the city, that a revolution was attempted within the place itself, and the cries of frantic women and all the tumult and terror prevailed, which is wont to occur in a town won by storm. In the end, however, the allies were roughly repulsed, and did not judge it expedient to renew the attack, but retired leisurely with an enormous booty into Arkadia, where Epaminondas restored the state and city of Messenia, which had been destroyed, and its people dispersed by the Lakedaimonians above two centuries before—a stroke of masterly policy by which he planted a perpetual thorn in the side of Sparta, thus establishing a domestic enemy, as it were, close to

* Polyb. Bellum Cleom. II. 65–8.

her very confines—this restoration occurred in the fourth year of the one hundred and second Olympiad B. C., and was celebrated with great solemnity, and the performance of sacred games. This done Epaminondas drew off his forces and returned into Boiotia, having inflicted the severest blow on Sparta that had ever yet befallen her; and having been brought to trial for retaining his rank of Boiotarch, in defiance of the law, beyond the expiration of the year to which his rank and military command were limited, was unanimously acquitted in consideration of his great services and the obvious necessity of the case.

In the mean time an alliance offensive and defensive having been entered into by the Athenians and Lakedaimonians, to the detriment of Elis, Argos and Arkadia, those nations solicited the aid of the Boiotians, who again took the field, when they found the isthmus fortified by a great trench and palisade from Kenchreai on the Gulf of Eghina, to Lechaion on the Gulf of Korinth, and defended by three times their own force of Peloponnesians, with their Attic and insular allies. In spite of this, after reconnoitering the works carefully, Epaminondas assailed the Lakedaimonian defences, which were the weakest, cut their guards to pieces, and, breaking through the lines, again entered the Peloponnesos, having thus accomplished an exploit inferior to none of his previous victories. On this occasion he was not, however, so successful as before; for, although he took Sikyon and Phlius, he suffered a heavy repulse from the walls of Korinth, at the hands of Chabrias, who defended it masterly with a garrison of Athenians; and a peace being again negociated by Artoxerxesto be general through all the states of Greece, except the Thebans only, he again returned home as rich as ever in military glory, but with no trophies or spoils of victory to display before his countrymen.

In consequence of this he fell, incomparable soldier as he was, unsurpassed by any then alive, into disgrace with his fellow-citizens, was deposed from his command and sentenced to serve as a private soldier, under Pelopidas and Ismenias his colleague, in an expedition into Thessaly against Alexander of Pherai, and well for them it was that he served in any capacity. For the army being forced to retreat, and reduced to the greatest extremities by the superior cavalry of the Thessalians, he was reinstated in his command by the unanimous voice of his soldiers, and reconstructing his rear guard, beat back the pursuers with loss, and brought off his own power scatheless.

His return was followed by his immediate reappointment to command, and the infliction of a heavy fine on the other Boiotarchai, so entirely futile are all Plutarch's efforts to make him out inferior to Pelopidas, who, however excellent an officer he might be as second in command, never evinced any genius as a leader, which should constitute him even a general of the second or third order: while Epaminondas is allowed by such critics as Frederick the Great and Napoleon, to have been a genius of first-rate splendor, and surpassed by no one, perhaps of any day, in —what both those giants in military science esteemed the greatest principle of war—the concentration of the greatest possible force, on a single point, in the smallest possible available compass.

Not long after this, in the third year of the one hundred and third Olympiad, in the Archonship of Kephisodoros, peace was at length established between Thebes and Sparta through the intervention, now for the third time of the Persian Artoxerxes; and a general peace prevailed for a few months throughout all Greece, from North to South, and from sea to sea, until in the course of the year next succeeding difficulties arising between Elis and Arkadia, paved the way for a fresh war in Greece. In the following summer worse troubles broke out between Elis and Pisa, concerning the Olympian games. Thebes, at the instigation of Epaminondas, turned her attention to gaining predominance by sea as well as by land, inflicted severe chastisement on the city of Orchomenos, which had rebelled from her authority, and utterly defeated Alexander, the tyrant of Pherai, though with the heavy loss of a good patriot and gallant soldier, Pelopidas, who died in the arms of victory.

But now the difficulty between Elis and Pisa inflamed all the elements of hostility, and involved Greece anew in a general and destructive war; for all sides armed at once, the people of Tegea and those of Mantineia, both Arkadian cities, acting as principals, the Boiotians assuming the alliance of the former, and the Lakedaimonians and Athenians of the latter city. Agesilaos with the Spartans being nearest to the scene of action, was necessarily the first in the field, and marching without a moment's delay, was engaged in the devastation of the territories of Tegea, when Epaminondas entering the isthmus with the whole available force of the Boiotians and many Euboian and Thessalian auxiliaries rallied to his standard, met within the Peloponnesos, the Argive, Messenian, and Arkadian allies of the Tegeatans. Here he learned that the Athenians had decided to send no troops overland, but by sea to Lakedaimon, and thence to send succor to the Arkadians, and that Agesilaos was in force in the neighborhood of Mantineia; and on this intelligence he caused his men to rest in their camps under the walls of Tegea* and then led directly, by forced marches, upon Sparta. And here it is seen at once, how much fortune has to do at all times in the affairs of war, and how little without her can be effected by the most consummate skill, prudence, and valor. Napier observes in his great work on the Peninsular war, the finest military history in existence, that the discovery of an unsuspected ditch, ten feet in width, has been known to prostrate the most scientific combinations, and overthrow the most perfect calculations; and in this instance the casual speed of a Kretan *hemerodromos*, or all-day runner, saved

* Xen. Hellen. vii. v.

Sparta; for Agesilaos warned the citizens by a horse-courier, that they should stand resolutely to their arms, for he would be with them not long behind the Thebans. And in fact he entered the city almost at the same instant from one quarter, that Epaminondas forded the Eurotas, and assaulted it on the other. The fight in the avenues and about the suburbs of the town was long and desperate; but the Spartans were doing battle for all that is dear to man, within the sight of their women and their children, around the hearths where even themselves had played when babes, among the graves of their fathers, before the temples of the Gods, and they were invincible. The feats of Archidamos, and of Isadas* the son of Phoibidas, who rushing from the baths with a spear suddenly caught up in one hand, and a sword in the other, fought in the front ranks, naked as he was, until the enemy retired, wounding and slaying many, but himself unwounded—must be read elsewhere, for my limits forbid that I should dwell on them.

After a furious conflict Epaminondas drew off his troops, leaving it to Agesilaos to erect a trophy, for it was not in his fortune or his fate to carry Sparta with the sword, though to him alone of living men it had been given twice to devastate Lakonia up to the very suburbs, twice to pass the Eurotas, and listen to the panic-stricken women, wailing through the city. It was his fortune alone that failed him; for even Xenophon, who gives him no undeserved or lavish praise, admits that, but for the speed of the Kretan runner, which was so extraordinary, that he ascribes it to divine intervention, he must have taken Sparta like a young bird in its nest, deserted of all who could defend it.

In no wise daunted, however, or disheartened by the failure of operations on which he had, and that of right, counted as almost certain, he retraced his steps with a celerity and decision so marvellous, that they remind us of the prodigious marches and

* Plutarch, Agesilaos, 42.

countermarches, and thunderstrokes dealt in every direction, of Napoleon during his Dresden campaign, and that final struggle in the heart of France. Fixing his head-quarters once more at Tegea he at once launched his cavalry against Mantineia, which he calculated on finding, as it indeed was, deserted by its defenders, who had marched with every man that they could muster to the rescue of Sparta. This blow again like the last appeared certain; and like that was defeated by an accident, for the Athenian horse had just come up from the isthmus as the Thebans entered the plain of Mantineia, and charging instantly preserved the territory of their allies from devastation, if not their city itself from capture. The loss was great on both sides, for they fought sharply hand to hand, and in so close a melée that there was no weapon so short that it was not used on either side. And the Athenians lost none of their own dead, but permitted the burial of the enemy's under a flag of truce.

But Epaminondas angry at the two repulses he had met resolved to deliver battle; and, having enrolled a thousand Arkadian clubmen he caused his cavalry to burnish their helmets, and all to grind their spear heads and sword blades, and furbish up their shields in readiness for instant action.

The scene was a plain at about thirty stadia, or four English miles' distance from Mantineia.

The action as usual commenced by a charge of the cavalry on each side, which was mutually arrayed on either wing of the hosts, the Thebans as usual holding the left wing of their own army opposite the Mantineians on the enemy's right supported by the Lakedaimonians, Eleans and Argives, with the Athenians on their extreme left.

In the cavalry skirmish, the Theban horse, who were mixed with a powerful body of Thessalian slingers and engineers, easily broke the Athenians, who all fled together to the left of their own infantry, without disordering it; but speedily rallying, fell violently on the Euboians, who had been sent with a body of mercenaries to occupy certain heights in that direction, and cut them off to a man. The victorious Thebans did not pursue the fugitives, but charged home on the flank of the Athenian foot, striving desperately to break into their phalanx, and had already thrown them into confusion, when the commander of the Elean horse, who had been placed in reserve with the rear-guard, charged in turn, and repulsing the Boiotians, restored the battle in this quarter.

And this, in my judgment, is the best, or rather the only good cavalry fighting that occurred during the Peloponnesian war; for in this instance they had evidently the true aim and object of war in view, beyond the mere breaking and chasing off the ground the horse directly opposed to them.

On the left wing the action was more decisive, for the superiority of the Theban and Thessalian squadrons was so manifest, that the Mantineian troopers were driven almost immediately, for shelter, to the rear of their phalanx. Then, with a mighty shout, the two main bodies charged along the whole front, and never, says Diodoros,* where Greeks met Greeks, were there such equal numbers opposed face to face on one field; nor ever were such leaders mated in renown and worth; nor ever were such soldiers set together. And where the Lakedaimonians and Boiotians came together, no man spared his own life, so he might take his enemy's; and first they thrust and strove at push of pike till their shafts were broken, and then fought it out with their swords and cutlasses, until their bodies were exhausted with wounds and loss of blood, but their spirits were inexhaustible. The battle long hung balanced thus, the whole air ringing with the clash and clang of blades on shield and helmet, for the combatants lacked breath to shout withal; when, seeing that the moment had arrived, Epaminondas, with his favorite tactic, obliqued from the

* Diod. Sic. XV., 86

left wing in deep and serried column, full upon the Lakedaimonian centre, and cut the phalanx in two on the instant; for even the Spartans could not endure the weight of that tremendous concentrated charge, but retreated in confusion, with the Boiotians pressing on their rear, and slaughtering them in heaps. At this moment a rush was made against Epaminondas by some of the bravest of the Spartans, who rallied and set upon him all at once; so that after a vigorous and heroical defence, one against many, he was struck down with a mortal lance-thrust through his corslet, from the hand, it is said, of Gryllos, the son of Xenophon, though it is by no means evident what he should be doing in the ranks of the Spartans, when his own countrymen were engaged in a different part of the field. Over his body the conflict again raged fierce and furious, but the Thebans, at length and with difficulty, prevailed, by dint of bodily strength alone, and having chased them a little way, returned sad and tearful, from their disastrous victory, to tend the body of their illustrious dead. The victory was in itself complete, yet it was unimproved, and followed up neither with carnage of the enemy nor advantage to themselves—for they had no general left who could pursue it, as he would have done, who had fallen in the arms of immortal glory.

He had fallen childless, it is true, as his weeping comrades exclaimed in their sorrow, but leaving behind him, as he cried himself, with his parting breath, two daughters to immortalize his memory—his twin victories at Leuktra and Mantineia.

And they did immortalize him, for to this day they survive, two of the most purely scientific battles ever won, and won by superior tactics only.

His greatest praise rests on the facts, that tne state, Lakedaimonia, against which his greatest efforts were directed, never recovered the pride of place from which he struck her down, when at her topmost pitch; and that his native country, which, with his rise, rose from obscurity, sunk into it again at his decease, never to shine again among nations. To add weight to the judgment of the critics I have quoted on his strategy or tactics, were impertinent as absurd; but were I to assign a place to Epaminondas among generals, it would be—as to an originator of a great system, ever opposed to the best troops in the then known world, and never beaten by them in the field—above Pausanias, above Alexander, above Scipio, above Julius Cæsar, above even Xenophon, and inferior only, of all masters in the art of war, to Hannibal, Wellington, and Napoleon, who are in my estimation the first men of the first class, unapproached, if not unapproachable.

As a man and as a patriot he was not to be excelled; for in either quality his character was as pure, as disinterested, and as spotless, as that of Washington himself.

Happy the state which can boast the production of an Epaminondas; and the possession of such a general as he, such a poet as Pindar, may well compensate for greater dulness of intellect than their enemies were wont to attribute to the breathers of the fat atmosphere of Boiotia.

VII.

ALEXANDER OF MAKEDON.

HIS BATTLES OF THE GRANIKOS, ISSOS, AND ARBELA; HIS CAMPAIGNS, CHARACTER, AND CONDUCT.

Three years only, after the battle of Mantineia, which put an end for ever to the supremacy of Sparta, and left Thebes the principal of the Hellenic cities, Philip, the son of Amyntas, succeeded to the throne of Makedonia, a vast district in the northern part of Greece, beyond the mountain chain of Oita, which, up to this period, had hardly been admitted by the pure Hellenes to be a Hellenic state, but had rather been considered, with the adjoining countries of Thessalia, Aitolia, Epiros, and more particularly Thraké, as semi-barbarous.

The kings of Makedonia, however, had, from the beginning, claimed descent from the heroic princes of the purest Hellenic blood; had been acknowledged as heirs of the Peleidan branch of the great Aiakidai, through Neoptolemos, the son of Achilles; and, till a very late day, they retained in their family the ancestral names of their race. From time almost immemorial, these princes had ruled with nearly absolute sway over the pastoral and hunter tribes who peopled their extensive plains, and who, to the days of which I write, had learned none of those democratic ideas, had acquired none of that thirst for freedom and jealousy of individual authority, which were the most striking characteristics of the southern Greeks. They maintained their courts with a sort of semi-barbarous pomp, not differing much, except that the heroic simplicity was gone, from the style of which we read in Homer; their government and many of their habits, that of polygamy especially, still savored strongly of patriarchal times, and were preserved long after they came to be considered pure Greeks, and were indeed the only independent sovereigns left in Hellas.

Hitherto they and their neighbors had meddled little with the affairs of southern or republican Greece; by whom, indeed, they were so nearly ignored, that, until the latter years of the Peloponnesian war, we scarcely find them mentioned in the page of history.

The time had now arrived, and the man, when and by whom they were to be brought into notice, and, in an incredibly short space of time—with little warfare, little bloodshedding, and one great battle only—to be placed at the helm of affairs in Greece; no part of which should ever be again, save nominally, independent. Of a truth, he was a very great man, this semi-barbarous Philip, son of Amyntas; a greater *man* by far, in my estimation, than his more famous son Alexander, and worthy of a place in this work, except that, like several others similarly omitted, I regard him rather as a statesman than a general; and in that light shall probably treat of him hereafter. He was a very great man, I say, and, with some vicious habits, which point particularly to the barbarian, and which Alexander shared with him, I allude chiefly to habitual excess in wine and fierce orgies of drunkenness—never a Greek, or indeed a southern, vice—he possessed many great qualities, far less apparent in the more showy but less solid character of his son; such as natural love of justice, constitutional dislike to bloodshedding, and willingness to hear even unpalatable truths, which, when added to his extraordinary political sagacity and great military shrewdness, eminently adapted him for the part he was destined to play, as the consolidator of an empire, and the pacificator of all Greece.

In the first year of the one hundred and fourth Olympiad, B. C. 360, he ascended the throne of Makedon; and, in four years afterward, there was born to him at the city of Pella in Thessaly—already famous as the birth-place of Achilles—of Olympias, his first wife, and daughter of Neoptolemos king of Epiros, Alexander, thereafter called the Great.

Of his youth and childhood I shall say nothing, as my portion of him is his military conduct and career; and as I never have believed that prodigious children necessarily make great men, or that great men were of necessity once prodigious children; but for those who adhere to such time-honored rubbish with the reverence ever attributed to nursery tales, I will indicate his life by good gossipping old Plutarch, who will sup them to satiety on anecdotes of his precocious growth and premature development.

All that it imports us to know, is, that he grew up much as any absolute young prince, under the care of an arrogant, masculine, imperious mother, and the tuition of an obsequious, adulating pedagogue, indulged in every whim, and taught all things save obedience, either to God or man, would naturally grow up; imperious, arrogant, self-willed, capricious, vain; impotent to restrain his passions, yet full of a fickle nobleness and fantastic generosity. Brave and high-spirited, he was by nature, even to excess; good-natured and merciful, when not crossed—for then he was a madman—and always liable to ingenuous and noble impulses, which never, unfortunately for his friends and himself, hardened into permanent impressions.

All that was good in him came of God's giving; all that was bad, of man's teaching. For it is probable that he never was instructed to question one impulse, to curb one emotion, to refrain from one action; and I seriously doubt whether, from the first day of his public career to the last of his life, he ever controlled one passion, resisted one temptation, considered the consequences of one action, or withheld his hand from the doing of one deed, once meditated, how bitterly soever he afterward might rue the doing of it.

When he was eighteen years of age, he first appears on the stage of public life at the battle of Chaironeia—three years older than Edward the Black Prince, when he won his spurs at Cressy; three younger than William Pitt, when he accepted the reins of government as prime minister of England. Nothing as yet, one may say, wonderful or premature; but not say so long; for thenceforth he blazed out into a sudden and splendid manhood.

Previously to this celebrated action, by a rare union of diplomatic sagacity and craft, with civil audacity and military skill, Philip had made himself master of Epiros, Thessaly, and all Thraké up to the Hellespont, as a tributary province; by mingling himself adroitly with the sacred war, he had annexed Phokis to his government, and had procured himself to be nominated general-in-chief of the Greeks, in the war undertaken to avenge the spoliation of Delphoi. This conflict having terminated in a general Hellenic peace, Philip suddenly broke it by declaring war on the Athenians, with scarce a pretext beyond the manifest cravings of his ambition for universal Greek dominion, which Athens had constantly and consistently resisted. Athens called upon Thebes for aid; and, once more for the last time, the two ancient enemies stood in the field, not now front to front, but shoulder to shoulder; contending not now for power or pride of dominion, but for their common liberty and independence stood as allies on the field of Chaironeia. But Iphikrates was no more, nor Chabrias, nor Timotheos; and only Chares the Athenian* was alive, superior in no respect of strategetic energy or

* Diod. Sic. XVI., 85.

counsel, to any of the private soldiers he commanded; and he led them—to slaughter.

Of Epaminondas, the great name alone survived; the tactics, by which he had so often conquered, had fallen into disuse, or, worse yet! had been adopted by the enemy; the veterans, whom he had taught to regard battle and victory as the same, slept with him the last cold sleep of oblivion. Of Pelopidas remained the memory—remained the Sacred Band, which he had instituted, and which alone did its duty on the day of "that dishonest victory."

In everything Philip was the superior, in strategy, in numbers, in the quality of his troops, and in the confidence, which, most of all things, tends to victory. In the action which ensued, he gave the command of one wing of his army to Alexander, whom he fortified with his best and oldest generals; and it is said that the crisis of the battle was his charge upon the sacred band of the Thebans, every one of whom lay dead where he fell, with his wounds all in front, worthy to the last of the name they had won under abler leaders; and in the days of Plutarch*—about 66 A.D., or three hundred years later—the oak-tree was shown on the banks of the Kephisos, beneath which his tent was pitched and hard by it, the *polyandrion*, or general tomb of the Makedonians, who fell in the engagement.

The details of this battle are nowhere very clearly stated, and even Plutarch gives the facts in relation to his hero as a rumor only; but the results prove how decisive was the victory, and that Alexander did here achieve high distinction, may be received as a historic truth.

In the following year all Greece having sunk into apathy and virtually snbmitted itself to his authority after the battle, Philip met the assembled delegates of all the Hellenic states at the isthmus, where he easily prevailed on them to declare war on Persia

* Plut. Vit. ix.

under the old pretext of revenging the desecration of the temples of Greece by the elder Darios, and was forthwith elected the autocratic general of the forces, in behalf of all Hellas. After this he set on foot great preparations for the invasion of Persia; appointed to every state the contingent which it should send; and returned to his own court to complete his armament.

There, surrounded by the din of martial preparation, and by grand pomps, processions, and games, in honor of the Gods who had given him what, though really indefinite and susceptible of two meanings, he chose to accept as a* favorable response from Delphoi, having already sent forward his lieutenants, Attalus and Parmenion, with part of his forces, to liberate the Ionian cities of Asia Minor, he was murdered by one Pausanias, as he went into the theatre; as some believed at the instigation of his repudiated wife, Olympias; and not, it is also hinted, without the connivance of Alexander.

It is pleasant, however, to be able at once to acquit the young man, and probably his mother also, of all participation in an act so atrocious, which may be attributed, on the concurrence of all trustworthy authorities, to private and personal motives on the part of the murderer, who was slain on the spot by some of the king's body-guard.

It was toward the latter end, therefore, of the first year of the hundred and first Olympiad, B. C., 336, that Alexander ascended the throne of his father; but his accession was surrounded with troubles and difficulties, and his throne was shared by a hateful participant—Attalos, the brother of Kleiopatra, the young wife of Philip, in behalf of whom he had repudiated Olympias, and who, either a few days before, or a few days after, the king's death—for authorities differ on the point—had borne him a son; so that, his own mother being repudiated, it was not unlikely that his succession would be disputed.

* Diod. Sic. XVI. 91.

Attalos, moreover, was in command of the veteran army sent into Ionia by the late king; and it soon became certain that he had shaken the allegiance of the troops, and was treating with the Athenians for the restoration of Greek independence—probably with a view only to his own interest and ambition. In other parts of Greece, a spirit of revolt was clearly manifest, the states believing themselves able to vindicate their liberty against a mere youth, new in office, and unskilled in judgment, and the arts of government.

The youth speedily undeceived them. In the second year both of that Olympiad and of his own reign, having taken vengeance of his father's murderers, he sent one Hekataios, his own confidential friend, with a few trusty soldiers to Asia, with orders either to bring Attalos, without delay, alive to Makedonia, or to take him off privately—the latter of which designs was speedily performed—and the army brought back to loyalty.

That was a bloody and a bad commencement of a reign. The act was a murder, and the manner of it scarce less exceptionable than the act. Yet it must be observed, in justice to Alexander, that in semi-barbarous royal families like his, tainted with all the corruptions of polygamous unions, and haremlike concubinage, and the co-ordinate curse of spurious relationships and kindred animosities, fraud and even murder appear almost of necessity to prevail; and that not to kill is in most cases to be killed by the heir apparent to the throne. More, therefore, of this his first crime may be ascribed to the morals, the manners, the necessities indeed, of his tribe, country, and station, than to any defect in his own temper or character. And it is very probable, that neither by himself nor by any one of his confederates was this deed ever regarded as a crime, but as an act of self-defence, and a legitimate assertion of just authority. And thus it is, to maintain true historic justice, that the characters of men must be meted, weighed, and judged of, by the measures, with the balance, according to the lights, which they had and used, not with others that they knew not of. Thus, therefore, I, in this case, would judge Alexander—almost innocent.

In the meantime the Athenians had heard of Philip's death with joy, and invited by their great orator and patriot Demosthenes, were ready to deny that they had ever yielded the supremacy of Greece to Makedon ; the Aitolians passed a decree to recall the exiles of Philip from Akarnania; the Ambrakiots had cast out the Makedonian garrison; the Thebans had voted to expel Philip's guards from the Kadmeia ; the Arkadians had never submitted to Philip, nor now submitted to his son ; and of the other Peloponnesians, the Argives, the Eleans, and the Lakedaimonians were all bent on the recovery of their independence, now that fortune appeared to favor an effort.

Then, at once, Alexander showed both of what race he came, and of what stuff he was made; for, without giving the revolutionists time to mature their plans, he speedily effected a reconciliation with the Thessalians and Ambrakiots ; and then, marching down with his Makedonian troops in full array of battle, entered the pass of Thermopylai, and persuaded the Amphictyonik council, there in session, to confer on him the leading of the Greeks by a unanimous vote. Thence he entered Boiotia, and encamping close to the Kadmeia, held the city of Thebes in immediate terror of an assault, until the Athenians, perceiving that their opinion of this young man was entirely contradicted by the decision, energy, and rapid enterprise, which they now perceived to be his characteristics, repented of their inconsiderate haste, and atoned for it by decreeing him General-in-Chief, and empowering him to make war on the Persians until they should have made atonement to Greece, for all the wrong they had done her. Content with this, he led back his power into Makedonia, and striking without notice or delay at the Thrakian malcontents, he reduced with unheard of celerity the revolted tribes of

Paionians, Illyrians, and other barbarians conterminous with them, to obedience; and, this scarcely accomplished, hearing that the Thebans were again mutinous and in arms, he bestirred himself with such rapidity that he actually sat down before the city, while the inhabitants were beleaguering the Makedonian garrison in the citadel, or Kadmeia, and before they were aware that he had a force on foot within the defiles of Thermopylai. Some of those who had instigated the revolt insisted for a while that the Makedonian army had come with Antipater, insisting that Alexander was dead; or, that, if any Alexander were present, it was the son of Aëropos, and not the king of Makedon.

On the day following his sudden appearance on the heights above Onchestos, near the Copaic lake, he descended to the sacred territory of Iolaos, where he again encamped, willing to give time to the Thebans to repent of their misdeeds; but so little desirous were they of conciliating, or even accepting his clemency, that they sallied with their light troops and cavalry, and advancing to his outposts, skirmished with them sharply and killed several of the Makedonians, until Alexander detached some targeteers and archery, who easily drove them back to their gates. Still, however, he would not attack them hastily, for he preferred conciliating to destroying them; and proceeded leisurely to encamp, a third time, close before the gates leading by Eleutherai to Athens, in order to be at hand to reinforce the garrison of the Kadmeia, which was blockaded by the Thebans with double lines of circum and contra vallation. But, in spite of the advice of their wisest and best citizens, the refugees and others, who believed that no mercy was to be had at the hands of Alexander, induced the Thebans to march out and offer battle. And even then Alexander would not attack the city; but, according to Ptolemy* the son of Lagos, Perdikkas, who com-

* Arrian. Anab. I. viii. Quoted by Arrian, I. viii.

manded the advanced guard of the army, not far from the palisades around the Kadmeia, assaulted and tore them up without awaiting orders, and fell upon the blockading force of the Thebans; being at once supported by Amyntas, the son of Andromenes, who was associated with him in the command of the outposts. Seeing this, Alexander led out his army to prevent their being cut off, and ordered the archery and Agrianians to charge and force their way into the palisades; but held the phalanx of *hypaspistai*, who were afterward called *argyraspides* or silver shields, and the foot life-guards, in hand without the works. Perdikkas, in endeavoring to force the second palisade, fell desperately wounded, and was carried to the rear; but his men together with the archers forced the Thebans into a hollow way leading to the Herakleion, and drove them up it, in confusion, to the temple; there, however, they rallied, and facing round with a great shout, broke the Makedonians in turn, killing Eurybotas, the captain of the Kretan archers, and about seventy of his men, and drove them back upon the lifeguards and the royal *hypaspistai*. In following up their advantage, however, they pursued too far, and disordered their own ranks, when Alexander seizing the occasion, charged with his phalanx, bore the enemy bodily back into the gates, which they had not time to close, and entering pell-mell with the fugitives, made himself master of the Kadmeia at a blow. The rest of the army perceiving that the ramparts were scantily defended, owing to the descent of their forces into the plain, scaled them at all points, and rushed in from all quarters toward the market-place; while the garrison of the Kadmeia breaking out at the same moment by an unguarded postern, after a short resistance at the Ampheion, completed the confusion of the enemy and the capture of the city. The Theban cavalry made their escape into the plain how best they might, and such of the infantry as could follow their example did so; but on all the rest, without regard to age, sex, or condition, resistance or submission, execution was done mercilessly; not so much by the Makedonian soldiery of Alexander, as by the Phokians, Plataians, and the other Boiotians, who had the fury of civil hatred and private vengeance to excite them. All perished by the sword's edge, whom on that day they encountered.

The terror and consternation spread abroad with the tidings of that terrible disaster and retribution, exceeds all description. Never before, within the memory of man, within the range of recorded history, had such a catastrophe, such an overwhelming destruction, befallen any Hellenic city. For the calamities of the Athenians at Syracuse and at Aigospotamos had befallen their armies only, but had left them a people, a city, and a state. The crushing defeats of the Lakedaimonians at Leuktra and Mantineia had deprived them of no foot of soil, nor robbed them of one political right; and, if the destruction of Plataia had been total during the Peloponnesian war, the smallness of the city and the scant numbers of the sufferers detracted from the magnitude of the occurrence and the horror it excited.

But here was a city, second to none in all Hellas, but rather the mistress and most powerful of them all—which alone, but the other day, as it were, had braved the united war of Attika and the Peloponnese; which, alone, had carried fire and sword to the banks of Eurotas and the inviolate gates of Sparta—on which destruction had descended like a thunderbolt, almost or ere the offence was committed, which had been expiated by so terrible a vengeance.

At dawn of day Thebes was a fair city, with green groves and verdant gardens, and fair sloping meadows, the greenest and the grassiest of all Greece, watered by sacred rivers, pure and perennial, Dirké, and Knopos, and Ismenos, crowned with cloud-capped towers and solemn temples, filled with glad homes and happy hearths. At dawn of day she was a powerful and independent state; she had a numerous and gallant army, that deemed itself invincible; she had a large and prosperous population, linked together by all fond ties of kindred, love, and country; and when the sun set she was—nothing.

The green fields scathed by the torch, the green groves felled by the axe, of the pitiless avenger; the pure waters of the sacred rivers crimsoned with the gore, and choked with the corpses, of a nation. Her state political dissolved for ever, her army slaughtered or dispersed never to be present under arms again as Thebans; her population butchered in their streets, about their hearths, in the secresy of their chambers, before the sanctity of their altars. Nothing had availed them, why they should not perish. And the dread decree of the auxiliaries had gone forth—for to them had the king committed the fate of Thebes—that the city should be razed to the very earth, and the territories divided among the confederates; that all the survivors of the inhabitants—men, women and children—all, should be sold as slaves, save the priests and priestesses of the Gods; and that, from the spoils of Thebes, Plataia and Orchomenos should be restored and fortified. The men of Plataia had not forgotten their own fate fifty years before; nor those of Orchomenos their own more recent, if less barbarous overthrow.

Terrible was the decree, but more terrible the execution, for it was carried out to the utmost letter; except only that

> " The Great Æmathian conqueror bade spare
> The house of Pindarus, when town and tower
> Went to the ground"—

and that the relatives of the poet were exempted from the sentence which delivered over all their countrymen to hopeless servitude.*

The shifting of this deed of cold political vengeance—for it

* Arrian I., ix.

was in fact nothing more; performed merely to intimidate Athens and the Peloponnesian cities—from his own hands to that of the confederated Boiotians, who, he was well assured, would be ruthless, as the once persecuted enemies of the fallen city, was but an empty and unsuccessful attempt to shift the responsibility from his own head also. But the awful eyes even of human justice will not be cheated; and the reproach, as the guilt, of this wholesale massacre and ruin, has clung ever, like a blight, to the renown of the great conqueror, not to be redeemed by fifty such capricious and personal shows of sympathy and tenderness, as the honors he paid to the captive ladies of Darios' house, or the tears he shed, too late, over the bleeding corpse of his royal victim.

To my mind, this extermination of the Thebans, and annihilation of their city, is the worst, and least to be palliated of all his evil actions—it was not a violent act of overboiling passion; it was not even an outrage suggested by fierce fanaticism, a cruelty prompted by the stinging sense of personal injury or the thirst of vengeance. The crime of the unhappy Thebans was a slight, was a most natural one, if indeed—which Americans will be little apt to grant—it were one at all. They had been recently conquered, deprived of independence, bitted with a foreign garrison in their own citadel; and, when the opportunity offered, they endeavored to liberate themselves from a yoke which it does not seem that they ever accepted. They were alarmed once into the relinquishment of their project, though it is not recorded that any treaties were exchanged or promises made for the future; occasion again offered, and again they accepted the occasion; yet even then they had scarcely proceeded beyond the premeditation and inception of an enterprise, which, if successful, must have been deemed proud and meritorious.

Time had not rendered her dependence prescriptive, nor had

she kissed the rod which smote her, or once accepted her subjugation to the yoke of Makedon. It is not even clear that, in her attempt to vindicate her rights, she had spilled the blood of a single Makedonian.

No more can be said of it, than this, that an independent city, for asserting her own independence, Thebes suffered at the hands of a fellow Greek, what no Greek city had ever before suffered, even at the hands of the Barbarian. The deed has, to my memory, but one parallel in history, and that parallel is the deepest blot upon the memory of a very great, and otherwise not cruel or unscrupulous man. I mean the massacre which followed the storming of Drogheda by Cromwell—like this, an act of accurst cold-blooded policy—not an act of punishment—not an act of vengeance—but an act, deeply calculated and done of malice aforethought, of pure intimidation.

Cromwell massacred the population, and hung the priests of Drogheda, in order to prevent the other Catholic cities of Ireland from resisting, and costing him men, time, and money. Alexander razed Thebes to the plough-share, in order that Athens, and Sparta and all the Peloponnesian cities might fear to raise the standard of revolt; which had they done in unison, not all his splendid military genius, not all the forces he could possibly command, could have compelled them to submission; but he must have returned to the semi-barbaric, semi-patriarchal pomp of his native kingdom, and given up for ever his ambitious dreams of Oriental conquest.

In this terrible affair the number of the Thebans slaughtered was not less than six thousand, while those sold into servitude exceeded thirty thousand persons; the plunder taken was immense, and more Makedonians fell than in any one of his great battles against Darios in after days,* for he buried no

* Diod. Sic. xvii. 14.

less than five hundred in the *polyandrion*, which was still to be seen in Pausanias' time, before the gates of the city called Electrai.

After this awful example, the Athenians tendered the most abject submission, and by the intervention of Democles were permitted to retain the Theban fugitives whom they had admitted, and whom the king had demanded of them; as well as the ten orators and statesmen, including Demosthenes, whom he had required to be delivered up as guilty of the rising before Chaironeia, and of the late revolt of Thebes; with the exception of Charidemos on whose banishment he insisted. The other states which had risen, as the Arkadians, Eleans and Aitolians, vied with each other in humiliating themselves before him; and Sparta alone standing sullenly aloof, all Greece now joined in the expedition against Persia, so that Alexander was at liberty to return to Makedonia, where he made all preparations for his departure.

In the spring of the third year of the one hundred and eleventh Olympiad, in the Archonship of Ktesikles and the consulship of Caius Sulpicius and Lucius Papirius, B. C., 334,* having left Antipater regent of Lakedaimonia, and governor of Greece in his absence, he set forth on the great expedition which, from that time forth, for above eight centuries, settled the question of Oriental invasion, much more, subjugation of Europe.

He marched by land over Thraké, crossing the Strymon and Pangaion hill, to Abdera and Maroneia, Greek colonies on the sea-shore, the latter of which still exists under the name of Marogna;† thence eastward across the Heros, now the Maritza, and the Melas, or modern Kavatza, at the head of the deep gulf of Saros, into what was then called the Thrakian Chersonese, where he took ship from Sestos to Abydos, near the entrance of the Propontis, or sea of Marmora, and transported his whole

* Diod. Sic. xvii. 17.

† Arrian. I. xi.

armament without loss or opposition to Asia Minor, although the Persian Satraps were at that very moment in command of a superior squadron in those waters. But the celerity of his motions had in fact taken them by surprise, and they were but now awakening, as if from a stupid sleep, to the sense of present danger. From Abydos he marched without delay southerly to the plain of Troy, where he performed funeral games in honor of his ancestor Achilles, and sacrifices to Priam, which should avert his wrath against the descendant of his slayer, Neoptolemos; as well as to the indigenous Gods of the place, Athene of the Ilias, and Zeus Herkeios, or the defender of walled cities. And here he made a muster and enumeration of the forces, with which he had come to attack a mighty empire, and a king, who, it was well known, could bring into the field above a million of men at a time Of Makedonian infantry, the flower of his whole army, these were found to be twelve thousand, of allies seven, and of Greek mercenaries five thousand; with five thousand Odrysian, Triballian and Illyrian targeteers and skirmishers, and one thousand Agrianian bow-men; of horse there were fifteen hundred Makedonians, led by Philotas, son of Parmenion, as many more Thessalians under Kalas the son of Hanpaios, six hundred other Hellenic cavalry, under Erigyios, and a corps of nine hundred Thrakian and Paionian guides commanded by Kassander. Besides these there were left in Europe with Antipater twelve thousand infantry, and eleven thousand five hundred horse.* I have chosen this enumeration, as it appears to be the most precise and elaborate, though the authorities differ but little; Arrian stating the forces at not much more than thirty thousand foot, and above four thousand horse;† while Plutarch says that the largest account‡ makes them thirty-four thousand foot and four thousand horse, the lowest thirty and five thousand.

* Diod. Sic. xvii. 17. † Arrian, xi. xii.

‡ Plut. Vit. Alex. xv.

So little discrepancy is rarely found among ancient authors, especially in regard of numbers, concerning which they are for the most part loose and incorrect.

With this apparently trivial force, he marched at once through an enemy's country, having few or no supplies on which to depend, and of course making war support war, except in so far as he was assisted by the Ionian cities, which would not seem to have been to any great extent, inasmuch as we do not hear of his being joined by any auxiliaries until after the battle of the Granikos. Their allegiance, however, appears to have sat very lightly on the provincial subjects of the Persian king, since we never hear of any resistance offered to any one of the various Greek invaders of the empire, unless by the organized forces of the different Satrapies; and if they lent no aid, at least they offered no opposition to an advance, or obstruction to a retreat. From the plain of Troy he now proceeded northward to Arisba, and thence to Percote, now Bergaz, on the Dardanelles; at the former of which places, according to Arrian, his army had been encamped during his visit to the Ilias; and it certainly seems far more probable that such should be the case, than that he should have marched thirty-five thousand men, a distance of over fifty miles, only to march them back again. With all the splendor of genius, however, Alexander possessed at least all its eccentricity; and it is by no means inconsistent with the known character, and subsequent pranks of the man, such as his march to the Oasis of Ammon, that he should have resolved to make his whole army participators in his sacrifices to the names of the ancestor whom it was his rage to imitate. No question, however, is involved unless it be whether the muster of the men was held at Arisba, or on the plain of Troy—a matter of no earthly import. From Percote he proceeded, still northward, to Lampsakos, at the issue of the Dardanelles from the sea of Marmora; and thence easterly along the sea-shore to the town of Kolonai, and the river Hermotas, near which he had learned that the Persians were encamped, and here he sent out a scouting party, consisting of the Apollonian squadron of the Royal companions, or horse life-guard, whose captain was Sokrates the son of Sathón, and four troops of the guides, the whole under the command of Amyntas, the son of Arrhabaios. From these he soon learned that the Persian generals, Rheomithres and Petines, and Niphates, and with them Spithridates Satrap of Lydia and Ionia, and Arsites governor of Phrygia on the Hellespont, lay encamped with all the Persian cavelry, and the Hellenic mercenaries, at the city of Zeleia, of which no traces have survived.

Here, it is said, when they held council what it was best to do —the arrival of Alexander being known—Memnon the Rhodian advised them to incur no danger in fighting there since the enemy were vastly superior in infantry, and animated by the presence of their king, while Darios was absent from his army—but, to devastate the country and retire, burning all the cities before the enemy; or, as Diodoros says—to take ship at once, embark all the troops, and transfer the war at once into Makedonia. Either counsel was sound and soldierly, but the latter—if, which I confess I doubt, it was ever given—would stamp Memnon the Rhodian as one of the first strategists of any day, as it would have been a diversion of the very highest order. Still I do not believe, according to my estimate of Alexander's character, that it would have produced the desired effect; since Antipater had a great power afoot, and it is certain that a renewal of Persian invasion would have produced a general Hellenik rising to the rescue.

It is almost to be regretted that it was not attempted, for we should then have had more certain proof, than we even now possess, of the real claims of Alexander to be considered, not only a great conqueror, but one of the world's greatest generals.

Whatever his advice was, at all events it was not taken; for, deeming it unworthy of Persians to retreat before an enemy, the chiefs determined to risk a battle in defence of the fords of the Granikos, a mountain torrent rising in the chain of Ida, and running across the Adrastean plain to the Propontis, into which it falls northward of Ryzikos. Anthon decides, on the authority of Chishull's travels in Turkey, that the Granikos is the modern *Demotiko*, and not, as is generally supposed, the larger river known as the *Ousvola.*

On hearing these tidings, Alexander drew up his infantry in a double phalanx, with his horse on his flanks and his baggage in the rear, detaching Hegelochos with a reconnoitering party in the van consisting of the horse called sarissophoroi, and five hundred light infantry. The armature of the sarissophoroi is not described anywhere that I can discover; but the sarissa was the famous pike of the Makedonian phalanx, from eighteen to twenty-four feet in length; a weapon which assuredly could not be hurled as a javelin, whence I conclude, that the cavalry armed with these must have charged them in rest like the men at arms of the middle ages, and have so ridden bodily in upon the enemy. These men soon gallopped back, reporting that the enemy were in force on the farther bank of the river, and apparently resolute to defend it; when Parmenion proposed to encamp at once, without attempting to force the passage, since, he said, and probably with truth, a Persian army would never dare to pass the night so near to a Greek encampment; proving, by his advice, that he was acquainted with the events of Xenophon's retreat, and had profited by the knowledge. But Alexander replied, that he had not crossed the Hellespont to be stopped by a paltry stream like the Granikos, and forthwith set his troops in battle order. And he did rightly in so doing; for his all was set upon a cast, and he well knew that he must carry every thing before him at a rush, or fail altogether. The prestige of a first victory was absolutely necessary to him, both for the confidence of his own men and the intimidation of the enemy. The least hesitancy on his part would have reversed the effect. There are cases in which seeming rashness is the surest prudence, and this was one of them.

The leading of the left he gave to Parmenion; retaining the right himself, in front* of which he set Philotas the son of Parmenion, with the royal companions of the life-guard, the archers, and the Agrianian javelineers; and to these he attached Amyntas with the *sarissophoroi*, or lancers, and the Paionian guides, with Socrates' squadron of the life-guard—all these on his extreme right, somewhat in advance. Next to these were ordered the Hypaspistai of the foot-guard, led by Nikanor son of Parmenion; and after these in regular succession, the phalanxes of Perdikkas son of Orontes, of Koinos son of Polemokrates, of Krateros son of Alexandros, of Amyntas son of Andromenes, and of Philip son of Amyntas. The first of the left wing, to the leftward, were the Thessalian horse, led by Kalas son of Harpalos; then the allied cavalry, under Philip son of Menelaos; and the Thrakians, whose leader was Agathon; and after these the infantry of Krateros, Meleager, and Philip, in phalanx, extending to the centre of the whole array.

The cavalry of the Persians were twenty thousand strong, and the Greek mercenaries little short of the same number; the former drawn up in front in a long phalanx upon the river banks, with the others in the rear; for the ground rose steep and commanding from the bank. But when they perceived Alexander—whom they easily recognized by the splendor of his arms, and the attention of those about him—advancing against their left, they strengthened that part of their line with many squadrons of horse. But when they were face to face on the adverse banks, the two armies stood still for a little space, in the awe and apprehension of that which was to follow; and there was solemn

* Anthon, Class. Dic., Art. Granicus. ‡ Arrian, I., xiv.

silence on both sides. For the Persians awaited the descent of the Makedonians into the river, that they might attack them as they issued from it on the further verge. Then Alexander leaped upon his horse, and calling to those about his person to follow, and show themselves good men that day, he desired Amyntas son of Arrhabaios to lead into the river with the guides and Paionians and one division of foot; and yet in advance of these Ptolemy the son of Philip, with Sokrates' squadron of the royal companions, to whose fortune it fell to lead all the cavalry on that day. Then himself, at the head of the right wing, he plunged into the stream, amid the blare of trumpets and the shout alalé for Enyalios, obliquing continually down the course of the river, that is to say toward the left; for marching from the west eastward, the Greek right was toward the mountains, whence the stream flows northerly to the sea—so that the Persians should not have it in their power to attack him in flank, as he ascended on the farther side, but that he might close as speedily as possible with their phalanx.

There is some difficulty in this passage, which is rendered almost word for word, with the exception of the parenthesis, from the Greek of Arrian; since, presuming the course of the river to be from south northwardly, as its general direction lies, and that of the Greek army from west eastwardly, and that the two armies stood face to face, as we are expressly told they did, to oblique from the right, down stream, or to the left, would be to do precisely what Arrian states the movement was intended to avoid. From this dilemma there is no escape, unless we understand the phrase " so that the Persians," &c., to have reference to the whole previous description, and not to the last clause relative to the obliquity of Alexander's own course.

The meaning would then be that he caused Ptolemy, with the life-guard, and Amyntas with the guides and others, who

* Arrian I., xv.

were in the advance, to charge perpendicularly on the Persian left, while he in person obliqued from their rear upon the centre, so that the attack of his van should cover his own flank, while crossing the torrent. This reading is also confirmed by what follows, since it is evident that Amyntas and Sokrates were in action long before the rest; the whole constituting a very fine specimen of an attack by the oblique method to the left; which, as I have previously observed, was first invented by Epaminondas, though in both his grand victories he operated contrariwise, or from the left to the right.

As Amyntas and Sokrates approached the bank, a great shower of javelins fell among them from the Persians above; and as they scaled it a fierce crush and concourse of horses followed, these forcing their way up, those pressing them bodily backward; and still the Persian missiles pelted them with arrowy hail, while the Greeks fought with charged lances. At first the Greeks suffered severely, for they were much inferior in numbers, and were fighting from lower ground, and the slippery river bed, and the whirling current; and, moreover, the best of the enemy were mustered there, Memnon himself, with his sons and followers. And the first of the Greeks who came hand to hand with the Persians, were cut to pieces, fighting gallantly, all but a few who fell back on Alexander.

For he was now close at hand, with the whole right wing, and he dashed, himself foremost of all, into the thick of the enemy's horse, where all their leaders fought, and the melée around him raged fast and furious; while one by one the other divisions of the Makedonians passed over with no further difficulty. It was now a cavalry action altogether, and yet it resembled rather the shock of infantry. For it was a complete melée, horses and men all closely wedged together, with room to strike and stab, but scant room to parry, the Greeks still bearing up to win the plain, the Persians struggling hard to force them down into the torrent. Great feats of arms were done that day, and the affair more resembled a passage of arms in the fourteenth century than a Greek cavalry affair; even as Alexander himself, in many respects, partook more of the character of a Norman Paladin than of a Hellenic general.

But still the Greeks won their way foot by foot, owing to their greater personal strength, and to their fighting with lances of cornel wood instead of javelins. Here it fell out that Alexander's spear was splintered to the grasp, and he called on Aretis, the royal equerry, to give him another, but his spear was shivered also and he was fighting brilliantly with the truncheon, which he held aloft, and bade the king ask another, when Demarates, a Korinthian, one of the Companions, lent him his own. With this, seeing Mithridates, Darios' son-in-law, fighting in the front, he rode at him, and striking him in the face unhorsed him. At the same instant Rhoisakes cut Alexander through the crest of his helmet, shearing away one of his long white plumes, quite down to the hair with his scymetar, but without injuring his head; him too, the king rode down, charging him with his lance through the corslet into the breastbone; but, as he did so, Spithridates was behind him with his scymetar uplifted to strike him through the broken casque, when Kleitos, the son of Dropidas, surnamed the Black, anticipated the blow, smiting the Persian on the shoulder with such a swordsweep, that his right arm fell to the earth, hewn asunder, with the hilt still grasped in the quivering fingers.

But other horsemen now came up apace, and the strife was equalized; and, as the cavalry was intermingled with light infantry which galled the Persians very severely, finding themselves unable to bear the brunt of the western lances, they gave way in the centre, where Alexander fought in person, and fled at speed, followed by both their wings. About a thousand of the horse fell, for Alexander would not pursue them far; but wheeled upon the phalanx of the Greek mercenaries, who had not moved from the place where they stood, rather through wonder at the fury of the onslaught, than from any resolute determination. And against these he brought up his own phalanx, and, at the same time, charging them with his cavalry on all points at once, cut them in two, as nearly as possible, in the centre, so that not a man of them escaped, unless it was one by chance who lay concealed among the slain; and of them there were taken but two thousand. Of the generals fell Niphates and Petines, and Spithridates, Satrap of Lydia, and the governor of Kappadokia, Mithrobarzanes, and Mithridates, Darios' son-in-law, and Arboupales, son of Darios, son of Artoxerxes, and Pharnakes, brother of Darios' wife, and Omares, leader of the mercenaries. But Arsites escaped from the melée, and fled into Phrygia, where he died by his own hand, fancying himself to be the cause of the overthrow of the Persian army. The Makedonians lost in all about one hundred and twenty men, of whom twenty-five were royal companions slain in the first onset, and sixty of the others cavalry, the infantry having been but partially engaged, and that only at the close of the action.

In this battle there are several things worthy of note; first—that it is the earliest battle on record, which was decided by cavalry, and more particularly by Greek cavalry, which were in general nearly as inefficient an arm of service as the Roman horse; and secondly—which is not generally understood in considering Alexander's victories, that beside the Persian cavalry he was opposed by a Greek force, unquestionably Peloponnesians, for they furnished nine-tenths of the mercenaries, nearly equal to the whole of his own infantry in number and not much inferior in quality, yet so ill were they led that their resistance was scarce worthy of notice.

But the fact is simply this that now, for the first time, war had so far advanced as to be, among the Greeks at least, a science; among the Romans it scarcely became one two centuries later. To be the bravest of the brave was no longer sufficient, nor to set men face to face in the field, and see who would bear the brunt the longest, the general aspiring only to be the hardest hitter, the height of strategy. Among the Greeks, as is the case in all free nations, every man was brave, and when the tug of war came between them, leading was everything.

In consequence of this, armies were properly constituted, and with a due proportion of cavalry to infantry, a point which never before had been attended to in Greece, and never was in Rome to the latest day of her existence. The army with which Alexander entered Persia was in fact formed nearly on the same principles and in the same proportions with Napoleon's divisions or rather *corps d' armèe*, each of which, complete in every arm of the service, consisted as nearly as possible of twenty thousand foot to four thousand horse, being in the rates of one mounted trooper to every five infantry soldiers, while in the legions even of the best period of Rome under Marius, Sylla, and Cæsar, there were but three hundred horse to six thousand foot, or in the ratio of one to twenty.

Under Alexander, also, artillery first came into general use, borrowed as it would seem from the Sicilian Greeks, who in that arm were never surpassed or even equalled. Sieges were no longer carried on by the slow and lingering operations of blockade, with walls of countervallation and circumvallation, but the ramparts were shaken by the ram, which operating on the principle, not of direct force, but of continuous vibration, produced effects almost equal to that of cannon shot; the parapets were demolished by stones of several tons weight, hurled from the potent machines, and the defenders swept from the battlements, by greater javelins than could be sent from any human arm, slung from the mighty catapults. A few years later than this field artillery was first employed by Machanidas, the tyrant of Sparta, in his battle against Philopoimen, but it was then proved unsuccessful, and never came into general use.

It is worthy of remark here that Alexander, like Hannibal and Napoleon, placed the greatest reliance in his horse, the former leading his own in person against horse or foot indiscriminately, contrary to the usual custom of his times, and both the latter almost invariably deciding the crisis of every action by a crushing charge of cuirassiers. The last and greatest of the three never hesitated to express his conviction that equal numbers of horse, equally well led, must overpower infantry, and certainly his splendid cavalry as led by Excelmans, Milhaud, and first in excellence though last in place, Murat, went far to justify the assertion; and the battle of Fere Champenoise, in which twenty thousand Russian horse, with horse artillery, annihilated an equal force of veteran French infantry duly provided with heavy guns, seems to place his opinion almost beyond dispute. The contrary idea, which has so generally prevailed since the origin of fire-arms and the decline of chivalry, seems to arise from the fact that the expense of keeping up large cavalry forces is so enormous that none but Nomadic tribes, the whole population of which are cavaliers from their cradle, or despotic governments can sustain it. The more democratic the governments, and the more impatient of taxation, the less powerful are they in cavalry; and to this reason is it that England and the United States, the people of both which countries are unquestionably and immeasurably superior as individual horsemen, to the French, have never been famous for this arm of service, and probably never will be so. During the whole peninsular war the British army accomplished little with their horse, and what they did chiefly by the Hanoverians of the King's German legion; and though at Waterloo the splendid exploit of Ponsonby's division which destroyed a column of five thousand foot and rendered eighty guns unserviceable for the day, and the splendid final charge of the heavy horse of the household brigade, are worthily distinguished among great cavalry affairs, still they are the exceptions to the rule which centuries have proved true from the days of Cressi and Poictiers to those of Alliwal and Sobraon, that it is on the infantry of England that her military power principally rests. To this it is that the true cause must be attributed of the small use made by Lord Wellington of this arm, which has led to the belief that he undervalues its utility and dislikes it in action—that he never possessed it in sufficient number to launch it effectually against the overwhelming superiority of his enemy; and precisely the same is the case with the United States, the dragoons of which alone of their troops, with the single exception of May's charge at Resaca de la Palma, achieved little distinction, simply because they had no opportunity of doing so, in consequence of their being so cruelly outnumbered; and even now, when it is obvious to every military eye, that one horse regiment on the frontiers of Mexico, and in the newly conquered provinces, is equal for real action, duty and utility, to three of foot, and that the equestrian Indians can never be put down effectually, without mounted rifles, and probably lancers also, so great is the senseless and absurd jealousy of expense in this vital matter, that instead of augmenting this valuable arm the recent legislatures have diminished it; and for a climax of absurdity have dismounted the superb horse-artillery, which was second to that of no other country, and which really won every pitched battle in Mexico, with the exception perhaps of Cherubusco.

After burying his own dead, to return to the field of the Granikos, with the most distinguished honors, and granting the rites of sepulture even to the bodies of the mercenary Greeks, whose prisoners were sent in chains, to be kept at hard labor in Makedonia, as traitors to the cause and name of Greeks, Alexander showed equal prudence and sagacity in his conduct both to the conquered country and to the independent nations of

Greece, treating the former with singular lenity and grace, and paying the greatest attention to those of the latter, whom he the most suspected of disaffection. For he did not attempt to alter the forms of their ancient polity, or even the time-honored names of their governmental officers, but contented himself merely with appointing friends of his own, in many instances native Asiatics, to the vacant Satrapies, and causing the same amount of tribute formerly paid to Darios to be paid into his own treasury. To this it is to be ascribed that in no instance was he troubled with anything like guerilla warfare, and that he never to the end of his career met any considerable inconvenience or detriment from the insubordination or rising of the provinces which had readily submitted to his arms, and which accustomed to be slaves, cared little whether they were called the slaves of Alexander or of Darios, no personal penalty or suffering being attached to either condition. In this respect he showed himself much wiser and more politic than his great successor, and only equal in the extent of conquest—Napoleon, concerning whom it has been justly observed that, the intolerable insolence and overbearing of the French prefects and officials who made every individual personally feel the degradation of his people, did more to alienate the minds of the conquered, especially of the Spaniards and Germans, than all the real grievances he inflicted on their countries, than all the deprivation of liberty and independence. To the Athenians he sent three hundred Persian Panoplies, which he directed to be offered to Athene in the Akropolis, with the inscription, "Alexander and the other Greeks, the Lakedaimonians excepted, these from the barbarians who dwell in Asia."

These things ordered, he marched southerly to Sardis, which being delivered to him on conditions, he suffered to retain its independence, though he garrisoned its Acropolis, which was a very strong place, and on which he erected a temple to Zeus

Olympios, with Makedonians, under Pausanias, one of the royal companions. The people of Magnesia and Tralles voluntarily surrendered their cities, and after sending out Parmenion and Antimachos the son of Agathocles, to reduce the Aiolian and Ionian cities, which were still subject to the Persians, under orders to subvert the oligarchies and establish democracies, under their own laws, and with the same tribute to himself which they had formerly paid to the Persians, he marched himself, by way of Ephesus, on the town of Miletos, now Palatska, which he took after a sharp resistance, enlisting the Greek mercenaries who had defended it, in his own army, and restoring their liberty to all the citizens who had not fallen in the storming of the city. There he disbanded his naval forces, and destroyed his ships, finding them overmatched by the Persian fleet, which he now resolved to put down by occupying all their maritime cities, so that they should have no place whence to draw their supplies or to procure sailors; and with this intent he marched through Karia to Halikarnassos, now Boudroun, on the gulf of Stanca, where he had learned that a large force of Persians and mercenaries was collected, taking all the cities on his route, and then laid siege to that important fortress and seaport. During the siege he attempted the neighboring stronghold of Myndos by a forced night march and sudden onslaught, but was repulsed; whereupon he resolved to waste no time on it, but turning on Halikarnassos, sat down in form before it. The defence was very long and resolute; for the garrison made constant and daring sorties, in order to destroy the works and machines of the enemy, and several times partially succeeded; and wherever the walls and towers were shaken by the rams, they built up stone curtains within, before the outer defences fell or the breaches became passable. Once they sallied in force at several points at once, and kindled such a blaze among the machinery as compelled Alexander to charge in person, when a terrible slaughter followed, and they were at length driven in, the drawbridge breaking down under the weight of the combatants, and the gates being all but carried by the Makedonians, who would have entered pell-mell with the fugitives, had not the portals been closed prematurely, to the exclusion of many of the men, who were slaughtered under the walls in great numbers. It appears that the city might have been carried at this time had not Alexander called off his army, not desiring to take it by storm, could he gain possession of it on conditions. But Orondobates and Memnon, the Persian leaders, finding that they could in no sort hold out much longer, fired the city and fell back into the citadel, when the Makedonians entered through the breaches made by the flames, cut the incendiaries to pieces, and took those to quarter whom they found in their own houses. Not choosing to waste time in reducing the heights, Alexander now razed the city to the ground, and passed onward, leaving Ptolemais, with three thousand foot and two thousand horse, all mercenaries, to keep Phrygia in subjection ; and appointed Ada, the daughter of Hekatomnos and the widow of Hydrieus, who had given up to him her town of Alinda, and named her son Alexander after him, to rule over the whole satrapy of Karia. From Halikarnassos he sent home all the newly married men of the Makedonians, to winter with their wives in their own country, under the command of officers who were themselves in the same condition, whom he entrusted with the charge of bringing back the men, and of levying a fresh force both of horse and foot, as large as they should find it possible, in that region. Thence he proceeded in person through Lydia and Pamphylia ; taking all the seaport towns, so as to render the navy of the Persians useless. On reaching Phaselis, where he lay encamped for a few days, he discovered a conspiracy against himself, at the head of which was Alexandros the commander of the Thessalian horse, who was brother of Heramenes and Arrhabaios, who had been participants in the murder of Philip, which was speedily suppressed, when he proceeded, by way of Perge, a short distance inland to Side, on the coast, and thence up the Eurymedon to Aspendos, a city the ruins of which have never been identified, though the river is well known as the Kapri Sou. From Aspendos he countermarched inland through the province of Pisidia and the passes of Mount Tauros to the city of Kelainai, on the Marsyas, a tributary of the Maiander, where stood of old the palace of the younger Kyros, encountering a stout resistance and some sharp fighting from the barbarian mountain, so far north as Gordion, a town on the river Sangaris, now Sakaria, flowing through Bithynia into the Black Sea, which stood probably not very far from the modern city of Eskiebecher, within sixty miles of the northern coast. Here he solved the oracle by cutting the famous Gordian knot, and met the men who had been absent on furlough, and who now returned, true to their time, with reinforcements of three thousand Makedonian foot, and seven hundred and fifty horse, of Makedon, Thessaly and Elis. While at this place he also received an Athenian embassy, praying for the liberation of the Athenian mercenaries captured at the Granikos; but though he treated the envoys with great courtesy, he denied their request, judging it imprudent, while the war with Persia was still at its height, to pardon Hellenes taken in arms against Hellas.* Thus ended the first year of the war; and immediately on the opening of spring, in the fourth year of the hundred and first Olympiad, B. C. 333, he broke up from Gordion, and proceeded south-eastward to Ankura in Galatea, now Angura, a large city and pashalick of Anatolia, to Mazaka in Kappadokia, now Kaisariah in Karaman, a fine town on the Halys, now Kizil Irmak or red river, flowing northerly into the Black Sea, and dividing Anatolia from Roum. From Mazaka, learning that Darios had now raised a great army, and was in full march to

* Arrian, I., xxx.

meet him somewhere about the passes between the Mount Amanos, Almadag of the modern geographies, and the gulf of Scanderoon or Aiasso, with a view to deliver battle without the confines of Upper Asia, he struck a direct southern course by Tyana, supposed to be the modern Ketch Hissar, at the foot of the central Tauros chain; and from thence, still in the same direction, to Tarsos, famous in later days as the birth-place of the great Apostle Paul, upon the river Kydnos—then a powerful stream, but now a mere rivulet, scarcely navigable even by small boats—being anxious to anticipate the Greeks, and occupy that noble city. Here he was detained several days by a severe illness contracted by bathing when over-heated in the ice-cold waters of that mountain torrent, down which three centuries later Kleiopatra sailed in her golden galley in such pompous state to meet the bold triumvir Antony. It was during this attack that he displayed one of those splendid gleams of magnanimous generosity which are the redeeming features of his variable and inconsistent character; for being warned by Parmenion that Philip his Akarnanian physician had been bribed to poison him, he calmly quaffed his potion while the astonished leech was reading the inculpatory letter. An act of generosity and confidence equally creditable to both parties, and justified by the result.

Between the Mount Amanos and the sea are two narrow defiles, with a plain between them, much broken itself by ridges of knolls and hillocks, and intersected by torrents flowing from the mountains. Of these the westernmost, just without Tarsos, is known as the Kilikian gates, the easternmost, near the town of Issus, now Aiasso, as the Assyrian gates, the word gates, *pylai*, being constantly used, as in the famous instance of Thermopylai, to signify a narrow gorge or defile between two mountains, or one mountain and the sea. To the second of these he despatched Parmenion to guard the passes, with all the allied and mercenary foot, the Thrakians of Sitalkes, and the Thessalian horse, and himself, so soon as he was sufficiently recovered from his illness, he advanced from Tarsos, which, though now merely a wretched Turkish village, retains its ancient name, to Anchialos, a city which being ill situated and without a harbor, has entirely disappeared from history. Here he saw the monument of Sardanapalos, with a statue of that prince in the act of clapping his hands, and an epigram in Assyrian verse, which is thus admirably rendered by Byron in his fine tragedy named from the royal voluptuary, whom he has chosen as his hero ;

Sardanapalos,
The king, and son of Anacyndaraxes,
In one day built Anchialos and Tarsos.
Eat, drink, and play. The rest 's not worth a fillip.

Leaving Anchialos he came to Soli, where he celebrated solemn games with musical and gymnastic exercises, and torch races, and a grand procession of all his forces under arms, in honor of Asklepios, and thence to Magarsis, where he sacrificed to the Magarsian Athene. Leaving Magarsis he again halted at Mallos, now Cape Malo, which was said to be an Argive colony, and to which he therefore remitted the tribute formerly paid by them to Darios. While he tarried at this place, tidings reached him that the king of Persia was close at hand with all his forces, at a place called Soki, said to be two days' march, fifty or sixty miles from the Assyrian gates, on hearing which he at once collected his army and marched past Issos, and through the defile to Myriandros, a flourishing town and seaport on the gulf of Scanderoon, the modern site of which is undefined, where he arrived on the second day after the receipt of the tidings, and where he was detained in his camp all the third by a violent storm of rain accompanied by a violent tornado.

And here, before detailing the second great battle of Alexander, it will not be amiss to pause a moment and observe with how consummate an union of military skill and political shrewdness the young Makedonian prince had proceeded. No rash impulse of inconsiderate valor, no greed of rapid and continuous victory, no undue thirst of present glory at the risk of future disaster, had tempted him to dash on in pursuit of his immediate object, the overthrow of the great king, until the whole country in his rear had been subverted, pacified, restored, and reinvigorated by just and merciful measures, and left in the secure and permanent occupation of a sufficient force of foreign Greeks to render any hope of counter revolution, particularly when backed by the contingents of the liberated Ionic and Aiolic cities, vain and impracticable.

All the western coast, from opposite Byzantion, or Constantinople, to the Levantine sea, all the southern coast, from Rhodes to the Syrian frontier, had been first taken into secure possession, thence by skilful marches and countermarches inland, the whole interior of Asia Minor, from the Dardanelles and Archipelago to the Kizil Irmak, or Red River, and the Syrian defiles had been conquered, and reduced to perfect obedience in the space of a single campaign. This tract of land, including the entire districts of Anatolia, Karamania, and a portion of Roum, or nine-tenths of the whole Peninsula, if it may be so called, between the Black Sea, the Archipelago, and the Levant, above five hundred miles in length by above three hundred in width, exceeded by at least one half the whole area of Greece, from the northern confines of Alexander's own dominions to the southern extremity of the Peloponnesos or Morea. It was occupied by a powerful, civilized, and highly cultivated race of men, was thickly strewn with the wealthiest and most magnificent cities and seaports in the then known world, and probably contributed the largest portion of the entire revenues of his empire to the treasury of Xerxes. This splendid territory he had not cursorily vanquished by the terror of his arms, to rise against him so soon as his back was turned, or take arms against his retreat if defeated; nor had he alienated the temper of the inhabitants by cruelty or wanton depredation; but by clemency, justice, and the imposition of moderate tributes, had converted it into his own property and his fast friend, a rich granary, storehouse, and treasury, from which to derive supplies of all kinds, a firm basis for future military operations, and a ready way for retreat should disaster overtake him.

How different from the wanton rapacity and savage pillage of the French marshals of Napoleon in Spain, by which they rendered every peasant in the land the mortal foe of France, ready to catch at the sound of the first passing bell as a war tocsin, and all athirst for vengeance till *Guerra al Cuchillo*, war to the knife, became alike their watchword and their battle cry! How different from the mad advance of the great Corsican himself, into the hostile heart of devastated but unconquered Russia, leaving Germany subdued, not pacified, in his rear, Hungary refractory, Poland unsatisfied, without a base of operations, without magazines, supplies, friends, in the country he had traversed, leaving to himself no alternative but complete victory or utter ruin, no retreat, but a flight through fifteen hundred miles of ravaged and exhausted country, with every city ready to become a Moscow, every river a Beresina, in his route.

The object of this great work he had accomplished at a loss of men certainly not exceeding three hundred, of all arms, in actual fighting, so that it is probable that after taking into consideration all the garrisons he had left behind him, and all the deaths of men whether under arms or by casualties, as well as the reinforcements he had received from Greece, and the enlistment of Greek mercenaries brought over to his own side from the adverse party, his army was increased rather than diminished, and that the force with which he stood prepared to dispute the diadem of Asia with Darios, was numerically larger than that with which he forced the passage of the Granikos, and now much stronger in that confidence in themselves, that proud and positive *morale*, which so often is the giver of victory.

Darios up to this time had determined, according to the advice of his best counsellors, to await Alexander's issue from the defiles, and give him battle in the open champaign country of Assyria, where the vast plains would allow him to deploy his almost innumerable hordes, and perhaps to overflank and surround the enemy, while the whole region would be favorable to the manœuvres of his powerful and splendid cavalry. And he was strongly urged by Amyntas, the son of Antiochos, who had deserted to him from Alexander, by no means to move from that district, and at first he took counsel and waited, though impatiently. But the tardiness of Alexander's movements, caused by his illness at Tarsos, his pomps and processions at Soli, and the sending out of an expedition against the Kilikian mountaineers, shook his resolve; and, with the characteristic arrogance of a vain barbarian, he came to the belief that Alexander was afraid of him, and would not advance against him, if he were not already in full flight. He determined, therefore, in spite of the reasoning and assurance of Amyntas, who insisted that Alexander was eager to meet not to avoid him, to march into the passes, where he was neither able to avail himself of his superiority in archers and javelineers, by deploying them in open order, nor to make use of his splendid horse, but gave himself, as it were, shackled into the hands of an enemy who certainly was not one into whose way one would willingly cast unnecessary advantages.

He entered, therefore, the defiles of Mount Amanos, known as the Assyrian gates, while Alexander was actually at Myriandros, to the southeast of the passes, and interposed between him and his capital, and marched to Issos, now Aiasso, having thus accidentally got into the rear of the Greek army. So soon as the Makedonian heard this intelligence, which at first he was inclined to doubt, as scarcely able to credit such an excess of good fortune, he embarked a few of the Royal Companions in a thirty-oared galley, and sent them by sea to reconnoitre, which could be done so, much more readily than by land, since the coast line here is much indented by deep bays and gulfs, from headland to headland of which it is but a brief sail. These soon returning with information that Darios was already, as it were, in the hollow of his hand, he was vehemently rejoiced and collecting all his officers harangued them on the nature of the contest which was now imminent, and encouraged them by the enumerated advantages he possessed, especially as compared with the deficiency of Xenophon's army in spite of which that gallant partizan had resisted all dispiriting influences, and conquered the Asiatics in every encounter, although he had no Thessalian, nor Boiotian, nor Peloponnesian, nor Makedonian horse, nor Thrakians, nor in fact any cavalry worthy of consideration, nor any archery or slingers, with the exception of a handful of Rhodians and Kretans.

Then having caused his men to dine and having sent forward a few horse and bowmen to reconnoitre the road, he retraced his steps with his whole army as soon as it became dark, and entering the defiles at midnight posted his sentinels on the cliffs and halted until morning, to give his men some repose before the terrible struggle to which he looked forward in the calm confidence of certain victory.

And now the time had arrived when the two royal rivals should meet in the field face to face, for as soon as it was daylight Alexander led his men, with his heavy foot in front, his cavalry following these and his baggage in the rear of all, through the defiles ; at first, where the pass was very narrow, in an exceedingly deep narrow-fronted column, as the nature of the ground compelled him to do; and gradually, as the gorge expanded, extending his front both to the right and left, by bringing up his rearward files, each by each, on the outside of either flank till the phalanx had acquired its due proportion both of rank and file. At this period, the usual depth of the phalanx, as constituted by Philip, was sixteen men in file; and it does not appear that any deviation ever took place from this formation, the old tactic by subdivision into enomoties, pentecostyes and lochoi, having been entirely discontinued, and remodelled in the recent or Makedonian phalanx. Kallisthenes, the sophist, who was present at this battle, states that in the first instance, the phalanx in defiling through these gorges was drawn up thirty-two deep, then sixteen, and lastly eight; but Polybios* has demonstrated, by measurement of the ground and comparison of numbers, that the whole of his description is an absurdity. He was himself no soldier, and of course wrote from hearsay. It is, moreover, evident that the phalanx *could* not be manœuvred in this manner; since the number of shields in file was invariably the same, and not that only, but the same men were invariably file-leaders and-rear rankmen; consequently, when it was necessary to contract the front, so many files as occasion required halted on either flank, while the rest marched onward, and then obliquing inward from the left and right, formed a second column, with as many shields in file as the first, and so on *ad infinitum*; and again, when it was desirable to extend the front, the second column obliqued to the left and right from the centre and marched up, on the outside, to their original places on the flanks, and so on with third, fourth, and fifth columns in succession to the end, till the proper front and formation was again recovered. Thus the depth of the *phalanx* was never really altered; though in passing bridges, defiles, or the like, it could be formed in

* Polyb. xii. 17.

column of any number of sub-divisions, each consisting of any given number of shields in rank, but immutably of the same number in file. I do not mean that the depth of *all* phalanxes was the same, since we have already seen them varying from eight shields of Athenians at Marathon, to fifty of Thebans at Leuktra, but that on whatever number of men in files it was resolved to fight, on that they invariably manœuvred.

For it must be observed that pivot movements were unknown to the Greeks, and that they never marched, as we say, by the flank, and bringing up this or that shoulder, wheeled into line to the front, owing to their method of hand to hand engaging, which made it absolutely necessary that the best man and steadiest soldier should be the leader, and the second best the rear rank-man of every file, whether on the march or in action. The field of battle it appears was about fourteen stadia in width from the sea on the left, to the mountains on the right, and according to Polybios,* one stadium will contain sixteen hundred men arrayed sixteen deep, when in open marching order—six feet being allowed to each soldier—or twice that number with their shields touching in the *synaspismos*, or close battle order.

The number of men requisite to form the true Makedonian phalanx was sixteen thousand men, or a thousand shields in rank by sixteen in file, although any number exceeding thirty-two and divisible by four could be formed on the principle of the phalanx. I conceive it probable, therefore, that, assuming the number of forty-two thousand assigned to Alexander's infantry as correct, the number of heavy foot was thirty-two thousand, or a double phalanx, the remaining ten thousand being archery, slingers, and javelineers, who did not fight in line. These men would in battle array have occupied ten stadia, leaving four more for the archery and horse.

These latter formed eight deep, which Polybios states to be

* Polyb xii. 17, &c., de Callisthenis Imperitia, Arrian, II. viii.

their true tactics, occupied a stadium to each eight hundred men in marching order, or half that distance in array of battle, leaving the necessary intervals for their manœuvres and counter-marchings. The whole force of cavalry would have required therefore about three stadia for their front, leaving one stadium, or something over, for the advance and retreat of the light troops to the van and rear, independent of the regular intervals.

I think, therefore, that we may assume this to have been Alexander's disposition in the battle of Issos. To himself, as usual, he retained the command of the right wing, giving to Parmenion the leading of the left, along the sea shore; for it must be remembered, that by the descent of Darios by the defiles of Mount Amanos into his rear, the natural position of the armies was reversed, so that the Greeks were fighting with their faces to the west and their backs to Babylonia, and the Persians *vice versâ.*

First on the right toward the mountains, the horse not having as yet deployed from the rear, he placed the companions of the foot-guard, and the hypaspistai under Nikanor son of Parmenion, next to these the band of Koinos, and next—forming the left of the right, and centre of the whole army—that of Perdikkas. On the extreme left was the band of Amyntas, then that of Ptolemaios; and last, touching Perdikkas' men in the centre, that of Meleagros. The infantry of the left, generally, were under the direction of Krateros, as the whole wing was under that of Parmenion, whose orders were on no account to leave an interval between himself and the sea shore, as it was certain that Darios would endeavor to profit by it, in his vast numerical superiority, to turn and envelop both flanks of the Greeks.

So soon as the pass opened out into a species of small plain, intersected by the mountain torrent Pinaros, now the Deli Son, Alexander brought up the royal companions of the life-guard, with the Thessalian and Makedonian horse, from the rear to his extreme right, and ordered all the Peloponnesian and allied cavalry to form on Parmenion's left along the sea. In the meanwhile Darios learning the approach of Alexander, pushed twenty thousand foot and thirty thousand horse across the river, using them as a screen wherewith to mask his movements and cover his army, while he was arraying it in line. And first he drew up his Greek mercenaries, thirty thousand strong, opposite to the phalanx of the Makedonians, and next to these on either hand sixty thousand Kardakians, who, like the Greeks, were armed as heavy infantry—for the ground on which they were marshalled sufficed for the formation of this number of men in single phalanx—and on his own left he pushed forward twenty thousand men along the crest of the mountains, who turned Alexander's left, and, as he marched onward, actually threatened his rear; but all the remainder of his innumerable multitudes, said to amount to six hundred thousand fighting men, archers, javelineers, and slingers, were drawn up in a huge, useless mass, in the rear of the Greeks and of those barbarians, who were formed in phalanx. This done, he recalled the thirty thousand horse who had cloaked his movements, and drew the greater part of them up in front of his right, where the ground was most suitable to cavalry movements, as being level along the sea, retaining a few squadrons on his own left, near the mountains, until finding the nature of the ground to be impracticable to cavalry, he detached them also to his right.

Immediately, on perceiving the immense force of cavalry to which Parmenion was now affronted, fearing that his left would be broken, he detached all the Thessalians to his support, causing them to ride around by the rear, instead of crossing his front; so that the movement might be unsuspected by Darios; in front of his own horse, on the right, he drew up the guides under Protomachos, and the Paionians led by Ariston, and the archery of Antiochos; but the Agrianians of Attalos, with some cavalry and archers, he sent against the enemy who had passed along the hills and occupied a projecting spur, completely in the rear of his right; so that his left wing was formed in two lines, one facing westward against the Persians beyond the river, and the others eastward, against the barbarians on the hills. He added also to his left the Kretan archery, and the Thrakians of Sitalkes; and behind the whole line he ordered the foreign mercenaries. But finding that his own phalanx was not sufficiently solid, he ordered up two regiments of the companions—that called the Anthemousian, commanded by Persidas the son of Menestheus, and that called the Leugaian, under Pantordanos son of Kleander, from the centre to the right, countermarching them secretly by the rear.

But now when the barbarians on the hill made no effort to descend upon his rear, he caused them to be charged by the Agrianians and some archery, which broke them with ease, and drove them up to the very summit of the cliffs, completely out of arrow shot of the army; after which he contented himself by observing them with a body of three hundred horse, which sufficed to hold them in check all day; and withdrawing the archers and Agrianians, supported by some of his Greek mercenaries, he pushed them forward on his right, in order to outflank the Persians.

Darios did not lead forward to the attack, but remained on the defensive along the steep and rocky banks of the river, which he had in some places protected by palisades; and observing this, Alexander galloped along his front, calling upon the men to show their valor, and addressing not only all the leaders, but the captains of squadrons and battalions, even of the mercenaries and foreigners, by name, when any one was conspicuous for peculiar courage or merit; and loud shouts went up on all sides, as they called to him not to delay, but to fall on at once.

Then he advanced, but very gradually, restraining the ardor

of his troops, and keeping them at a slow march, lest the front of the phalanx should be disordered by a more rapid movement; but soon as he came within the range of missiles, he led in person with his right wing at an impetuous and fiery charge, in order to come quicker hand to hand, and so to evade the shot of javelins and arrows, and he crossed the river in one headlong rush, and scattered the Persians of the left as with a thunderbolt. But the Greek mercenaries of Darios charged home against the Makedonian phalanx, where it was left uncovered, in consequence of being separated from the right, which had charged so furiously with Alexander that it could not keep abreast of them, owing to the pace of its advance, which was of necessity more leisurely, and the broken and rocky nature of part of the ground which it had to traverse; and the conflict here was both furious and stubborn, for the mercenaries of Darios fought desperately to prevent the Makedonians from ascending the river banks, and to retrieve the victory, jeopardized by the flight of their left wing. The Makedonians, on the other hand, were inspired by a desire to emulate the splendor of Alexander's onslaught on the left, and by the pride of maintaining their reputation, as hitherto unconquered and unconquerable in the field. Besides this, moreover, there had always been a rivalry of races, between the Makedonians and the pure Hellenic races. And the struggle between them was long and desperately maintained at push of pike, with the bronze bucklers clanging in the shock of the close conflict, and the loud pæans echoing in the Greek tongue on both sides, and the wild battle clamor, *alale*, and great mutual slaughter. And there fell Ptolemaios son of Seleukos, and many others, most valiant and distinguished men of the Makedonians, to the number of a hundred and twenty; nor did the Greeks yield a foot, much less turn to fly, until the victorious right of Alexander having pushed their left bodily off the field, so that their whole flank was exposed, wheeled upon them, seeing that its own centre was hard pressed, and charging home full on their shield arms, cut them to pieces with a frightful carnage.

Up to this time the Persian horse opposed to Alexander's left had fought with exceeding gallantry, for not waiting the advance of the Greeks, they had dashed forward, crossed the river in full career, where it rushed over a shallow bed near the sea, and charged manfully upon the squadrons of the Thessalians. These in like manner charged, and to the shock of spears succeeded a close and terrible melée, with broadsword, scymetar, and battle-axe, until, Darios having already fled, and the Greek mercenaries been cut to pieces on their left, they too turned rein, and fled headlong, in the utmost rout and confusion. The roads were bad, as after the heavy rains which had lately fallen they were all poached up and trampled into mire by the march of the myriads who had passed over them; and the horses, oppressed by the weight of their own ponderous armature, and the burthen of their riders, armed all *cap-a-piè*, labored fearfully in the flight. And the fierce Thessalians pressed on them savagely—for they had suffered in the battle, and now had vengeance, which they worked out with bloody execution—and as it was no retreat, but an entire rout, the Persians were disorganized, and as many died trampled to death by their own comrades as fell beneath the bloody spears of the Thessalian lancers. Darios himself did not his duty on that day as a general, a soldier, or a man—for so soon as his left wing was broken by Alexander's headlong charge, long before the best portion of his forces were beaten; almost, indeed, before they were in action—he turned his chariot, and fled in it, so long as the ground was level, at the utmost speed of his horses; but, so soon as he got into broken ground, on a led horse; leaving his shield, his bow, and his royal robe behind him; and what is far more discreditable to his name and character—since even the weakest and most cowardly of animals will fight to the death in defence of their females—abandoning his mother, wife, and daughters, who, according to the Persian habit, had followed him in the campaign, and were taken with his treasures in the forsaken camp.

Alexander pursued him hotly with his cavalry until it was dark night, but was unable to overtake him; for his pursuit had been delayed by the sturdy resistance of the Greek force and of the Persian cavalry—for with sound judgment and soldierly coolness, he did not withdraw a man from the immediate front of battle until the whole force was broken and destroyed.

In the conflict and the carnage which followed it, there fell of the Persians, Arsames, and Rheomithres, and Artizues, the leaders of the cavalry at the Granikos; and Sabakes the satrap of Egypt, and Boubakes, a Persian of high distinction; and besides these, it is said, of common men not less than a hundred thousand, of whom ten thousand were of the brave horse. So that Ptolemaios the son of Lagos, who pursued in person with Alexander, states that a ravine, across which they had to follow, was so completely bridged by the dead that they charged over it as on level ground.

Such was the battle of Issos, fought in the month of Maimakterion,* corresponding to the latter part of November and the first of December, in the Archonship of Nikostratos, at Athens, in the fourth year of the one hundred and first Olympiad, B. C. 333. It was fought on the oblique method, like that of the Granikos; the Greek left and centre being partially retired, until Alexander had forced back the Persian left with singular advantage, which put it in his power to take all the other divisions of the barbarian army successively in flank, and so to destroy them absolutely. It was won almost entirely by the tactics of the general, since it is perfectly evident that even his Thessalian cavalry on the left, with the single exception of the royal companions, his best horse, had gained nothing, and were barely able

* Polybios xvii. 29.

to maintain their ground against the spirited exertions of the Oriental cavalry, while the Makedonian phalanx, having the disadvantage of the ground against them, if anything had the worst of it in their conflict with the Greek mercenaries of Darios—all Peloponnesian republicans and soldiers of the first order—until the thundering charge of Alexander with the guides and life-guards upon their naked flank, pierced that gallant band through and through,* and made such a carnage in their broken ranks, that scarce two thousand of them rallied on the following day about the person of the fugitive king.

In the meantime the camp of Darios had been captured, with its vast treasures in plate, garments, armors, furniture, coined and uncoined gold, and all the profuse and lavish luxuries of Oriental royalty; and, in addition to all this, the mother, wife and sister of Darios, together with two grown-up daughters and an infant son, were made prisoners, beside a few other Persian ladies of rank, but not many, since most of the nobles of Darios' court had sent their women to Damaskos, whither the most part of Darios' treasury had been sent likewise.

It has been made the most of, as a very great and noble trait of Alexander's character, that he offered no indignity or violence to these captive beauties; I cannot, however, but regard these as mere rhetorical flourishes; since, although it certainly was the custom of the time to sell whole communities into slavery, the capture of the families of sovereign princes, or even generals of high rank, was a most unusual occurrence; and I cannot but believe, arguing from the habits of that day, not from the higher morality of our own, that to have subjected ladies of that quality to any disgrace or dishonor, particularly in cold-blood, after they had escaped unscathed from the tumult and terrors of the sack, would have reflected infinite reproach and shame upon the conqueror. Indeed, it is my conviction, that acts of licentious vio-

* Arrian II., xiii.

lence on the part of generals or others in high command toward female prisoners were as rare, and would, if committed, have been esteemed as infamous, as in our own times.

Alexander detained these ladies, however, in captivity, although he caused them to be served by their own attendants, and with all the luxury due to their birth and title as queens and princesses, which he allowed them to retain ; he even carried them about with him in all his marches, and in one of the latest, before the fatal battle of Arbela, the unhappy wife and mother died in durance, leaving her marriageable daughters in durance, and the heir to his father's throne at the victor's mercy. It is evident enough that his object in this was to intimidate Darios, by working on his feelings in behalf of those helpless treasures, into early and absolute submission. Surely, there was little magnanimity or generosity in this ; nor did his practice in this instance accord well with the principle of which he constantly boasted, that he waged war not on women but on warriors ; and on Darios himself, not as enemy on enemy but as rival against rival, for national and individual glory, and for the honor rather than the possession of empire.

It is evident that the distinction is not a difference, for to subject women of the highest rank to the penalties of war, by detaining them close prisoners, is in effect to make war on them ; and to have done them farther wrong would have overthrown at once all his pretensions to a sort of chivalry, which though fickle and fantastic, does appear in some sort to have regulated his conduct. To conclude, I fear we must attribute what there was of generosity in his conduct toward these unhappy ladies to his love of appearances and vain thirst of glory, while all that was stern and selfish must be assigned to his natural temper and disposition.

On the day following the battle he decorated those of his officers and men who had distinguished themselves, and added large gifts of money. Balakros the son of Nicanor, he appointed Satrap of Kilikia, and filled his post in the body-guards by Euenes the son of Dionysios, and to the command of Ptolemaios son of Seleukos he promoted Polyperchon son of Simmias. Then without a moment's delay he sent Parmenion forward with a sufficient force to make himself master of Damaskos, where the amount of wealth taken was so prodigious that the relation of it almost exceeds the limits of credibility, for the amount of coined money is said to have been two thousand six hundred talents, nearly a million sterling, besides five hundred pounds weight of wrought silver, and other booty beyond calculation, in tents, chariots, tapestries, house furniture, vases, statues, and goblets, of gold.* The loss of the Makedonians, by which this decisive victory was won, seems to have been three hundred hoplitai, on whom in this action the hardest fighting fell and a hundred and fifty horse,† by whose efforts in the battle and the flight which followed it, at least a hundred thousand of the enemy were slain. Of Darios' Greek mercenaries, about eight thousand men under Amyntas the son of Antiochos, Thymondas the son of Mentor, Aristomedes of Pherai, and Bianor the Akarnanian, all deserters from Alexander, fled the moment the action commenced and made their way through the mountains to Tripolis in Phoinikia, where they made themselves masters of shipping and escaped first to Kypros and thence to Egypt, where Amyntas was shortly afterward put to death by the natives.

At Damaskos were taken several revolutionary agents, sent from the Greek cities as envoys to Darios, but all these Alexander prudently and politically, not in my apprehension mercifully,‡ pardoned; for his victories had now placed him above all fear of danger from them, and he felt that after the cruel blow he had stricken against fallen Thebes, conciliation rather than intimidation was his game. An embassy from Darios soon after reached

* Quintus Curtius, iii. 34. † Polybios, xvii. 36. ‡ Arrian. II. xv.

him, praying for the liberation of his family, and offering him splendid conditions of peace, but to them he returned a stern refusal, couched in savage and imperious language, forbidding him to presume again, to treat with him as equal with equal, king with king, but as a slave with his lord and master.

It has ever, I confess, been a marvel and a mystery to me, in what part of this man's conduct or character it is, that his eulogists discover anything magnanimous, generous, or chivalrous; unless it be in a sort of mad-headed, inconsiderate courage which prompted him ever to be the first where blows were going, often to the serious detriment of the service, and endangering of the army; and which seems to have arisen rather from the fiery excitability of his temper and his constitutional insensibility to danger, than from anything rational or moral, without which nothing can be in truth heroical.

In the meantime Darios, who had made his way with the relics of his power through the passes of Mt. Amanos into the open plains beyond, fled with the utmost speed to Thapsakos, where he lost no time in interposing the broad and powerful stream of the Euphrates between himself and his enemy, although the precaution seems to have been needless, inasmuch as Alexander showed no willingness to interrupt or even hurry his flight; since immediately on hearing of the capture of Damaskos with its imperial treasuries, he turned in a diametrically opposite direction, marching down due south along the shores of the Levant, where he laid siege to the powerful and wealthy city of Tyre, which had refused him admission within its walls, and had gone so far as to murder the heralds, whom he had sent to require their submission. The cities of Byblos and Sidon surrendered at his approach, but Tyre being strongly situated on an island, powerfully fortified and protected on the sea-side by a great flight, made a most desperate and stubborn resistance. Alexander's first attempt was to build a mole across the channel from the continent to the island, so as to bring his engines to play upon the walls, but his mole was constantly impeded, and once actually destroyed by the fierce sallies and counter-engines of the besieged, assisted by storms and adverse weather, of which they took the utmost advantage. Machinery and military engineering was brought into play to a greater extent than had ever before been attempted, and in no respect can any other sieges be compared to it, in antique history, but those of Syracuse defended by Archimedes against Marcellus, and of Jerusalem against that most odious and cold-blooded of all Roman butchers, Titus the son of Vespasian.

For seven long months it foiled all the efforts of the Makedonian to reduce it, nor is it in the least degree probable that he ever would have taken it, had he not again collected a naval force with which he ultimately stormed it in the eighth month after assailing it. From this time forth, whatever there had been before of good or tolerable in the character of Alexander, disappears altogether, and unless it be in the capricious and unavailing tears which he is said to have shed over the ashes of Darios, we find nothing in his nature that is not hateful, disgusting, and almost superhumanly revolting and atrocious. Of the Tyrians, eight thousand men fell in the assault and the carnage which followed it, and of this slaughter we may in some degree acquit the king, as it is probable that, if he had endeavored to check or pacify his soldiery, maddened by the losses they had undergone and the unexampled severity, and length of the defence, he would scarce have succeeded; but it is not to be denied that in cold-blood he sold all the old men, women, and children, except such as were stealthily saved by their neighbors, the Sidonians, into hopeless slavery, and crucified two thousand of the youth around the walls of the place. Thence, insatiate of blood and unglutted with gore and booty, he pursued his path of devastation to the frontiers of Egypt, where he again met stern resistance at the walls of Gaza, that city of Gaza, the gates of which had been borne away in ages gone, by the giant strength of Samson. The siege of this place again cost him time, and human life, and his own blood—for he was dangerously wounded here, as he had been twice before Tyre, and, in the carrying the two cities, incurred a greater loss of men than his two great pitched battles cost him. The capture of this second stronghold he took advantage of, whereby to disgrace himself immortally by the base and barbarous murder of Boitis, the gallant governor of the place, who, guilty of no crime but the brave maintenance of the liberties of his native place, was brought before him covered with wounds and loaded with chains, was insulted brutally by the unkingly and unmanly conqueror, and then by his orders dragged by the heels, perforated and secured with thongs, behind a chariot's wheels around the walls, yet living, while Alexander, it is said, exulted openly over his success in imitating his great ancestor, Achilles, in his vengeance on his enemies. On this paltry plea it is useless to comment. The very existence of Achilles is hypothetical, and this brutal deed ascribed to him by Homer is related as an act of signal individual vengeance taken for the death of his brother in arms Patroklos, and in direct contrast to his ordinary demeanor which is represented as kind, generous, courteous and placable, alike to friend and foe, so soon as the rage of battle had subsided in his bosom.

Whether this base and felon deed was committed in a frantic emulation of the hero of the Iliad, or—which is far more probable—in cold, calculating, merciless policy, to deter other governors of towns from a like pertinacity of defence, it is equally detestable and accursed—after that, overlooking all his jealous slaughters of his best and bravest generals in fits of tyrannical suspicion, or in orgies of bestial drunkenness, I regard it almost a crime in the Historian who dares apply to this capricious, jealous, cruel and fantastical despot, the degraded title of a hero. Brave he unquestionably was, as every bull-dog is, and as ninety-nine of every hundred men—for of all others, this much admired and over-rated gift of mere physical courage, is the commonest and cheapest; and it is owing to the extreme rarity of cowardice, no less than to its loathsomeness, that men regard a coward as a monster, rather than a man—and with that one exception of bravery, I can see no other quality that he possessed which should preserve him from the utter execration of mankind.

From Gaza he passed downward into Egypt, which, never a willing vassal to the Persian kings, surrendered voluntarily to his arms, and after founding Alexandria—which must, I think, be regarded, in connection with the other details of this portion of his expedition, rather as an act of regal ostentation than of policy or patriotic foresight—rushed away, dragging his army after him, through wastes of burning sand, in search of the temple of Hammon, whose venal priests he easily induced to proclaim him the son of the god, and himself a divine king, and one to be approached, not with human reverence, but with sacrifice and adoration.

The battle of Issos was delivered, as I have stated above, in the beginning of the winter B. C. 333. Tyre and Gaza were carried in the following year, in the month Hecatombaion, corresponding to the latter part of July and the beginning of August, in the archonship of Aniketos,* according to Arrian—or, as Diodoros says, of Nikeratos;† and it was not until the month of Pyanepsion, corresponding to the end of October and commencement of November, in the second year of the one hundred and twelfth Olympiad, B. C. 331, in the archonship of Aristophanes,‡ after a lapse of two years, that he returned from this absurd, if not insane, career of superstitious folly and childlike vanity, to follow up his advantages, and decide the contest for

* Arrian II., xxiv. † Diodoros xvii. 40.
‡ Arrian III., xvi. Diod. xvii. 49.

the crown of Persia on the plains of Arbela. A graver military error than this diversion from his true course and true purpose I cannot conceive, or one that casts a greater doubt upon the reality of Alexander's ability as a strategist. As a mere tactician and fighter in the field he was certainly of the first strength; but, judging from this movement, undertaken for no conceivable reason, and from which no possible benefit was derived, I consider him liable to the charge, not only of want of fixity of purpose and soundness of judgment, but of serious strategetical incapacity.

It is idle to speak of the danger of leaving such places as Tyre and Gaza in his rear, or of suffering such a granary and store-house as Egypt to continue in his possession; for in the first place, their geographical position, separated by leagues and hundreds of leagues of barren and burning deserts from the regions into which Darios had betaken himself, rendered it impossible that either those cities or that province could have made any effectual diversion in his favor, even if they had desired to do so. And secondly, none of the tributary cities or remote dependencies of the Persian kings ever served them voluntarily, or, if they did so at all, from loyalty; and Egypt, as the result showed, was far better disposed to revolt herself from the arms of Darios than to strengthen him against his enemies.

The consequence of this faulty and unmeaning movement to the southward, when he ought to have been following Darios up with the utmost promptitude and perseverance—which had he done, that unfortunate prince must have lost his capital, and, probably, his whole empire, without the possibility of raising an army to strike another blow for it, and that long before Tyre had fallen—the consequence, I say, of that absurd movement and expedition was his being compelled, almost two years afterward, to fight a third and most unnecessary battle against a much larger army than he had yet encountered, in ground exceedingly adverse to himself, and as advantageous to the Orientals, who had gained experience from disaster—and, in fact, to risk the defeat which he very narrowly escaped—his left wing being very nearly defeated, his rear turned, and his encampment actually sacked by the barbarians, at Arbela.

No one, however ignorant of military affairs, but must perceive that an army of a million of men cannot be brought together, armed and embodied, in a moment; and, in fact, we find that it was not until after Alexander's return from the great oasis in the African desert, above two thousand miles distant, and after a lapse of two entire years, that he was enabled to take the field against him. We have seen that his forces were completely dispersed; that on his arriving at Thapsakos, after the battle, the Persian king could muster only four thousand men under his standard; so that a vigorous pursuit, even had it failed to capture him, could not have failed to drive him into the extreme north-eastern provinces—to which he fled after Arbela—and to leave his capital, and all the wealth and power of his empire in the hands of the conquerors. His communications were all safe with Makedonia and Greece at large, through Asia Minor, which afforded him an admirable base of operations against Lower Asia, governed as it was by his own officers, and secured him a safe retreat, should the worst have occurred. But when we consider, in war above all things, the immense advantage of dealing successive blows, each after each, before the stunning effect of the last has passed away; the importance of acting against a people demoralized and dispirited by defeat, and despairing even of safety by arms, rather than of giving them time to recover courage, growing out of the assailant's tardiness and want of energy; and last of all, the great influence which the fall of their capital produces on any nation—but more especially upon the Orientals—we cannot fail to see that Alexander threw away a chance, if not a certainty, of terminating the war at a blow; and so far from gaining any adequate advantage by the delay, weakened his own army, exposed it to needless toils and perils, and alienated the people of Syria by his ruthless cruelty, with no possible object that I can discover, unless it were the spoils of the proud and wealthy Tyre, so long the mistress of the seas.

It was early spring of the year 331, when Alexander took his departure from Memphis, and returned, through Phoinikia, by the same way he had come, receiving congratulatory embassies from all the Greek states, regulating the tributes, and accepting the submission of the conquered provinces, as he passed; but he did not reach Thapsakos and the fords of the Euphrates, which Darios had crossed a few days after the battle of Issos, until the month Hecatombaion—the same in which, on the previous year, he had taken Tyre. Here he found Mazaios, with three thousand horse and two thousand Greek mercenaries, appointed to defend the passage of the river, but they made no offer at defence, flying without drawing a bowstring, leaving the Makedonians to cross the stream unmolested. Hence he marched up the Euphrates, keeping the river on his left, through Mesopotamia, in a northerly direction, with his back toward Babylon, having learned from some scattered prisoners of Darios' army who were taken on the march, that his rival was encamped on the Tigris, with a much larger army than he had in Kilikia, and intended to make a stand there, to obstruct his passage. Thither then he followed with all speed, as if to make up for the time he had wasted during the two past seasons; but when he reached the banks of the river, he found neither Darios nor any forces left to confront him, and crossed the Tigris, without any opposition from the enemy, but with great difficulty, owing to the strength and rapidity of the current.

On the following day a few horse showed themselves on the

plain, when Alexander instantly charged with the body-guard, and one squadron of the Companions, and the guides, and though they fled without striking a blow he pursued them so sharply that he killed a few and made several prisoners, from whom he learned where Darios lay, and of what troops his army was composed. For he had now called in all the wild and barbarous tribes from the shores of Kaspian to the Persian gulf, Indians and Baktrians, and Sogdianians, under their Satrap Bessos, and Sakians of the Skythian race, horse archers, serving not as subjects of Darios, but as allies of Darios; and Barsaentes their Satrap had brought the Arachosians and the hill-tribes of India, and Satibarzanes brought the Arkians. The Parthians, and Hyrcanians, and Tapuroi all cavalry, were then under Phrataphernes. Atropates led the Medes, and with the Medes were enrolled the Kadusians, the Albanians, the Sakesinai; but the tribes from the Persian gulf were commanded by Orondobates, and Ariobarzanes, and Otanes. The Uxians and Susians followed Oxathres, the son of Abulitos. Bupares led the Babylonians, and the scattered tribe of Karians and Sitakinians, mustered with the Babylonians. Mithraustes and Orontes commanded the Armenians, Ararakes the Kappadokians, and Mazaios the troops of Koilesyria, and Syria between the rivers. Their whole force amounted to forty thousand horse, a million foot, two hundred scythed chariots, and fifteen elephants, which had been brought thither by the Indians proper from beyond the Indos. And with this enormous armament, Darios was awaiting his approach in the plains of Gaugamela on the river Bumodos about seventy miles distant from the city of Arbela, now Erbil, in a country perfectly level and free from the slightest inequality of surface; for Darios had been advised that his defeat on the Issos was caused by his wanting the room to display his forces, and by ruggedness of the surface hindering the action of his cavalry, and believing this—as it was indeed in good part true—had em ployed his numbers in cutting away every hillock, and filling up every hollow, so that the whole field was practicable for his chariots, and for the charge of his admirable horse.

On gaining this intelligence Alexander halted his army, and remained where he was four days, which he spent in fortifying an entrenched camp with a fosse and a palisade, within which he determined to leave all his baggage and supernumeraries, and all the soldiers who chanced to be *hors de combat*, while he would advance himself with the fighting men, carrying nothing but their arms, and deliver battle on the spot. The armies were at this time about eight miles asunder; but there was a range of low hillocks between them which intercepted their view, nor until Alexander had marched half the intervening distance and ascended the hills, did he discover the countless multitudes of the enemy filling the plains almost beyond the reach of eyesight with all the gorgeous glitter and barbaric pomp of Asiatic warfare. And here, it is said, Parmenion advised him to attack the enemy by night in his camps, and that Alexander refused, saying that he came to fight battles not to steal them.

He decided well, although that unquestionably was not his reason; though it was well too that he should give it as such, since it was likely to encourage the soldiers, who were not, it should seem, in such high spirits as usual, having fallen into a panic once, when no enemy was within miles of them, as they marched through Mesopotamia, and having been again so much disordered in fording the Tigris that had they been attacked by Mazaios they would surely have been defeated. But Alexander well knew that in a night attack, the least disorder or want of combined action must be fatal, and that the risk must be greater to a small force like his own, the only chance of which was perfect unity of movement, and intelligent concert. He deferred the battle, therefore, to the next morning, and spent the afternoon in carefully reconnoitring the ground, which he suspected to be perforated with pitfalls, and strewn with calthrops and crowsfeet, to lame his horses. It is said that in the morning of the battle he slept so late and so soundly that Parmenion had hard work to arouse him, so anxious had he been of late, lest the enemy should persist in refusing action, and devastating the country behind him as he retreated.

And well he might be anxious, and self-reproachful, for it was entirely his own fault that Darios had an army there at all, to encounter him; for not one man of all the myriads there assembled came from the regions which he had traversed, but had been brought up at vast labor and expense of time and money from the extreme regions of the east, the north, and the south, almost from the limits of the frigid to those of the torrid zone. Doubtless he now felt and acknowledged to himself that for the idiotic vanity of being styled the son of Hammon, he had lost the opportunity of being actually king of Asia, and that he had in consequence all his battles to fight over again here at Arbela, and that except in being so far advanced into the bowels of the land, and having in his favor the prestige of victory, he was not one iota the better, than he was on the eve of the Granikos. Had Napoleon won the battle of Issos in November, he would have been crowned in Babylon before the new year. Nothing in war is of so much consequence as time, and the best judge and economist of time is the greatest general. But now Alexander was in the field, and there, as is admitted, he had few superiors —he had desperate valor, he possessed the full confidence of his men, he was in command of as fine an army as ever marched to victory, and, last not least, his fortune never failed him, though certainly he tried it to the utmost. The army of Darios was thus arrayed, for the plan of his battle was taken in the original draft as Aristokelos states. On the left were the Baktrian cavalry, the Daai, and the Arachosians, and next to these the Persians, horse and foot commingled. Then counting from the right the

Susians and to the right of these the Kadusians up to the centre of the whole array. To the extreme right of the line the Medes were ranked with the men from Koile Syria, and Mesopotamia; the Parthians and Sakians, the Hyrcanians and Tapiroi, the Albanians and Sakesinai closed up with the centre, where Darios fought in person, with the corps known as the Kinsmen of the king, and the Persian immortals having golden balls on the reverse of their spears, and the Indians and the Karian exiles and Mardian archery. The Uxians, Babylonians, Sitakinians and nations from the Persian gulf were drawn up in deep masses behind the centre. On the left, opposed to Alexander's right were the Skythian cavalry, with about a thousand Baktrians, and a hundred war chariots; the elephants were opposed to the body-guard with fifty chariots, and on the extreme right of the Persians stood the Armenian and Kappadokian horse with the last fifty of the scythed cars; but the Greek mercenaries, who could alone hope to withstand the shock of the Makedonians, were stationed in the centre, on either hand of Darios and his Persian body-guard.

Against this formidable array Alexander ordered his men thus. On the right of his line were the Royal companions of the horse life-guard, the first of whom were the squadron of body-guards, commanded by Kleitos son of Dropidas, then the squadrons of Glaukias, of Ariston, of Sopis son of Hermodoros, of Herakleides son of Antiochos, of Denetrios son of Athamenes, of Meleager, and, last of the royal squadrons, of Hegesilochos son of Hippostratos. But Philotas the son of Parmenion commanded the whole body of the household cavalry. Next to the horse was the royal foot guard of the *hypaspistai*, and then the remainder of those troops. After them, who were under the command of Nikanor, a second son of Parmenion, stood the regiments of Koinos, Perdikkas, Meleager son of Neoptolemos of Polyperchon of Amyntas under command of Sinmias, that day—for Amyntas was on recruiting service in Makedonia, and lastly, to the left of the whole phalanx, of Krateros son of Alexandros, who commanded all the infantry of the left.

Next to the phalanx were the allied horse, under Eriguios son of Larekos, and the Thessalians of Philip son of Menelaos; and Parmenion had the leading of all the cavalry of the left, and kept about his own person the best of the Pharsalian horse and most of the Thessalians. Such was the array of the front line, but in the rear of these he had formed a second line, whose leaders had orders to form front to the rear, in case of the enemy's turning their flanks and attacking them in reverse. On the right, supporting the royal squadron, were half the Agrianians, led by Attalos, the Makedonian bowmen under Brison, and what were called the old bands of mercenaries under Kleander. In the van of these were the guides, and Paionian horse, led by Aretes and Ariston; and again, in the van of these the allied cavalry under Menidas. But, in advance of the royal squadron, and the other Companions, were the rest of the Agrianians and the archery, and the javelineers of Balakros opposed to the scythed chariots; and Menidas had orders, in case the enemy should turn that flank, to take *them* in flank with a flying charge as they wheeled; so was the right wing ordered. But in the rear of the left, to guard against a flank attack, were the Thrakians of Sitalkes, the allied cavalry of Koiranos, the Odrysians under Agathon son of Turimma, and, in the van of all these, the mercenary troopers commanded by Andromachos the son of Hiero. With the baggage guard, the Thrakian infantry were posted in reserve; the whole of Alexander's forces amounting to forty thousand foot, and seven thousand horse—a small force, indeed, as it would seem, to contend in the open field against a million of men. But in truth, as all these Oriental battles show, the Greek soldiers were only actually opposed to so many men as could be brought to bear upon them at one instant; for the moment the first struggle was over the battles were ended, since the Orientals could never be made to act in succession as reserves, but when those who were exposed to the first brunt turned their backs, all fled in headlong rout and irretrievable confusion. So that in reality the vast numbers of these Asiatic hordes rather swelled the carnage of their own ranks, and enhanced the glory of the Greeks, than increased their difficulties or added to their danger.

So soon as the armies were fairly front to front, Alexander as usual charged first with the cavalry of his right wing, and the Persians met him in full career, greatly outflanking him to the right, and the Skythians, who were wheeling round his flanks, were engaged with the troops set to oppose them; and still Alexander led at full gallop to the spear-hand, and was almost beyond that part of the plain which was levelled, when Darios fearing that his chariots would be rendered useless, directed all the advanced cavalry of his left to turn Alexander's right, and prevent his farther progress to that hand. And, as they did so, Alexander launched Menidos with the mercenaries against them; but the Skythian and Baktrian horse charged Menidos home, and broke his squadrons by the vast superiority of their numbers, when Alexander brought up Ariston's Paionians, and the allies, who broke the barbarians in turn. These again were supported by fresh squadrons of Baktrians, and rallying on their supports, fought hand to hand furiously with the Greeks, and Alexander's men fell fast—for they were sorely overmatched, and the Skythians were better accoutred with defensive armor—still the Makedonians could not be forced off their ground, and charging constantly in open column of squadrons, at last bore the enemy bodily out of their lines. Then the barbarians launched their chariots, hoping to dislocate the phalanx, and cut it to pieces with the formidable scythes. But in this they were sorely disappointed, for the Agrianians and the javelineers of Balakros, who were in front of the royal companions, received them with a shower of missiles, which they could not brook, and seized the reins; dragging the drivers down, and surrounding the horses, cut them to pieces. Some few passed through the ranks, which opened to receive them; and these ran away, doing no damage, to the rear, where they were mastered by the grooms and horse-boys of Alexander's army.

But as Darios now advanced along his whole front, Alexander ordered Aretes to charge the horse who were wheeling round his right; and as this charge succeeded to perfection, and separated the cavalry from the barbarian phalanx on the right, Alexander himself charged with all his cavalry of the Royal Companions and his phalanx full into the gap, at a tremendous pace and with the terrible battle-cry. For a short space the strife was stubborn and hand to hand; but, as Alexander and the life-guard charged in, irresistibly, plunging their spears into the faces of the Persians, and riding them down with the sheer weight of their horses, and as the Makedonian phalanx fell in upon them, solid as a wall, and bristling with the terrible sarissai, the Asiatics could endure it no longer, and Darios himself was the first man to turn and fly. And at the same moment the Skythian horse gave way before the onset of Aretas, and in that quarter of the field all was utter ruin and carnage among the Persians; for the Makedonians trampled them under foot and slaughtered them at pleasure.

But Simmias, with his regiment and those to his left, was unable to join in the pursuit, but halted his phalanx, and maintained a standing fight; for intelligence had reached him that the Makedonian left was worsted. And thus the front being opened, some of the Indian and Persian horse broke through the centre and cut their way to the camp and the baggage-guard; and there was desperate fighting there, for the barbarian prisoners of war rose on their captors, and, taking up arms, made a great slaughter of the unarmed camp followers; and the cry went through the tents that victory was with the Persians, and the hearts of Sisygambis the mother of Darios, and her captive granddaughters, beat high between hope and terror. But the hope was soon ended, for the troops who were drawn up for that purpose in the rear of the front line, wheeled instantly, and forming face to the rear, took the plunderers of the camp in reverse, and making a fearful slaughter of them, recovered all that was lost in that quarter.

But in the mean time, the Persian right, ignorant of the flight of Darios, had completely turned the left of Parmenion; so that, far from being able to assist Alexander or to press the flying foe, he was unable to hold his own ground, but sent to the king for aid. He, having no enemy in his part of the field who was not already in headlong flight, turned most unwillingly from his pursuit, for he had strong hopes of capturing Darios and terminating the war with a thunderstroke. He knew, however, too well the consequence of leaving a field half won, and wheeling hard to his own left, with all the cavalry of the Royal Companions, charged, as hard as they could spur their horses to the shock, on the right of the barbarians. The first whom they encountered were the worsted Parthians and Indians, and the bravest of the Persian horse, retreating from the Greek camp, and this was the heaviest and fiercest conflict of the day; for finding themselves cut off, and seeing no hope of safety unless by dint of sheer blows, they charged up face to face against Alexander, without hurling a javelin or turning a charger, but struck each man at the man opposed to him, and slashed and hewed, and were slashed at and hewn down, unsparing and unspared. In the end, however, Alexander and the Greek valor prevailed, though sixty of the Companions were killed outright in that short melée, and Hephaistion and Koinos and Menidas were wounded.

And now Alexander was on the point of attacking the extreme

right wing of the enemy, having swept their whole front from the extreme left, when he perceived that his work was done to his hand by the gallantry of his Thessalians, who never failed him, so that he was enabled to return to the pursuit of Darios—whom he followed on the spur so long as there was light to see—but when he had crossed the Lykos or Great Zab, not far from the spot where the Greek leaders were murdered in the expedition of Kyros, he halted for a few hours at midnight, to recruit his men and horses; and on the following morning resumed the chase as far as to Arbela, seventy miles distant from the field of battle, hoping there to take Darios; but he had again escaped—perhaps unfortunate that he did so, for he might have found the compassion of his enemy a surer stay than the loyalty of his false friends. Of Alexander's personal attendants there fell in the conflict and the pursuit a hundred men and above a thousand horses, half of them belonging to the Royal Companions, between wounds and weariness; the entire loss of the Makedonian army being about five hundred, while that of the enemy was counted at three hundred thousand killed, and more prisoners than slain, with all the elephants and camels, and all the wealth and treasures of the camp.

And this action, in fact, terminated the war; for from Arbela Alexander marched straight to Babylon, which sent out a deputation of the priests and chief men of the city to meet him, with gifts and the keys of the city, acknowledging him conqueror and king. Thence, after a short pause, which he spent in ordering the government, appointing officers, regulating tributes, and establishing everything on a solid foundation, he marched in twenty days to Susa, the royal city and seat of government, where he became master of all the treasures accumulated by the Persian kings for ages—including all the spoils carried away from Greece by Xerxes, and fifty thousand talents of silver—equal to fifteen millions sterling—and virtually king of Asia. From Suza he pressed hard on the traces of Darios, through India, and, sending out his generals in all directions to complete the subjugation of the country, pursued himself day and night, with his light troops and horse—chasing the more earnestly when he knew that Darios was in peril from the treachery of Bessos—killing horses and wearing out men, but himself indefatigable; until at length, when he had but five hundred soldiers left about him, he found his hapless rival breathing his last, pierced with numerous wounds, and having endured, as the climax of all agonies, that of expiring by the treacherous hands of false friends, without a friendly hand to wipe the death sweat from his brow or to close his dying eyes.

His enemy and conqueror, they say, wept over him; certainly he buried him with all the honors due to a king, and in a kingly sepulchre; but not till after he had robbed him of all that makes life valuable—family, friends, station, country, life—for if it was not by his hands or by his orders, it was by his instrumentality, that he died.

So after making him a widower, fatherless, and a beggar, he wept over him, and buried him as a king. The king's tears and the kingly burial availed the senseless clay about the same. But they were in truth offered to the vainglory of the living, not to the memory of the dead, and so their purpose was answered.

The death of Darios occurred in the third year of the one hundred and twelfth Olympiad, 330 B.C.; so that four years only had elapsed between his passage of the Hellespont and his succession to the undisputed throne of Asia, which, had he used ordinary foresight and energy after the battle of Issos, he might have grasped two years sooner.

And here I leave Alexander—for it is not his life nor his character that I am relating, but his military and strategetical career, which I regard as terminated here; so far, at least, as to enable us to form a judgment of his qualities, merits, and defects, as a strategist.

It is true that his life lasted four years longer, and that those four years were passed in almost incessant warfare; that he overrun the countries, shedding human blood like water, from the shores of the Kaspian Sea, which he looked upon the first of Greeks, perhaps of Europeans—to the banks of the Indus, down which his galleys sailed triumphant to the Persian Gulf, and thence ascended the Red Sea to his Egyptian province—that he gained fruitless victories, barren of all but slaughter, whithersoever he went, and founded cities, the very names of which have perished; that he risked his own life and that of his followers as recklessly in the storming of some paltry Indian village, as when all was at stake on the fields of the Issos or Gaugamela.

But beyond desperate fool-hardy courage and the admirable discipline of his unrivalled troops, there is little to observe and nothing to admire in the details of his latter campaigns. His cruelties, his debaucheries, his capricious jealousy, and almost insane tyranny, are so well known that I need not dwell on them as a counterblast to the dazzling splendor of his glorious career, as it is called, of victory and renown.

He died, as it has generally been stated by historians and almost universally received, of the consequences of a more frantic orgy of drunkenness than was usual even for him—but as it is now pretty satisfactorily ascertained, of one of those devouring and fatal fevers peculiar to the Punjaub and the banks of the Scinde, whither he had pushed his frantical pursuit of glory. So that the drunkenness was the consequence of the burning thirst which accompanies that peculiar fever, not the fever the consequence of the drunkenness. So he died, but not with him died the evils he had done, for he bequeathed his empire on his death bed to the bravest—he might as well have said with Pyrrhos of Epiros, to the sharpest sword, for that was the arbiter appealed to through many an age of blood and barbarism among his successors.

His career has been compared, in my opinion most unjustly, to that of Napoleon—there being but two points of resemblance between them, the extent of the territories they overran and devastated, alike without consolidating an empire, or founding a dynasty—and the oceans of blood they shed to gratify, not satiate, their boundless ambition. As a general, Alexander cannot for a moment stand in juxtaposition with the mighty Corsican, who never took a leaf out of any man's book of strategy whereby to win a battle; but where the difficulties waxed the greatest and the dangers, thence drew the most splendid inspirations, thence produced his most marvellous resources. The history of his battles is as various as the battles themselves are numerous, and each is a study and a lesson in itself. Alexander's battles were all cast in the same mould, all won on the same principle, and that principle not his own, but the oblique method of Epaminondas; overpowering the enemy's left by his own personal attack, with his centre and left withdrawn, and then wheeling to his own left and enfilading the ranks opposed to him by a flank attack. Nor did he do this as Epaminondas did—by a concentration of force on a single point, so that his onset must to a mathematical certainty succeed—but by reliance on the prestige of his great name and the vehemence of his personal onslaught. In any one of his battles, had the enemy been able to make head against him for half an hour longer than he did, the Makedonian army would have been beaten to a certainty. Never was a won battle nearer lost, unless we except Marengo, which was not one but two battles fought in one day, than that of Arbela, for the day was lost on the left, more than doubtful on the right, and the camp taken in the rear, when Alexander's personal rush upon the centre carried all before it, and the flight of Darios gave him a victory which might even then have been long contested, if not won, by Persia. His own death while leading would at any moment have lost all, for it was his own fiery courage and the terror that attached to his name, not his plans or his tactics, that conquered.

As a daring soldier and superb cavalry officer he was undeniably great, and with but two rivals, one of the middle ages, one of these latter days—Cœur de Lion, and Joachim Murat, whom in very much of his military character he most resembles.

As a man, he stands so immeasurably below Napoleon that I am almost ashamed to mention them together, for Napoleon, though stern, inflexible, and careless of human life where policy required its taking off, was as far removed as possible from cruelty, while Alexander was barbarous beyond Henry VIII. and Nero, in his fits of frenzy, sacrificing like the former his nearest friends to his moods of tyrannical suspicion, and rejoicing like the latter in strange, unusual, and hideous tortures of his victims.

For the rest, he has left no Simplon and no Code Napoleon to stand up perdurable monuments of beneficent genius above his sea of bloodshed he has literally left nothing beyond

> A name at which the world grew pale,
> To point a moral and adorn a tale.

He was, however, a great and appointed instrument, as I believe all the world's great conquerors have been, in the hands of the Almighty, either for the preservation or for the punishment of nations.

I believe that to him mainly it is due that Europe was not enslaved by the Asiatics; for the Greeks, divided as they were by intestine feuds, could have offered no resistance to their combined power, except when themselves combined—as they could only be by the iron hand of a military despotism. The Romans had not yet emerged from their small Italian struggles, nor attained such national weight or military science in those days, as could have enabled them to turn the scale, had Asia, once possessed of Hellas as she was of the Ionian cities, and added to her Tyrian, Sidonian, and Carthaginian fleets—for in such a war Carthage would have gone hand in hand with Persia—the terrors of the Makedonian Phalanx, the Peloponnesian Hoplitai, and the invincible triremes of Attika.

Therefore, in some sort, we owe gratitude to the wild conqueror, and it may be that we are in some sort indebted for the language we speak, and the liberty we enjoy, in a hemisphere he never dreamed of, to the victories of Alexander of Makedon.

It may be thought that the judgment I have expressed in this instance, is over severe; for so our nature appears to be constituted, that the eclat and splendor of great personal valor, the extent of mighty countries overrun and subdued, produces such wonderful effects on the minds of men, that the gorgeousness and glitter of feats of arms and the palms of victory efface all considerations of mortal suffering on the battle field, in the dungeon or on the scaffold, and live forever conferring a false and fitful immortality, long after the groans and sorrows of the victims have sunk into the silence of oblivion and the tomb. Yet, if we consider calmly the atrocities committed by his orders and under his authority at Thebes, at Tyre, at Gaza, and the barbarous torments inflicted in cold-blooded policy, alike on the good and gallant Britis and on the brutal and bloodthirsty Bessos—if we remember the unrelenting, if not undeserved, slaughter of the high-spirited and brave Parmenion, the ruthless slaughter of the hardy Klutos, who had saved his own life in the desperate melée of Issos—if we recount the woes inflicted on the brave population of a loyal country, fighting in defence of their own liberties, the fearful waste of blood in his reckless and fruitless battles, we shall have no reason, I think, to doubt the correctness of the verdict which condemns him as the rashest of conquerors, and the cruellest of all who have laid claim to the much misapplied title of hero.

ONSET OF NUMIDIAN HORSE.

p. 334

VIII.

HANNIBAL,

HIS BATTLES OF THE TICINUS, TREBBIA, THRASYMENE, AND CANNÆ.
HIS CAMPAIGNS, CONDUCT, AND CHARACTER.

It cannot fail, at first sight, to strike even the most unobservant reader of ancient history with something of wonder, that we know so little distinctly, and, if I may so express myself, individually, of this man, the greatest captain, beyond all question, of antiquity; perhaps—his means and the then state of military science considered—the greatest of all ages.

The causes of this general ignorance are manifold; but the most important are the entire absence of any Carthaginian narrative of the circumstances of the Punic wars; and the ignorance or favoritism of the Greek and Roman writers on the subject—Polybius having been a personal friend of Scipio and Lœlius; and Livy, writing so long after the occurrence of the facts which he describes, that it was not much easier for him, than it is for us, to arrive at the real truths of what he received as history, or its materials; the legends, namely, of the illustrious Roman houses, and the funeral orations of consulars and senators, which, for the most part, contained as many falsehoods as they counted lines.

It is more remarkable, however, that, until the Colossus Niebuhr came upon the stage, no modern historian was clear-sighted enough to discern, through the thick mists which prejudice, blind error, or intentional falsehood, have accumulated over the ages of Roman republicanism, even a glimpse of the transcendant genius, unrivalled military foresight and resource, unwearied perseverance, and indomitable patriotism, of this great captain, this great politician, and, in spite of some defects, which were those of his age rather than his own, this great man.

Niebuhr, it is true, lived not to bring down the history of that wondrous nation, on whose early ages he first poured the light of intelligence, to the days of the hero, whom I shall endeavor briefly to set before my readers in his true light; but from one passage in his third volume it is clear that, had he lived to write of the second Punic war, he would have done justice to the incomparable greatness and genius of this much-belied and unappreciated leader. In that passage he speaks of "Scipio as towering above his nation, as much as Hannibal above all nations," and to any person who has carefully studied the career of the great Carthaginian, in the graphic pages of Arnold's magnificent history—alas! like Niebuhr's, left incomplete, by the untimely death of the author—it will be evident that in this phrase there is nothing of hyperbole.

Professing, myself, to adduce no new fact, scarce even theory, concerning this remarkable soldier, it strikes me that a short digest of his campaigns, divested of the dry details which render historical studies displeasing to the superficial reader, and combined with some comparisons of his deeds with those of other greatest soldiers, may prove neither unpalatable nor unuseful to the perusers of ephemeral literature; while it may tend to clear the memory of a much misrepresented hero, from the prejudiced opinions naturally instilled into us by our school readings of Horace's immortal odes, and "Livy's pictured page."

Hannibal was, it would seem, born a general—his father, Hamilcar, was the greatest of his nation and his day; to him succeeded Hasdrubal his son-in-law, to him Hannibal, the greatest of his race, supported by his brothers, Hasdrubal, the younger, and Mago, both generals of extraordinary ability, and with the exception of Scipio alone, both superior in *coup d' œil*, resource, and strategy, to any Roman leader. Never did one family produce such a galaxy of military splendor. It must not be understood, however, that they were merely born, for they were constantly bred, soldiers; the camp was their home from their early childhood; the clang of arms and the din of martial music, was the lullaby of their almost cradled sleep; and, when they came to the years of adolescence, the battle field was alike their playground and their school, and their great father their tutor in the rudiments of strategy, which none could better teach. Hannibal was but nine years old, when he accompanied his father to Spain, that father having first made him swear upon the altar that he would never be the friend of Romans. "Hannibal* swore, and to his latest hour never forgot his vow." The boy swore ignorantly at the time, though he forgot not; but it must not be supposed that the father dictated that vow ignorantly, nor even in the bitterness of blind hatred, or the darkness of political prejudice and passion. The man probably, even then, discovered dimly the future greatness of the child; the patriot assuredly had discoved the inherent and eternal antagonism of Rome and his country, the immutable necessity that one of those two must fall and leave the other the world's mistress.

Rome had just come off conqueror, and humbled Carthage to almost the lowest degradation, after a long and doubtful strife of two-and-twenty years, waged upon sea and land with changeful fortunes. Carthage had lost her wealthiest colonies, and above all the dominion of the seas; for the time she could maintain the conflict no longer, but the genius of Hamilcar saw where her vital energies might be renovated, and whence a mortal blow might

* Arnold, II. 257.

be dealt against her now triumphant. To Spain he sailed, and in Spain he laid the plans, and began the system, which his far greater son carried out, and by which he shook Rome to its foundation.

For two-and-twenty years peace lasted between the rival states; and during those two-and-twenty years, thanks to the absence of Carthaginian and the paucity of Roman annals, we know but little of the individual progress of the great Punic family, except that they had conquered and consolidated a vast and wealthy Carthaginian empire, including almost the whole of Spain south of the Ebro, abounding in rich mines of gold and silver, and swarming with a martial population which formed the very flower of the Punic armies. On the death of Hamilcar he was worthily succeeded by Hasdrubal, his son-in-law, whose progress in farther consolidating the Punic power in Spain, and whose eminent abilities displayed in the foundation of New Carthage, at that time the Gibraltar of the Mediterranean by its commanding and central position, so far alarmed the Romans that even then they would have renewed the war with Carthage, had they not been deterred by the terrors of a Gaulish invasion. Three years had elapsed, when Hasdrubal was assassinated in his tent, and by the common voice of the army, ratified by the decree of the Senate, the youthful Hannibal was chosen in his place.

Up to this time we know nothing of the future hero, except his parentage and vow; for the next twenty years he filled the world with his renown, and had his fortunes matched his greatness and his glory, the world to-day would be no more like that it is, than it would, had the Saracens over-run and subjugated Europe in the day of Charles Martel.

Scarce any one at all familiar with history can have failed to observe the extraordinary parallelism between the campaigns, the military conduct, and the fortunes of Hannibal and Napoleon.

That parallelism is thus strikingly touched upon by Arnold. "Twice," he says, "in history has there been witnessed the struggle of the highest individual genius against the resources and institutions of a great nation; and in both cases the nation has been victorious. For seventeen years Hannibal strove against Rome; for sixteen years Napoleon Bonaparte strove against England; the efforts of the first ended in Zama, those of the second in Waterloo." The extraordinary similitude of the genius, conduct, and military character of these two giants in arms, is far from ending with this general resemblance. Almost from point to point, their destinies are similar. At the age of twenty-six, Hannibal was elected to the supreme command of the Carthaginian armies, and thenceforth to the close of the war he disposed at his will the resources, and held in the hollow of his hand the councils of his country. At the age of twenty-six, Napoleon assumed the command of the army of Italy, and from thence his fortunes and his will were those of France. The scenes of the glory of both were the Alps and Italy. Both had the faculty of seeing at a glance where the blow must be planted, which should cripple the enemy; both delivered that blow instantaneously and irresistibly. Both had the same reliance on their cavalry as an arm of service; Hannibal winning by it all his greatest victories, and Napoleon insisting to the last, that cavalry in equal force, equally led, must conquer infantry. Both vanquished every leader in the field, whom he personally encountered, save the very last; and there is probably no one so prejudiced as to assert at this day that either Hannibal or Napoleon found in his conqueror a superior in strategy or in military genius. Nor does the similarity end even here; for both found their final vanquishers in generals made in Spain by conflicts with their own lieutenants, who were in no wise superior to other eminent leaders of their enemy; and both ultimately perished miserably, in exile, victims to the countries which they had kept so long in awe and perturbation.

In a military point of view, the correctness of their *coup d'œil;* the lightning speed with which they followed up conception by execution; the power of concentration, by which constantly inferior on the whole, in force, they were ever superior at the point of action; the marvellous foresight, by which they showed seeming rashness to be real prudence; the thunderous crash with which, when they delivered battles, they annihilated, not conquered, their antagonists; nay, the unerring certainty with which they threw themselves on the communications of their enemy, and defeated at a blow the most skilful combinations, were identical in these two mighty captains—none other, in my opinion, ever have possessed the same qualities, or used them with the same effect. Both were the makers of their own systems, the founders of their own schools; but on the whole, I must consider Hannibal as the greater strategist of the two; because, in the first place, he was the prime originator and inventor, while his great eulogist, and in some points imitator, had the benefit of his example, as well as that of other mighty conquerors; and in the second place, because with means infinitely inferior, against obstacles infinitely greater, and without the aid of modern science, he accomplished, what may be held to have been, in the then condition of the world, results nearly equal.

As men of genuine greatness—I shall observe only, that no single act of Hannibal's life ever subserved to any selfish motive or ministered to his own aggrandizement; and that no single act of Napoleon's did not so. The consideration of self would seem never to have occurred to the one; to have been ever present to the other. Both were fanatics for glory; the one because his own was his country's; the other, because his country's was his own. Both were accused by their enemies of great moral crimes and turpitude; and both, in the main, unjustly. It is one of the sad truths concerning warfare, but no less a truth; that, in playing the game of war, with nations for playthings and the world for a field, expediency must be in a great degree the moral rule; and that, if the game is to be played at all, the sufferings or the lives of individuals, even if those individuals be counted by thousands, must not be considered, where the sufferings or the lives of millions are in question. The sin lies in the playing the game at all, not in the details or the practice of the play. Both these great men were stern and unrelenting in carrying out the lines which they held it true policy to lay down; neither, so far as history shows, was tainted in the least degree by anything resembling personal cruelty. Both have been accused of faithlessness—a charge never in any case to be much regarded, as brought between nations; for nations are ever prompt to reclaim loudly, when the losers, against deeds, the like of which themselves commit readily, when the winners. In the case of Hannibal, the Romans had all the history-writing to themselves; thence, Punic faith is to this day the proverb for entire faithlessness. Had the French writers alone made the world's annals of the late great struggle, "perfidious Albion" had gone down a byeword to all ages. Had the English held the like station, the utter faithlessness of Napoleon would have become proverbial with posterity.

But to return, from this striking parallel, to our immediate hero, we find that he devoted the two first years of his chief command, to completing the subjugation and pacification of Spain; and the third to the conquest of Saguntum, a city allied to the Romans, situate on the river Ebro; a city, therefore, which the Carthaginians were bound by treaties not to disturb; a river which they had no just right to cross. Hence, the sole cause of the charge of perfidy against Hannibal. A treaty *was* unquestionably violated by Hannibal; as the Romans had violated another treaty far more flagrantly, at the close of the first Punic War; and as they would unquestionably have violated any that existed now, had it been to their interest to do so. The truth is simply this, that the two nations had been at peace as long as either deemed it very essential to be at peace. Both were preparing for war; Hannibal was ready the first, and therefore struck the first blow. He wished to serve his country; his country deemed that he was serving her, and therefore sustained him; and so well, in truth, did he serve her, that had the genius and character of Carthage borne any relation to those of Rome, such as the genius and character of Hannibal bore to those of the ablest Romans, Rome must have succumbed in the unequal contest; and the world to this day would probably, if not certainly, have been Semitic or Phœnician, and Asiatic, not Roman and European, in its language, its civilization, its religion.

But of this Hannibal thought not; nor, had he thought, would have cared anything. His business was to provoke a war with Rome, and then to deal her one home-stricken blow, that should paralyze her at once and forever. This was his business, as he saw it; and he was one to do that which he saw his business, as thoroughly as Cromwell or Napoleon.

Hannibal's plans were now fully laid, and without further delay he put them into execution. It was already late in May, when he set out from Carthagena for the Ebro, having to cross five degrees and a half of latitude before reaching the Pyrenees, and to conquer the whole half-Romanized territory north of that river, before entering Gaul—then an unknown, unexplored, and barbarous, though highly warlike country, the geography of which was less familiar to the Roman or Carthaginian of those days, than is that of Central Africa to us at this period. His force, on crossing the Ebro, was ninety thousand foot and twelve thousand horse, besides elephants, which was reduced by detachments and losses in the field to fifty thousand foot and nine thousand horse, before he crossed the Pyrenees. In those days, field artillery there was none, nor its equivalent; but engines for casting huge stones and beams into beleaguered cities—as effective, perhaps, against the imperfect fortifications of those days as our battering artillery—did exist; and of these Hannibal was unable to carry any with him, if he had any in Spain, or even if the Carthaginians knew the use of them, which seems to be doubtful; and to his weakness in this arm, the failure of his ultimate attempts against Rome is, I believe, wholly to be attributed. It is a proof of his wonderful power of adapting himself to circumstances, and of his tact in dealing with barbarians, that he actually traversed the whole of France, from the Pyrenees to the Rhone—a tract of vast forests and difficult morasses, swarming with fierce and warlike savages—with little loss and no serious opposition. So rapid had been his motions, and so incredulous were the Romans, though forewarned, of the possibility of such a march, that, although the consular armies had time to have disputed the passes of the Pyrenees with him, he had actually crossed the Rhone, and gained three days' march toward the Alps, after a slight skirmish with the Roman light-horse, before the Consul Scipio was aware of his arrival in Gaul. That general, finding himself anticipated, did good service to his country, and acted on sound military principles, sending his consular army on to Spain by sea, under his lieutenant, while he himself took ship for Pisa, crossed the Appenines, and, having command of the Prætorian armies of twenty-five thousand men, between Placentia and Cremona, before Hannibal had descended from the mountains, was in readiness to receive him, on his appearance in the plains.

Hannibal, in the meantime, had plunged into the passes of the Alps, in so far as we can judge, by the valley of the Isere, with thirty-seven elephants, in addition to the force of infantry and cavalry as specified above. Now, it appears to me, that to compare Napoleon's passage of the Alps with that of Hannibal, is much as it would be to compare the voyage of Columbus to the passage of an Atlantic steamer—the former travelled over roads, difficult indeed and dangerous, but still *roads*, with bridges, depôts of provisions, and friendly inhabitants, through a country perfectly known, thoroughly explored, and accurately surveyed for his own purposes by his own incomparable engineers. The latter forced his way through unknown passes, over bridgeless ravines, with no aid of modern science, no pontoons or devices of engineering, no provisions or forage save what he carried with him, fighting his way, inch by inch, through hordes of hostile barbarians, and that with men and animals from the almost tropical climate of Africa, who perished, in thousands, by the inclemency of weather unendurable to southern constitutions. Add to this, that it is an undoubted fact, that the limits of eternal snow lay far lower down the mountain sides in those days than now, and that much of the great Carthaginian's line of march lay within and above those limits. Napoleon's celebrated passage was made at the expense, to use his own words, "of a few accidents"—Hannibal's at the cost of thirty-three thousand men out of fifty-nine thousand, and all the elephants but eleven. The terrible disparity of loss shows the disparity both of difficulty and audacity. The merit of the conception rests incontestably with Hannibal; who did what no man had ever dreamed of doing before him, and which it might not be possible to do at all. Napoleon did, with splendid ability, certainly, and prodigious celerity, what he well knew had been done before, and *could* therefore, unquestionably, be done again.

The results, in both instances, were precisely similar. It is now nearly certain that Hannibal crossed the Isere, followed the upward course of the Rhone, surmounted the Alps by the pass of the little St. Bernard, descended the Val d'Aosta, and thence marched eastward into the country of the Insubrians, where he expected to find allies, and to raise the Cisalpine Gauls against their old enemies the Romans. Their country lies north of the river Po, in the neighborhood of Placentia and Cremona—Roman colonies on that great river—and it was on the banks of the Tesino, a northern tributary of that stream, that the two rival nations first came into contact. This affair of cavalry has been magnified into a battle, though it was but a skirmish, except in the prestige of success, and in the proof it gave of the superiority, never again doubtful during the whole war, of the African to the Roman cavalry. The Numidians were the Cossacks of that age, mounted on incomparable barbs and Arabs, unequalled as horsemen and lancers; the heavy-armed Carthaginian horse were complete cuirassiers, fighting with charged lances and long cutting sabres. The Roman cavalry, never a favorite or successful arm of their service, wore no cuirasses, and, for weapons, carried weak, inefficient javelins, and the short stabbing sword of the infantry, which was entirely inefficient as a trooper's weapon. In this affair of the Ticinus, the heavy Carthaginians met the Roman horse in front with a steady charge, while the wild Numidians broke in upon both their flanks, and routed them in an instant. The country was entirely open and favorable to the movements of cavalry; the Romans, therefore, crippled in that arm, were forced to retreat; re-crossed the Tesino, breaking the bridge behind them; crossed the Po also, and posted themselves under the walls of Placentia. Hannibal, without pursuing, passed the Po higher up, by a bridge of boats, and being rapturously received by the Gauls, descended the right bank of the river, and offered battle to the Romans. But they expecting reinforcement by the other consular army, of Sempronius, declined it; and in a few days afterward retreated several miles southward, up the valley of the Trebbia, and encamped among the first spurs of the Appenines, where they were comparatively safe from Hannibal's tremendous cavalry, which they had already learned to dread. The Carthaginian had, in the first instance, taken post to the eastward, in order to intercept the expected approach of Sempronius from Rimini, on the Adriatic; but now, learning, perhaps, that this consul had given, or anticipating that he would give him, the slip, by turning aside into the hill-country to the southward, far below Cremona, he threw himself at once upon the main communications of the Romans, placing himself directly between them and the magazines, on which they were subsisted, at Placentia and on the Upper Po, precisely as Napoleon did by the Austrians at Marengo; thus straitening them of supplies in their camp, while his own cavalry swept the plains in every direction, keeping all his communications open, and the friendly Gauls abundantly supplied him with provision, as he lay on the right bank of the Trebbia.

Meantime, the junction between the two consular armies was effected, and by this means the effective force of the Romans was raised to above forty thousand men; while that of Hannibal had been so much swelled by the accession of Gaulish recruits, that he was anxious to deliver battle almost on any terms; the rather, that the subsistence of his army had weighed heavily on the Gauls; who, fickle and treacherous, even beyond the wont of barbarians, were showing symptoms of impatience at his protracted sojourn among them. His great superiority of cavalry, moreover, both as regards quality and numbers, rendered him confident of success in the extensive plains of the Po. Sempronius was now in command of the whole Roman forces, Scipio being still *hors de combat* from a wound received in the affair of cavalry on the Tesino; and as this general had no taste as yet of Hannibal's quality, and found himself cut off from his magazines, which the Carthaginians were now beginning to master, and insulted in his very camp, on his own side of the river, by the Numidian horse and Balearic slingers, he merits no reproach for having determined to give battle on fair ground; for with such a force as he commanded, purely homogeneous and Roman; such a force, in a word, as had never within a century encountered an equal foe, he was justified in expecting victory over any troops in the known world. He was falling short of provisions, moreover, and there was great danger of a general Gallic rising, in case the population should be encouraged by the protracted inactivity of the Romans.

To deliver battle, under such circumstances, was therefore soldierly and justifiable on all sound military principles; to do so rashly, however, and hastily, and that, too, on ground and at time of the enemy's choosing—such an enemy too, and so superior in horse—was unpardonable. Yet, just this thing did Sempronius.

It was now mid-winter, for neither of the belligerents had thought of going into winter quarters—Hannibal, from the imminent necessity of striking quickly and decisively, and the Romans, from the impossibility of suffering him to keep the field unwatched. Even now, the climate of the plains at the foot of the Alps, included in the districts of Lombardy and Piedmont, is severe and inclement in the winter season; but in those times, when the country lay in great part uncleared and covered with primitive forest, it was far more tempestuous and cold than at present.

The Trebbia swollen with snow-water, ice-cold from the frozen Appenines, ran now a breast-high torrent, though in the summer droughts its pebbly bed might be crossed almost dry-shod. Across this paralyzing stream Sempronius suffered Hannibal to allure him, on a wild morning, with flying sleet storms and snow gusts, by a false attack and feigned retreat, to his own side of the river; and that too without allowing his men to breakfast; while the Carthaginians, expectant of what was to come, had fed heartily, and armed themselves in their tents by blazing fires.

In addition to this advantage, an ambuscade of two thousand horse and foot had been concealed, under Mago's command, in an old watercourse covered with brushwood and coppice, which Sempronius, negligently or disdainfully, left in his rear, as he hurried on to attack the enemy, who had drawn out from their camp, and formed line of battle, facing the river, to oppose him.

The order of battle was simple, and on both sides the same; indeed, it was the only order then in use, the centre being formed of the heavy infantry, covered by their light troops and skirmishers, with the cavalry on either flank. So far as I can observe, this form was rarely deviated from by the ancient military nations; the cavalry were invariably directed against cavalry; and, after an equestrian combat which generally terminated in the chase of one party, for miles, perhaps leagues, from the field by the other, a second engagement followed between the solid infantry which often led to the occurrence of drawn battle. The same defect of strategy is observable in all Prince Rupert's fighting, during the English civil-war, who, in four or five different pitched battles, had he wheeled on the flanks and rear of the Parliamentarian foot, after scattering their horse by his headlong charge, would have terminated the war at a blow. Hannibal, who made more use of his cavalry arm than any other general of antiquity, never appears to have attacked infantry in front with horse, or even in flank, until the enemy's cavalry were in flight; and yet the Roman foot—as foot the best undoubtedly in the world—were from their armature of heavy missile javelins and short stabbing swords, not differing much from the larger bowie knife, peculiarly unfitted to resist the charge of cavalry, which their loose and open order was calculated to invite.

The result of this battle was as must be foreseen from the preceding events which led to it. In the fight itself there was little strategy; the great abilities of Hannibal had been displayed in the manœuvres by which he compelled the enemy to deliver battle, and then induced him to deliver it, at disadvantage, and on ground selected by his enemy. The rest he left to his soldiers, confident that they would do their work to his satisfaction; nor was his confidence disappointed. He was, moreover, in the open field greatly superior to his enemy, even without taking the exhaustion and ill-plight of the legionaries into consideration, who fought wet to the skin, chilled, and fasting, against men full-fed, fresh, and warm, from their recent campfires. His cavalry, ten thousand strong, six thousand of whom were incomparable African cuirassiers and Numidians, could not be checked by the feeble legionary cavalry of four thousand, for a single instant. The Balearian slingers and African archery were as much superior to the Roman light troops, who fought only with slender javelins; the Italians never having been famous for the use of the bow. The velites of Sempronius, therefore, were driven in upon the legionaries at the first onset, and passed through the intervals of the Manipules to the rear, while the cavalry were scattered, as by a thunderbolt, on both wings simultaneously, by the Carthaginian elephants and horsemen. The soldierly qualities of the Roman foot did not fail them in this emergency—in fact never did fail them throughout the war, for when opposed to foot they were never beaten—for they maintained the fight, exhausted as they were, with advantage, until Maharbal, whom Arnold styles not unjustly "the best cavalry officer of the first cavalry service in the world," leaving the pursuit of the flying horse to his Numidians, unequalled in such operations, thundered on both their flanks with his elephants and cuirassiers, and to complete the whole Mago, bursting from his ambush, broke down upon their rear, horse and foot, pell-mell, and pierced them through and through. The legions of the centre, still undismayed and unbroken, cut their way straight through the African foot before them, and reached Placentia in safety, though the whole Carthaginian army was interposed; the rest were slaughtered ruthlessly and unremittingly, according to the usages of ancient warefare, until the ice-cold waters of the Trebbia checked the pursuit of the victors, and saved the residue from slaughter. During the same night Scipio with the shattered relics of the army, re-crossed the Trebbia and joined his colleague in Placentia; whence in a few days they retreated separately, Scipio on Rimini, Sempronius across the Appenines into Etruria, leaving Hannibal at the close of his first short campaign the master of all Cisalpine Gaul, or, in other words, of all Italy, north of the Appenines.

Hannibal, politic ever, and fearing to distress his new and fickle allies, by wintering among them, and so compelling them to subsist his troops, made an effort to cross the Appenines, but the cold was too severe, and the passes were impracticable to his hot-blooded southern cattle, so that he was forced in his own despite, after losing all his elephants but one, to return and winter among the reluctant and faithless Gauls, from whom he appears to have apprehended even assassination.

In the following year, new consuls having been chosen at Rome, Caius Flaminius and Cneius Servilius Geminius, soldiers were levied very vigorously and an immense force set on foot; two several consular armies, each consisting of four Roman legions, or about twenty-four thousand men, besides an equal force of allies of the Latin name, were opposed to Hannibal, covering the two different roads which led to Rome, the Flaminian by the Adriatic coast, and the Emilian through Tuscany. Servilius took the command in lieu of Scipio at Rimini, on the Adriatic, and Flaminius that of Sempronius, at Arezzo, a town of Tuscany, situated among the Appenines on the confines of the states of the church, about a hundred and twenty miles due north of Rome. So that apparently Hannibal could not advance upon Rome, without encountering the one or other of these two powerful hosts. Many reasons had induced both parties to open this campaign at an early season, and in fact Flaminius was in the field so soon as the 15th of March. Hannibal, however, had no idea of affronting the might of Rome in her own central Latin territory, much less of attacking her walls, when he had no means adequate to the storming of such petty garrison towns as Placentia, Cremona, and the other Roman colonies planted in the half subjugated districts of Cisalpine Gaul. His game was to rekindle the ancient feuds of Samnium and Campania, against their haughty mistress, and, subsisted on the wealth of the rich plains of La Puglia and the Terra di Lavoro, to wear out the patience of the Roman allies by devastating their territories, until he should be able to raise all Southern Italy in one common league against their common mistress; and then, and not until then, to strike a home blow, which should be at once irresistible and decisive. Skilfully avoiding, therefore, both the main roads he marched almost due south, down the valley of the Serchio, through a tract of almost impassable morasses, among which his army suffered severely, upon the Valdarno, which he entered some twenty miles westward of Florence, and plundered it with extreme severity, compensating his men for their previous toils by the enjoyment of those rich districts. Thence, finding that Flaminius moved not from his post at Arezzo, he advanced rapidly through Tuscany, turning that Consul's left to the west and southward, and passing onward, with Cortona's mountain citadel unmolested on his own left, direct upon the Lake of Perugia—better known as the fatal Thrasymene—which he approached on its northern side, as if it were his intention to strike the waters of the upper Tiber, and so enter the very heart of the Latin country, and descend on Rome itself, leaving both her consular armies far to rearward. To effect this he had made a long and circuitous flank march close under the position of a concentrated enemy; a manœuvre singularly hazardous if executed in the face of an alert and active foe. It was such a manœuvre which lost Austerlitz to the Russians, and Salamanca to Marmont; but Hannibal's superior cavalry enabled him to execute it in the plains without fear of molestation from an enemy whom he had now completely outwitted.

Satisfied by this that Hannibal desired to avoid him, Flaminius broke up from Arezzo, and pursued, in hot haste, fearing only that his fugitive enemy, as he vainly imagined him, would have already entered the basin of the Tiber, and commenced the devastation of the especial territory of the city. But Hannibal had foreseen the movement, and prepared a trap, more terrible than that even of the Caudine forks, for his unwary pursuer.

The road, which passes to the northward of the lake Thrasymene, or Perugia, into the Latin country, traverses at first a narrow defile between steep cliffs and the deep waters of the lake, and then turns abruptly to the north, crossing a little lap of land between low hills to the left and right. Within this gorge Hannibal had paused, and crouched like a lion, for his spring. With his Africans and Spaniards he barred the road in front, on the crest of the ridge, where the road wound upward from the lake. His Gauls he posted with his cavalry on the left of the pass, among the low hills; his archery and slingers on the right, while he garnished the tops of the cliffs, above the pass, with light troops and the Gaulish auxiliaries. Fortune and the weather favored him, no less than the ground. Flaminius arrived late, after a forced march, at Passignano, just without the passes; encamped, and before daybreak entered the defiles, without reconnoitering or sending forward an advanced guard; thinking only how best he might overtake his flying enemy. A thick mist from the lake covered all the low grounds and defiles, while the heights above were bright in the clear atmosphere; still onward marched the doomed column, crowded in dense array, and marching at their fastest pace, emulous to fall on the rear of the enemy. Not a sound was heard, not a bowstring was drawn, until the head of the column was ascending the last height, whereon the Africans and Spaniards were posted, and the rear was entangled in the defiles, and overlooked by the Gallic auxiliaries. Then at once, before, behind, and on both flanks, broke on their ears the slogan of the Gauls, the clang and clatter of the Numidian horse, and the fatal whistle of the bullets, slung like hail into their ranks by the fierce barbarians. The van alone cut its way clear through the troops that opposed them, and escaped for a while, six thousand strong, to one of the neighboring villages. They alone—for of the centre and the rear of that doomed army not one man escaped to tell the tale of the disaster. The thirsty lance of the Numidian, the claymore of the Gaul, and the deadly missiles of the Balearians did their work thoroughly. Flaminius died like a soldier, in the field which he had lost, and although Hannibal sought for his body, to which he would have given honorable sepulture, it never was discovered whether it was engulfed in the deep waters of the lake, or was confused in some pile of mangled corpses. He slept soundly, and his countrymen forgave his rashness for his valor. It is said, that an earthquake made the soil to reel, unheeded, under the feet of the combatants, so deadly and despairing, on both sides, was the conflict.

Before the sun set, the six thousand men, who had escaped, were prisoners to Maharbal and his indefatigable horse. Of fifty thousand men, fifteen thousand only were left alive, and these prisoners; of whom the Italians were discharged, free and without ransom, while the Romans were kept in strict custody, to be sold as slaves or slain, according to the pleasure of their captors; so ran the laws of antique warfare.

There was no force between the conqueror and Rome; but no rash impulse, no overweening confidence induced that wise leader to deviate from his preconcerted plan, or to enter the Latin country, in which he well knew that he should find a bare and devastated country, a deadly enemy in every male inhabitant, an impregnable fortress in every Latin town. Even on the day succeeding the defeat, the little borough of Spoleto shut its gates against his horsemen, and he had neither the means nor the inclination to assault it. He devastated, however, the whole rich plain from the Tiber to Perugia and Spoleto; and then, leisurely crossing the Apennines in the direction of Ancona, descended the shores of the Adriatic, through the country of the Abruzzi, into La Puglia, even to the Gulf of Manfredonia; possessing the whole country, from the Apennines eastward to the Gulf of Venice; and from Ancona southward to the Ofanto, in what is now the kingdom of Naples. During this long excursion, he put to the sword every Latin and Roman who was taken; a policy bloody indeed and cruel, but of which the Romans could not at least complain, since their own practice was the massacre of every living thing, even to domestic animals, in captured cities. Living with his troops on the fat of the land, he recruited his invaluable cavalry with rich herbage of the fertile plains of the south, and so made war feed war, at the greatest cost to the enemy. Still no state joined him; no city opened its gates; nor had he the means of forcing, either by storm or blockade, even the meanest of the Roman colonies:—this is sufficient answer to those empty declaimers who would censure so consummate a master of the art of war, as Hannibal, for want of energy in not storming Rome itself.

At this time, though the Romans had no individual man who could be compared for a moment with Hannibal, the spirit of the people was admirable and heroic to the utmost. Not a word was spoken of surrender; not a soldier was withdrawn from any foreign station; only a Dictator was appointed, fresh levies were drawn together, Rome herself was put in a state of defence, and the whole country was ordered to be devastated, the corn destroyed, and every house and hamlet burned to the ground, wherever he should turn his march.

This doubtless, as well as the hope of driving the allies into revolt against Rome, so soon as they should find Rome helpless to protect them, induced him to avoid the Latin country, and to bide his time patiently and with stern perseverance. The people of La Puglia would not join him; therefore, he crossed the Apennines again, into the Samnite country, a hundred years before so deadly hostile to the Romans. But Benevento, its capital, was now a Latin colony, and like all its sister towns, steadily shut its gates against him. Laying its territories waste on every side the terrible invader rolled the tide of devastation onward, ascended the Voltorno till he found it fordable, then crossed it, and rushed down like a torrent of lava, sweeping all before him with pitiless conflagration into the very garden of Italy, the glorious Falernian plain, the pride of Campania. Summer had scarce yet commenced; a long campaign was still before him; Fabius the Dictator was in the field watching him from the hills where Hannibal could not assail him; for unaided by their invincible horse, the Carthaginian foot could not cope with the legionaries—the rawest levies beating them with ease, when fighting from behind intrenchments. Hannibal, it must be remembered, had no base of operations, no fortified garrisons, no guarded magazines, no hope of reinforcements from the rear; his hospitals, his magazines, were necessarily in his camp; his granaries and store-houses were in the fields of his enemy and her allies. Thence it became a trial of patience between Fabius, the Delayer, as he delighted to be termed, and Hannibal, who, perhaps, deserved the title better, for prompt as he was to strike when a blow was to be stricken, he never once struck a blow untimely. Hannibal waited patiently the time when the allies should desert Rome as unable to defend them; or when Rome, conscious of their near defection, should descend to fight in a fair field, in order to defend their loyalty. Fabius waited patiently the time when Hannibal should expose a weak point to an attack, or should attack at a disadvantage—but that time never came.

Once Fabius thought that he had taken his great antagonist as in a net, and that he could not escape one more example of the Caudine Forks; but by a simple stratagem his wily enemy baffled his deep laid schemes; extricated himself from the toils, without the loss of one man; and returned into his old quarters, east of the Pyrenees, loaded with plunder, to pass the autumn and winter at his ease, leaving the Dictator and his system, a stumbling-block to his friends, and a laughing-stock to his enemies. So discontented indeed were the people, that a bill was passed at Rome, giving equal power to the master of the horse, Minutius, and the Dictator, and dividing the armies between them; but it soon became apparent that if the system of delaying was ineffective, the system of delivering battle to Hannibal was fatal. For Minutius, venturing to do so, was very severely handled; and a second route of the Trebbia was prevented only by the timely rescue of the slow Dictator.

No farther action marked that autumn; Hannibal went into winter quarters, well assured that one of two things must occur in the ensuing campaign—either the Romans must deliver battle to retain the fealty of the allies, when he looked forward confidently to an overwhelming rout of their forces, which itself would induce defection of the allies—or they must again abandon them yet another season to plunder and devastation; when they would assuredly rise in revolts unsolicited.

The steadiness with which this great captain adhered to his first system, is worthy of all praise, as a quality of the highest strategetical ability; and scarcely second to it, the military observer must rate the care with which he nurtured, cherished, and preserved his great resource, his invaluable cavalry, never to be replaced if once lost. Nor will the tactician fail to remark, in this connexion, the difference between the conduct of the Carthaginian, and that of the great French Emperor; who, by recklessly sacrificing in the morning of the 18th of June, his incomparable cuirassiers and dragoons against the immovable English squares, suffered that to be converted into an utter rout, which might have been only a severe check, had his retreating columns been covered at night by the fourteen thousand unrivalled cavalry, the bulk of whom were uselessly expended in vain charges on an impenetrable infântry, and lay cold on the red clay of Waterloo.

At Rome, in the mean time, there was discontent from within and clamor from without. The hot spirits within cried Shame, that Roman armies should avoid any enemy in the field; the cold spirits without cried Shame, that Rome should see her allies suffer the extremities of war, without striking one blow to aid or deliver them. The crisis, for which Hannibal had been so long waiting, had arrived.

The consuls of the year were elected with a direct reference to the question of giving battle, or no; and the choice decided the question in the affirmative. The consular armies had lain during the winter at Canusium, a small town to the south of the Ofanto, deriving their support from a large magazine, which they had established at Cannæ.

In this campaign Hannibal took the initiative, and again threw himself suddenly on the communications of the enemy, getting unexpectedly into their rear, and surprising their magazines at Cannæ; in the citadel of which, as a place of some strength, he established himself. The campaign had not opened so early as usual in this season, for the corn was already ripening; yet the consuls had not yet reached the camp at Canusium, when the proconsuls sent for instructions from the senate how to act, after their supplies had been thus cut off.

The answer was the arrival of the consuls, Terentius Varro, of plebeian, and Lucius Æmilius Paullus, of the highest patrician blood, with reinforcements—raising the Roman force to about ninety thousand men—and orders to risk a battle. On their arrival, they marched upon Hannibal, and found him encamped on the left bank of the Ofanto, at about nine miles distant from the sea, on very open ground, highly advantageous to cavalry operations. Perceiving this, the Consul Æmilius was desirous to retreat farther from the sea, into the hill country, where the Carthaginian cavalry would be less efficient, and whither he supposed Hannibal would be compelled to follow him, so soon as the crop on the seaboard should be exhausted. Varro, however, of a bolder and more sanguine temperament, when his day for command arrived, took steps which must needs bring on an action, by interposing himself between Hannibal and the sea, with his left on the river and his right on the town of Salapia. Hannibal at once marched down upon the Roman camp, and offered battle, which Æmilius, in his turn being in command, declined. Some unimportant manœuvring followed, in which the Romans were somewhat the sufferers. A few days elapsed, when Varro forded the river and drew out in battle array, on the right bank, upon which his right flank now rested. Hannibal immediately followed his example, and crossing the Ofanto at two points, drew out opposite to him.

This battle is the most worthy, of any in ancient history, unless perhaps it be that of Leuctra, of the attention of both the scholar and the tactician; for it is the prototype, and very counterpart, in its arrangement and results, of those of the greatest pitched battles the world has ever witnessed—Fontenoy, Aspern, and Waterloo. And, if I do not err, the result must ever be the same, where, of two armies, equally matched for courage and strength, and equally well led, the one rushes in solid column of attack into the centre of the other; which, if steady enough to fight in line, must envelop and overwhelm it. Such was the fate of the all but victorious square of the Highlanders at Fontenoy; such of the terrible column of Lannes at Aspern; such of the terrific final onslaught of Ney with the young guard on the heights of Mount St. Jean; and such, even more markedly, was the result of the battle now under consideration.

For some inexplicable reason, the Roman army, which was infinitely superior in numbers and quality of infantry, and the habit of which was to fight ever in line, was crowded into deep, narrow columns, on this occasion.

On the extreme right of the Roman line, next to the river, were the Roman knights, and next to these the legions; on their left the allied infantry, and on the left again the cavalry of the Latin name.

Opposing these in order, stood, next to the river, the Gaulish and Spanish horse; then half the African foot, armed like the legionaries; then the Gaulish and Spanish foot, and to their left the remainder of the Africans, with their left covered by the Numidian horse.

Thus far all was even; but Hannibal had purposely arrayed the Carthaginian army, precisely as the English army was drawn up at Waterloo, owing, in the latter instance, to the formation of the ground; that is to say, in a great convex line, with the apex toward the enemy.

On the signal being given, the cavalry charged on both sides; and, although the Roman knights fought stubbornly, they could not resist the onslaught of Hasdrubal, who chased them up the river bank, slaughtering them unsparingly, till seeing them utterly dispersed and broken, he wheeled across the whole rear of the Roman host, and falling on the Latin horse, who still held their own against the Numidian skirmishers, scattered them like a thunderbolt. Meanwhile, the Roman legions, seeing the Carthaginian infantry advancing in a wedge—instead of withdrawing their own centre, as they should have done—rushed in toward the centre from the flanks, till they were all crowded into a vast dense single column, which forced its way onward by the weight and fury of its own desperate charge. Thus, the Gauls and Spaniards in the centre of the Punic line were pushed back bodily into the rear, so that the Africans on the wings, who had been originally withdrawn, were now in advance; and the whole Carthaginian army, from being a convex, had become a concave line, overlapping and tearing to pieces the flanks of the long unwieldy Roman column, with their assailing wings.

Precisely similar to this catastrophe, was that of the British column at Fontenoy, where the French and English forces reversed their usual mode of fighting—the latter attacking in column, the former resisting in line. Precisely similar was the check and overthrow of Lannes' terrible column at Aspern. And, with but one exception, precisely similar even to the smallest details, were the whole tactics of the last decisive charge at Waterloo. The exception is this, that whereas the Punic line of battle at Cannæ became concave, from convex, by the retrogression of the centre; the British line at Waterloo underwent the same change by the advance of its flanks. In both actions the attacking column plunged into a concave line, carrying all before it; until its head was checked by the steadiness of the resisting centre, its flanks ravaged by the onslaught of the wings, and, to complete the parallel, in both cases, its rear torn to pieces by a charge of cavalry, its own cavalry having been long before expended—for at the close of the bloody day of Cannæ, Hasdrubal, returned from the slaughter of the Latin horse, broke in upon the rear of the still struggling legionaries, and closed the conflict by such a butchery as history but seldom has recorded.

Strange results followed this catastrophe. All the Southern allies deserted from Rome's authority, except the Latin name; and, even of these, twelve colonies refused their contingents. Still Rome disdained to treat; and Hannibal, unable, for want of artillery or of sufficient disciplined and steady infantry, to attack her walls, was compelled to maintain the war in the Southern provinces. From that day forth the Romans fought no more pitched battles; and, having regular supplies, while Hannibal was compelled to forage for his subsistence, they could rarely be forced into action. Whenever he did so, indeed, his superiority of resource and ability inevitably told; but the war was henceforth changed into a war of sieges; and in these Hannibal fought at disadvantage, for his cavalry could not be brought to bear, and his infantry were, as I have before observed, inferior to the legions. Still, never were the talents of the great Carthaginian so conspicuous as in these later campaigns, when the Romans selected none but soldiers of proof, and those soldiers had learned strategy even through being beaten by Hannibal. His manœuvres about Tarentum; his marches to and fro, dealing tremendous blows on all hands; his presence seeming almost ubiquitous, cannot fail to remind the reader of Napoleon's finest campaign, in my opinion, which terminated with the abdication of Fontainbleau.

His reappearance before the walls of Capua, when confident that he was leagues distant before Tarentum, the Romans, by a vast combined movement, had surrounded that city, and already exulted in the sure prospect of its fall, only to vanish like morning shadows before the mere splendor of his presence, seen on the distant summit of Tifata, surrounded by his veteran invincibles, is so complete an antecedent to Napoleon's similar reappearance at Dresden, and the scattering of the allies, that if the names and geography were changed one narrative might do for either.

When on his removal to the south, the Romans gathered

again about the fated walls of Capua, and fortified themselves in their leaguer with lines of circumvallation and countervallation which mocked his army's strength, what decision could be sounder, what conception grander, what execution more masterly than that of his forced march upon Rome itself, in the hope of drawing them from their half-won prey? What more romantic than his actually hurling his javelin over the Colline gates of Rome, and wasting the immediate territory of the city with the sword and fire before the very eyes of her Senators? It is true the Romans did not raise the siege, and that to his great regret they did take Capua; but that in no wise detracts from the correctness of his military principles, or the magnificence of his military achievements.

This was in the sixth year of the war; for five years more he struggled on with varying success, but unvarying courage and conduct; in the eleventh year Hasdrubal, his brother, followed in his footsteps from New Carthage to the Alps, passed them, and entered Italy with powerful reinforcements, which might well have changed the fortunes, would certainly have protracted the duration, of the war. But he was intercepted by vastly superior forces, concentrated against him by means of Claudius Nero's splendid forced march from one to the other end of the Peninsula, utterly defeated and killed.

This was the great, the *one* great Roman achievement of the war; and it was disgraced by a deed of the foulest atrocity. Hannibal's first information of his brother's defeat, was that brother's pale and bloody head cast over the entrenchments of his camp. Yet he had sought for Flaminius' body to give it honorable burial; and when Marcellus was slain he buried his remains with all honor, and sent his inurned ashes to his son.

The defeat of Hasdrubal was the real downfall of all Hannibal's prospects of success; for it had long been evident that his single army could not effect the destruction of the Roman Republic;

and Carthage, with Spain now wrested from her grasp, could offer him no aid. Indeed she was, ere long, to be so hard pressed at home, as to require his all-powerful arm, alas! no longer powerful to preserve her. All he could now do, was to act on the defensive; and he did that as brilliantly and effectively, as he had before assumed the offensive. Before he was recalled to fight at home for the very existence of Carthage, he had maintained himself for seventeen years in the heart of an enemy's country, without reinforcements, supplies, or moneys except what he took from the enemy; he had traversed and retraversed every portion of the peninsula, from the Po to the Gulf of Tarentum, wasting it with fire and sword at his own will; he had won three pitched battles, which are to this day the admiration of all strategists; he had beaten every force that ever met him in the field; he had never suffered a defeat; and when he withdrew from the shores of Italy, he did so, not that the Romans drove him thence, but that Carthage needed him elsewhere. At Zama he was overpowered, not vanquished; for the Romans were superior, in both numbers and quality, of both horse and foot. And the Numidians, to whose irresistible onset and impetuous horsemanship Hannibal had, in great part, owed his previous successes over the Romans—for with their thundering charge he terminated the crisis of almost every battle, crushing their indomitable infantry under foot, after having broken and exterminated their weak cavalry—were now arrayed under the savage and revengeful veteran Massinissos on the side of Scipio.

There was little manœuvring in this action, but much hard fighting; and it was won in the end by the stubborn hardihood of the Roman reserve of Triarii brought fresh into action with their long spears, after all the forces of the Carthaginians had been successively wearied out and cut to pieces.

Scipio gained no laurels by that victory beyond the barren

honor of being styled the conqueror of Hannibal, whom all men of all countries knew to be his better.

And Rome earned eternal disgrace by her persecution, even unto the death, of the aged, friendless, helpless exile, during whose life-time she could not but tremble.

Take him for all in all, not looking for virtues incompatible with the times, the country, and the state of society in which he flourished; weighing what he did against the means with which he did it; judging his acts by his motives, and his character by his conduct; I think we shall not err in pronouncing him, one of the purest patriots, and THE GREATEST CAPTAIN, without exception, whom this world has yet seen, or perhaps will see for ever.

HERBERT'S NEW WORK.

THE CAPTAINS OF THE OLD WORLD—Their Campaigns—Character, and Conduct as compared with the great modern Strategists—From the Persian Wars to the end of the Roman Republic. By HENRY W. HERBERT. 1 vol. 12mo., with illustrations, cloth. Price, $1 25.

CONTENTS.—The Military Art among the Greeks and Romans—Miltiades, the son of Cimon—His battle of Marathon—Themistocles, his sea-fight off Salamis, &c.—Pausanias, the Spartan; his battle of Plataia, &c.—Xenophon, the Athenian; his retreat of the Ten Thousand, &c.—Epaminondas, his Campaigns, battle of Leuktra and Mantinela—Alexander of Macedon, his battles of the Granikos, Issos, and Arbela, &c.—Hannibal, his battles of the Ticinus, Trebbia, Thrasymene, and Canæ.

"The theme is full of interest, to which Mr. Herbert's known literary ability and classical taste may be expected to give due exposition. The work is an original one—the material of which he claims to derive, not from modern books, but from the ancient authentic sources of history which he has examined for himself."—*U. S. Gazette & N. American.*

"Mr. Herbert has succeeded admirably—and has produced a work that will entitle him to a high rank with the best authors of his native and his adopted country."—*Syracuse Star.*

"The exploits of those captains are detailed, whose achievements exerted the most powerful influence on the destinies of the world. The author is a well-read historian, and has contemplated the events he describes with the eye of a philosopher and scholar."—*Philadelphia Presbyterian.*

"This is a powerful and brilliant delineation of the captains of the Old World—it opens with the three great Wars of Greece, and traces the course of Hannibal in the most captivating style."—*Albany Spectator.*

"To a nervous and pointed style the author adds the research of a scholar and the enthusiasm of a man of action. The strategies of warfare—the arming of troops, and the stern conflicts of man with man, are of course congenial subjects to one whose knowledge of skill in woodcraft is proverbial, and Mr. Herbert consequently enters into them with gusto and with clearness of perception."—*The Albion.*

"This volume which is intended to be the first of a series, includes seven of the greatest generals of antiquity, beginning with Miltiades and ending with Hannibal. The facts are all drawn from the most authentic sources, and the characters displayed with uncommon skill and effect. It was a bright thought, the bringing together of these illustrious names in one group."—*Albany Argus.*

"The writer draws a comparison between them and the great modern strategists, and gives an exceedingly interesting and graphic picture of the celebrated conflicts of olden times from the Persian wars to the Punic wars."—*N. Y. Observer.*

"This is an unique and able work. It displays sound and varied scholarship, united with a knowledge of the military art rarely possessed by a civilian. There is a truth and freshness about the descriptions that show the author to be no second-hand compiler, but one who has drawn his knowledge from a careful study of the Greek and Roman historians in their native garb. We would recommend this work to the attention of the young student, as a better manual of antiquities relative to the military art, than any set treatise on the subject, while its views of historical epochs and political relations are equally valuable and trustworthy. His analysis of the character and strategy of the great captains of antiquity is full of interest and instruction."—*N. Y. Recorder.*

VAGAMUNDO; Or, THE ATTACHE IN SPAIN. By John E. Warren. 1 vol. 12mo. Price, $1 00.

"The author of the volume before us has evidently many of the necessary qualifications for a traveller in Spain. Light-hearted and gay, his good humor never deserts him, and he is disposed to view everything through a *couleur de rose* medium. Much of this illusion may perhaps be ascribed te the *senoritas* who appear to have exercised unbounded sway over the susceptible heart of our Attache. In his eyes Spain is a paradise of houries of bewitching beauty."—*London Literary Gazette.*

"The Attache, enjoying peculiar advantages frem his official position, made the most of his privileges, and has given us a daguerreotype of that singularly romantic country and people in a style at once lucid, lively and readable."—*The Leader.*

"We have seen more elaborate works upon Spain than this, but few abound more with agreeable incidents and pleasant descriptions. The writer's imagination revels amidst the soft and beautiful scenes in which he finds himself, and he contrives to make the objects which pass before him almost as visible and palpable to his readers as they were to himself."—*Albany Argus.*

"He seems to have made good use of his means, for the book is full of incidents, told in a rather lively manner, and with due sensibility to the romantic scenery as well as to the romantic history of Spain"—*N. Y. Evening Post.*

"The author is a man of unquestionable talent and keen observation. He paints with great power, and sketches manners and men with the hand of a master. There is an intenseness and earnestness throughout the entire book remarkable in these days of literary foppishness and superficiality."—*Oneida Herald.*

THE FALL OF POLAND. Containing an Analytical and Philosophical Account of the Causes which conspired in the Ruin of that Nation—Together with a History of the Country from its Origin. By L. C. Saxton. 2 vols. 12mo. With Illustrations. Price, $2 50.

"The entire work is no hasty utterance of crude opinions, for the auther has evidently fitted himself for the task he has undertaken, by a study of history generally, and particularly by a careful collation of those writers that bear upon the subject. In order to be more complete, the various topics are arranged under different heads: as Religion, Government, Great Men, Civilization, Society, &c., thus enabling the student to refer directly to the subject which he may desire to see, and fitting it, with its appropriate index, to make a valuable work for the library."—*Newark Daily Advertiser.*

"It is the product of great thought and research, and presents a complete and accurate view of the history, government, laws, religion, popular character, and in short everything connected with Poland that can have an interest for the scholar or the statesman. It is a solid, symmetrical, and glowing incorporation of all the great points of interest of one of the most interesting nations of modern times, and deserves to be placed among the enduring ornaments of American literature"—*N. Y. Courier & Enquirer.*

"He has gone into his subject with thoroughness—having been many years in gathering his materials, and giving them symmetry and form."—*Boston Transcript.*

'The author has set himself to the task with great zeal, and with quite an extensive knowledge of the accessories of his subject."—*Cincinnati Daily.*

LECTURES ON ART—AND POEMS. By WASHINGTON ALLSTON. Ed... Richard Henry Dana, Jr. Contents—Lectures on Art, pages 3–167—Aphorisms, sentences written by Mr. Allston on the walls of his Studio, pages 167–179—The Hypochondriac, pages 179–199—Poems, pages 199–317. 1 vol. 12mo. Price, $1 25.

"There is a store of intellectual wealth in this handsome volume. It is a book of thought. Its contents are the rich and tasteful productions of the scholar and artist, who had mind to perceive and skill to portray much that is unseen by ordinary minds, as well as intelligence and power to exhibit whatever is grand and beautiful both in the physical and moral world."—*Christian Observer.*

"These are the records of one of the purest spirits and most exalted geniuses of which this country can boast. The intense love of the beautiful, the purity, grace and gentleness which made him incomparably the finest artist of the age, lend their charm and their power to these productions of his pen. * * * There are in his poems feeling, delicacy, taste, and the keenest sense of harmony which render them faultless."—*N. Y. Evangelist.*

"As a writer we know of no one who in his writings has exhibited such an appreciation of what constitutes beauty in art, correctness in form, or the true principles of composition."—*Providence Journal.*

"We commend them to the intellectual and the thoughtful, for we know that no one can read them without being wiser, and we believe the better."—*Albany State Register.*

"The production of a most ethereal spirit instinctively awake to all the harmonies of creation."—*Albany Argus.*

"The exquisitely pure and lofty character of the author of these lectures and poetic fragments is well expressed in them. It gave their structure a freshness and calmness, and their tone a purity that remain to charm us, and that are equally admirable and delightful."—*The Independent.*

"His lectures possess great attractions for every one aiming at cultivation of mind and refinement of taste, while his poems, which elicited so high praise when published singly, are sure to receive it when as now embodied in a more classic form."—*Natchez Courier.*

"The lovers of American literature and art will rejoice in the possession of these matured fruits of the genius which seemed alike skilled in the use of the pen and pencil."—*Newark Daily Advertiser.*

POEMS AND PROSE WRITINGS. By RICHARD HENRY DANA. 2 vols 12mo. Price, $2 50.

"Mr. Dana's writings are addressed to readers of thought, sensibility and experience. By tenderness, by force, in purity, the poet paints the world, treading in safety the dizziest verge of passion, through all things, honorable to all men; the just style resolving all perplexities, a rich instruction and solace in these volumes to the young and old who are to come hereafter."—*Literary World.*

"Mr. Dana is evidently a close observer of nature, and therefore his thoughts are original and fresh."—*True Democrat.*

"In addition to the Poems and Prose Writings included in the former edition of his works, they contain some short, practical pieces, and a number of reviews and essays contributed to different periodicals, some of them as much as thirty years since, and now republished for the first time—as the expression of the inmost soul, these writings bear a strong stamp of originality."—*N. Y. Tribune.*

"No one, we predict, will ever lay down the volume with that common exclamation on his lips—'I can't get interested in it,' for it grapples to the reader with hooks of silver, which hold him quite as fast as if they were made of steel."—*Boston Gazette.*

FRESH GLEANINGS, or a New Sheaf from the Old Field of Continental Europe. By IK. MARVEL. 1 vol., 12mo.

"This book should be read by all who can appreciate a style full of grace, in a composition replete with original and striking thoughts."—*Boston Journal.*

"Agreeable, quaint, humorous, philosophical, pathetic, charming, glorious Ik. Marvel! It is as refreshing to the mind, wearied with the thrice-told insipidities of continental travel to dip into his fresh sparkling pages, as a plunge, this hot weather, into the cold, diamond, deer-haunted waters of some mountain lake. We have turned over his soft, thick, dainty pages, and our eye has glided along the stream of his bright descriptions, pleasant thoughts, humorous expressions, and characters painted with a few light touches, like daguerreotype portraits—very Sterne-like and exceedingly fine—until arriving at the end we are startled at the rapidity with which the feet of Time, flower-muffled, have trodden."—*Albany Atlas.*

"A series of the liveliest, newest, most taking and most graphic sketches of out of the way scenes, character and incidents, that were ever done up between a pair of bookbinder's covers."—*Commercial Advertiser.*

"This is decidedly the most agreeable book of the season. It reminds one by an occasional association of ideas, rather than resemblance, of imitation of Sterne's Sentimental Journey, and some of Longfellow's transatlantic sketches; but its freshness, its variety, graphic descriptive power, and genial sympathies, are all its own."—*Buffalo Advertiser.*

THE BATTLE SUMMER. Being Transcripts from Personal Observation in Paris during the year 1848. By IK. MARVEL. With Illustrations by DARLEY. 1 vol., 12mo

"It is a series of pictures—sketches of scenes which passed under the author's eye. It is most ably done, and shows the hand of one gifted with genius and destined to make his mark on the literature of his country."—*N. Y. Courier and Enquirer*

"The book is filled with a series of pictures and sketches more graphic it would be difficult to find."—*New York Recorder.*

"Like a talented and enthusiastic artist, he placed himself in the best positions, and caught the lineaments of each scene to be transferred to his canvas. * * * In truth, he has furnished a gallery of portraits which are very life like."—*Presbyterian.*

"An elaborate history would fail to convey so vivid and truthful a conception of the rise, progress and manner of the 'second reign of terror' as is to be obtained from this work.' —*Portland Transcript.*

"It is by far the most able and most impressive account of the scenes in Paris, and reveals a power of description that will give the author a name."—*N. Y. Evangelist.*

THE LORGNETTE, or Studies of the Town. By an Opera-Goer (IK. MARVEL) 2 vol., 12mo. Set off with DARLEY'S Design.

DREAM LIFE. By IK. MARVEL. 1 vol., 12mo.

THE FRUIT GARDEN. SECOND EDITION. A Treatise intended to Illustrat and explain the Physiology of Fruit Trees, the Theory and Practice of all operations connected with the Propagation, Transplanting, Pruning and Training of Orchard and Garden Trees, as Standards, Dwarfs, Pyramids, Espaliers, &c., the laying out and arranging different kinds of Orchards and Gardens, the selection of suitable varieties for different purposes and localities, gathering and preserving Fruits, Treatment of Disease, Destruction of Insects. Descriptions and Uses of Implements, &c., illustrated with upward of one hundred and fifty figures, representing different parts of Trees, all Practical Operations, Forms of Trees, Designs for Plantations, Implements, &c. By P. Barry, of the Mount Hope Nurseries, Rochester, New York. 1 vol. 12mo.

" It is one of the most thorough works of the kind we have ever seen, dealing in particular as well as generalities, and imparting many valuable hints relative to soil, manures, pruning and transplanting."—*Boston Gazette.*

" A mass of useful information is collected, which will give the work a value even to those who possess the best works on the cultivation of fruit yet published."—*Evening Post.*

" His work is one of the completest, and, as we have every reason for believing, most accurate to be obtained on the subject."—*N. Y. Evangelist.*

" A concise Manual of the kind here presented has long been wanted, and we will venture to say that, should this volume be carefully studied and acted upon by our industrious farmers, the quantity of fruit in the State would be doubled in five years, and the quality, too, greatly improved. Here may be found advice suited to all emergencies, and the gentleman farmer may find direction for the simplest matters, as well as those which trouble older heads. The book, we think, will be found valuable."—*Newark Daily Advertiser.*

" It is full of directions as to the management of trees, and buds, and fruits, and is a valuable and pleasant Book."—*Albany Evening Journal.*

" The work is prepared with great judgment, and founded on the practical experience of the Author—is of far greater value to the cultivator than most of the popular compilations on the subject."—*N. Y. Tribune.*

This Book *supplies* a place in fruit culture, and that is saying a great deal, while we have the popular works of Downing, Thomas, and Cole. Mr. Barry has then a field to himself which he occupies with decided skill and ability.—*Prairie Farmer.*

A DOMESTIC HISTORY OF THE REVOLUTION, by Mrs. E. F ELLET. 1 vol. 12mo. cloth, $1 00.

This is a new work, entirely different from the Women of the Revolution, by the same author. It embraces a complete outline of the History of the American Revolution, but illustrates more particularly the Domestic History of that eventful period. In this respect it is absolutely an original contribution to American History, and will be found to be interesting as a book for general reading, suited for private and public libraries, and as a class book for reading in schools.

www.ingramcontent.com/pod-product-compliance
Lightning Source LLC
LaVergne TN
LVHW020118110826
845151LV00001B/202

* 9 7 8 1 4 2 5 5 4 2 4 8 1 *